T0347524

European Union and the Making of a Wider Northern Europe

Since 1990 the European Union has enlarged to incorporate much of northern Europe including Finland, Sweden, Estonia, Latvia, Lithuania, Poland and the former East Germany. It has become the entity towards which the minor, small and great powers in the European north, and many regional agents and organizations there, tend to look before anything else, and towards which regional political and economic activities increasingly tend to gear themselves.

This book provides the first comprehensive account of the emergence of the EU as a northern European power. It not only places the EU as an international actor in the context of northern Europe but also creates a new understanding of (inter-)relations between the EU and the states of the region. This unique study provides:

- a fresh approach to the under-theorized field of EU foreign policy;
- key empirical material, including hundreds of documents, interviews and field experiments;
- in-depth case studies of relations between the EU, Nordic states, Baltic states and Russia with its northwestern regions.

This book will be of strong interest to scholars of European politics, foreign policy studies, Russian studies and international relations.

Pami Aalto is Research Fellow at the Aleksanteri Institute, University of Helsinki, Finland.

Routledge Advances in European Politics

European Union and the Making of a Wider Northern Europe

Pami Aalto

Routledge
Taylor & Francis Group

LONDON AND NEW YORK

First published 2006
by Routledge
2 Park Square, Milton Park, Abingdon, Oxon, OX14 4RN

Simultaneously published in the USA and Canada
by Routledge
270 Madison Ave, New York NY 10016

Routledge is an imprint of the Taylor & Francis Group, an informa business

Transferred to Digital Printing 2008

Typeset in Times New Roman by
Prepress Projects Ltd, Perth, UK

British Library Cataloguing in Publication Data
A catalogue record for this book is available from the British Library

Library of Congress Cataloging in Publication Data
Aalto, Pami, 1972–
  European Union and the making of a wider northern Europe/Pami Aalto.
  p. cm. – (Routledge advances in European politics; 38)
  Includes bibliographical references and index.
  1. European Union countries–Relations–Europe, Northern. 2. European Union countries–Relations–Russia (Federation). 3. Europe, Northern–Relations–European Union countries. 4. Russia (Federation)–Relations–European Union countries. 5. European Union–Europe, Northern. 6. European cooperation. I. Title. II. Series.
  JZ1570.A54A48 2006
  341.242′2–dc22
  2005035886

ISBN10: 0–415–39342–6
ISBN13: 978–0–415–39342–3

Contents

Figures

Tables

Acknowledgements

This book represents work that was started in 2001 and at first carried out whenever time permitted alongside other projects. During 2003–5 the primary research was conducted and the book manuscript written up more systematically.

The site for starting the work was the Copenhagen Peace Research Institute (COPRI), where I worked as a Visiting Research Fellow during February–March 2001. During that time some of the central ideas for the new theoretical approach to EU foreign policy studies that is introduced in this book, and which is applied to the EU's northern European engagement, were initiated. Pertti Joenniemi kindly functioned as my academic host. He provided a lot of inspiration as well as supplying me with piles of literature and interesting papers, and in that way helped me to develop my idea of conceptualizing the EU in terms of geopolitical subjectivity. The very busy work in Copenhagen yielded a working paper, 'Structural geopolitics in Europe: constructing geopolitical subjectivity for the EU and Russia', *COPRI Working Papers* 22/2001. A considerably revised version of the paper was later presented in a seminar session of COPRI's famous 'European security' (EUR) research group hosted by Barry Buzan and Ole Wæver. I am extremely grateful for that opportunity, which helped me to fine-tune the piece that contains the most important theoretical propositions advanced in this book and that was ultimately published as 'A European geopolitical subject in the making? EU, Russia and the Kaliningrad question', *Geopolitics*, 7: 143–74.

My interest at the time in geopolitics-influenced theoretical approaches and EU foreign policy studies had a fruitful feeding ground in my membership in an international network of scholars including Simon Dalby, Vladimir Kolossov and Gerard Toal, with Vilho Harle, Mika Luoma-aho and Sami Moisio as its most important Finnish members. It was a memorable northern summer night in 2003 involving these three Finnish scholars at Vilho Harle's countryside place in northern Finland, sitting on an old sauna terrace overlooking a river, where I got the necessary encouragement for continuing on the theoretical path I had chosen. During that night my colleagues convinced me to continue applying my geopolitical subjectivity approach to this book on EU foreign policy, which was then still in its early stages of preparation. Promoting this new approach emerged as an opportunity to contribute something different to EU foreign policy studies, a field of research with which I had back then been familiarizing myself for a few years. Later Vilho Harle kindly read and commented on the whole manuscript, as did Pekka Korhonen from the University of Jyväskylä and Tuomas Forsberg from the University of Helsinki.

I received further encouragement for the idea of the book from Jean Monnet Professor Jyrki Käkönen in the Department of Political Science and International Relations, University of Tampere, Finland, where I worked during 2001–5. Jyrki read a draft introductory text to the book. His comments were instrumental in expanding it into the final product. My sincere thanks must also go to the department and the rest of the staff there, who together formed a very good working environment where I lacked nothing I needed for this research. And the good international student body of the department must be mentioned as well, thanks to their interest in listening to many of the ideas and arguments presented in these pages. They often provided vital feedback by posing questions that made me think harder. Similarly I wish to thank the Academy of Finland's funding through the projects 'Identity politics, security and the making of geopolitical order in the Baltic region' (2001–3, no. 50882) coordinated by Vilho Harle and myself, and 'Russia, the Russians and Europe' (2003–5, SA decision no. 103049), which was my own solo project.

Some invited presentations that were particularly instrumental in helping me to get feedback on the project were made in the northern European locations Alfried-Krupp Wissenschaftskolleg, COPRI's successor institution the Danish Institute for International Studies, the University of Turku and Södertörns Högskola. For the invitations I am grateful to, respectively, Aino Bannwart, Pertti Joenniemi and Christopher Browning (now at the University of Birmingham), Marko Lehti (now at Tampere Peace Research Institute) and Egle Rindzeviciute. Andres Kasekamp from the Estonian Foreign Policy Institute (now at the University of Tartu) invited me to a project on Estonian foreign policy that helped me to fine-tune aspects of the Estonia chapter to this book. Russia-related parts of this book were presented in a workshop on Russian and East European Studies chaired by myself and Krista Berglund in the Annual Meeting of the Finnish Political Science Association at the University of Jyväskylä in 2002.

But there are also many other individuals who should be specifically mentioned. They have provided valuable comments, critical remarks on my texts and presentations, and good intellectual company and useful exchange in the fields of EU foreign policy studies, northern European, Baltic and post-Soviet studies, at the intersection of which this book is situated: Eiki Berg at the University of Tartu, the well-known methodological author Steven Brown and his colleague Richard Robyn at Kent State University, Hiski Haukkala at the Finnish Institute for International Affairs, Alexey Ignatiev at the Kaliningrad representation of the East–West Institute, the noted EU scholar Niilo Kauppi at the University of Helsinki, Vahur Made at the Estonian School of Diplomacy, Viatcheslav Morozov at the St Petersburg State University, Sirke Mäkinen and Vesa Vares at the University of Tampere, Gediminas Vitkus at the Vilnius University, Henri Vogt at the University of Helsinki, and Anders Wivel at the University of Copenhagen.

Small but useful professional support also came from Clive Archer, Manchester Metropolitan University, Richard Mole, School for Slavonic and East European Studies, David Smith, University of Glasgow, and Jan Zielonka, then at the European University Institute but now at St Antony's College, Oxford. Likewise, I wish to acknowledge having been influenced by the well-known perspectives of the Danish scholars Hans Mouritzen and Ole Wæver. Of course, not all or even many of these individuals might share all the arguments offered in this book but, then again, useful intellectual exchange and debate is the way social science moves forward.

Institutional support for the finalization stages of this book was received from the Aleksanteri Institute, University of Helsinki, where I moved in August 2005. There is definitely a need to acknowledge the interest shown towards this book by the institution's leadership, as well as the senior and junior staff. The good reception at Aleksanteri helped me to continue my work for this book uninterruptedly. The Department of Political Science, University of Helsinki, should also be acknowledged for granting access to Robyn Milburn, who helped me to compile the index to this book.

Finally, I have enjoyed the warm support of my two families: one consisting of my parents, who have been instrumental in supporting my academic work, as well as my brother, who has always assisted me when I have needed it; and the other comprising my wife Freja, who has tolerated my sometimes unsociable intellectual wondering and provided very unconditional and warm support, and her parents and the extended family from whom I trust to have learned something different in the form of the cosy lifestyle of the Swedish-speaking population of Finland.

From my heart I trust all of these northern European and wider encounters and learning processes will continue – also after this book, the field of EU foreign policy studies will continue to need further input and inspiration from various directions in order to develop better theoretical approaches.

Abbreviations

BSR	Baltic Sea region
BEAC	Barents Euro-Arctic Council
CBC	cross-border cooperation (programmes of the EU)
CBSS	Council of the Baltic Sea States
CEE	Central and Eastern Europe
CEES	Common European Economic Space
CFSP	Common Foreign and Security Policy
CIS	Commonwealth of Independent States
CSR	Common Strategy on Russia
EBRD	European Bank for Reconstruction and Development
EC	European Community
EEA	European Economic Area
EEC	European Economic Community
EFTA	European Free Trade Area
ES	English School
ESDP	European Security and Defence Policy
ESSR	Estonian Soviet Socialist Republic
EU	European Union
FCMA	Friendship, Cooperation and Mutual Assistance (Treaty)
FEZ	Free Economic Zone
FSU	former Soviet Union
FTD	facilitated transit document
GDP	gross domestic product
IR	international relations
NATO	North Atlantic Treaty Organization
NCM	Nordic Council of Ministers
ND	Northern Dimension
NDEP	Northern Dimension Environmental Partnership
NEI	North European Initiative
NGO	non-governmental organization
OSCE	Organization for Security and Co-operation in Europe
PCA	Partnership and Cooperation Agreement

QMV   qualified majority voting
SSR   Soviet Socialist Republic
SEZ   Special Economic Zone
SVOP   Sovet po vneshnei i oboronnoi politike [Council of Foreign and Defence
       Policy]
USSR   Soviet Union (Union of Soviet Socialist Republics)
WTO   World Trade Organization

1 Introduction

This book examines the processes by which the European Union (EU) has become a northern European power. In doing so, this book portrays the EU as *the* most important power in northern Europe towards which most other international and regional agents need to, and will, look. That such a very strong claim can now be advanced was not really foreseen in many analyses that were published at the turn of the millennium regarding future patterns of order in northern Europe.

For example, in 1998, in an excellent comparative study of northern European countries bordering Russia, Hans Mouritzen and his colleagues thought it unlikely for the Baltic states and former Soviet republics Estonia, Latvia and Lithuania to attain membership of both the EU and the North Atlantic Treaty Organization (NATO) during the coming decade. That would only be possible in the improbable case that Russia, the successor state to the Soviet Union after it collapsed in 1991, would accept it in return for concessions in one or another area from these 'western' organizations (Mouritzen *et al.* 1998: 191–3). In an earlier study, Mouritzen even introduced a scenario in which out of the Baltic states Lithuania might not be attracted enough by EU membership to try and make the necessary sacrifices (Mouritzen 1996a: 297; cf. 1996b: 305). In Mouritzen's analysis, some reservations towards the EU's pull were seen as necessary regardless of his postulating it as the primary source of order in the northern European region.

In 1999, Peter van Ham also supposed that the often expressed foreign policy goal of the Nordic states Denmark, Finland and Sweden, of securing a place for the three Baltic states in forthcoming EU expansion, would not be easily attainable. In his view, at that time the European Commission and the Union's citizens seemed too reluctant to include the Balts. Russia's tendency to consider these countries as part of its self-declared sphere of influence or 'near abroad' served to keep the EU – which still at that time had a very vague identity in relation to the provision of security – cautious about any plans for incorporating them (van Ham 1999: 237). And according to Helmut Hubel, any steps towards including the Baltic states should be accompanied by measures directed at increasing trade and other cooperation with Russia in order to keep it engaged constructively. Moreover, efforts at constructing a 'European peace order' that would include Russia could not rely on the EU model of integration alone (Hubel 1999: 242–52). Many observers were of the opinion that, as long as Russia had great power or imperial pretensions, the EU would have to manoeuvre carefully and diplomatically within the EU–Russian borderlands (e.g. Wæver 1997a: 80).

The Baltic states were in this manner often seen as being caught between 'two political cultures' – 'Russian' and 'European' (Hubel 2002: 7). Russia was conceived of as a potentially revisionist great power intent on keeping the Balts under its thumb and on blocking any uncontrolled expansion of European organizations into its northern European sphere of influence. Interesting aspects of the envisaged regional order were captured by Olav Knudsen, who suggested two theories applicable to the situation: great power rivalry and imperialism. The great power perspective postulates inherent instability in relations between the minor/small powers of the region (Baltic states and Nordic states), and the great powers present in the region (Russia, Germany and, with reservations, the United States). Theories of imperialism, for their part, suggest that the main question for the twenty-first century is whether Russian or German imperialist impulses will regain their historical significance in northern Europe (Knudsen 1999: 3–13). In these images, the EU does not even figure. The prevalence of a fairly traditional and realist, state-centric view of northern Europe's political determinants, like Knudsen's, is present even in a recent account focusing on north European region building efforts since the early 1990s. Here the future prospects of integration within the region depend on whether state agents or sub-state agents/non-governmental organizations (NGOs) will gain the upper hand in ordering regional developments (Hedegaard and Lindström 2003: 12–13). In this scheme, the EU is considered a mere intergovernmental organization. This image stands in stark contrast to its depiction in this book.

The scheme introduced in this book has the benefit of hindsight in arguing that many analyses seriously underestimated the ability of the Union to exercise power in northern Europe and include the Baltic states as part of its enlargement into Central and Eastern Europe (CEE) and, thus, closer to the sphere of influence that Russia more or less willingly inherited from the Soviet Union. This book focuses on these processes by questioning purely state-centric accounts of northern Europe and especially of the EU as an organization that merely provides a framework for regional cooperation of northern European states. In other words, our tendency to think of the EU in terms of conventional notions of political agency will be exposed in this book.

Our imagination tends to be locked into the category of *Westphalian nation-states* and other entities we are used to identifying around ourselves and speaking of, like *Westphalian-federal states* and *international organizations*. In an ideal-typed Westphalian nation-state, the power of the centre is uniformly distributed across all territorial and functional dimensions. The power of the centre reaches all corners of the state equally and is not territorially and functionally differentiated, unlike in the case of the EU. In Westphalian-federal states like Germany and the United States (US), the constituent units maintain more independence, but their ties to the centre are identical to each other across both territorial and functional dimensions.[1] The debate about launching a European federation is an old one (e.g. Heffernan 1998: 125–31), and it resurfaced again in the 1990s and at the turn of the millennium (Chapter 4). However, since then the idea of European federalism has failed to gather sufficient strength, and the prospects of its dramatic resurgence remain rather dim in light of the findings outlined in this book. International intergovernmental organizations, for their part, consist of nation-states, or federal or other types of states that are all equally bound by the common rules, if any, typically pertaining to a limited sector of policy. For this reason international organizations usually have very little autonomy from their members. These features do not quite clearly apply to the EU, where member states remain variously integrated with the common rules whilst remaining greatly affected by EU integration practically across all sectors of policy. Remarks that 70–80 per cent of national legislation originate in European law are not uncommon.

Instead of the conventional notions and loci of political agency a new theoretical approach is offered in this book. It postulates that the recent, to many of us somewhat surprising, turning points in EU–Baltic and EU–Russian relations represent only a part of wider and more long-term processes whereby the EU is becoming the *main geopolitical subject* of northern Europe. What I mean by this is briefly introduced in the remainder of this chapter, before I outline the recent historical background for the EU's rise in Chapter 2 and present a more conceptual discussion in Chapter 3.

The opening up of the EU's wider northern Europe

For the EU, events such as Denmark's EU membership in 1973, the reunification of Germany in 1991 and, most decisively, Finland's and Sweden's membership in 1995 opened up a new view onto northern Europe. These more or less northern EU members were also instrumental in gradually engaging the Union in their efforts of overcoming some of the remaining Cold War era divisions in northern Europe by means of regional cooperation. The main targets of these region-building efforts were Estonia, Latvia and Lithuania, and the northern parts of Poland, as well as northwest Russia. Moreover, as implied, the target countries themselves each started developing closer relations with the EU. The Baltic states and Poland filed membership applications in the mid-1990s and joined the EU in May 2004, and Russia is increasingly closely bound to the EU direction by a 'strategic partnership' with the Union. And along Russia's northwestern interface with the enlarged Union – bordering Finland, Estonia and Latvia – the EU's regional cooperation framework, the Northern Dimension (ND), was launched in 1997–8. The ND policy deals with questions of 'soft security' ranging from the environment to economy and education, and is now becoming part of the Union's new neighbourhood policy towards its 'wider Europe' that is opening up as a result of the EU's enlargement rounds. Taken together, these developments manifest a powerful northern European opening to the EU due to the pressure for EU accession states and applicants to converge with EU legislation and policy priorities, while a less binding but clearly observable pull applies to the EU's neighbours with market and other interests in the EU area.

This all implies that the EU has become the entity towards which the minor, small and great powers in the European north, and many regional agents and organizations there, tend to look before anything else, and towards which regional political and economic activities increasingly tend to be geared. But this should not lead us into rushed comparisons as to what extent the Union is taking the traditional place of states like Russia and Germany in exercising power in the region. Neither should it lead us to take for granted northern Europe's belonging to a Westphalian-federal European superstate with sharp borders and a modern territorial form. Although since the 1990s there have undeniably been important pressures for federal development in the EU that will also be discussed in this book, I suggest that it will be theoretically more fruitful to understand these de-velopments as part of socially constructed processes by which the EU is acquiring what I call geopolitical subjectivity. This is about *ordering*, i.e. the ability and willingness to create and maintain order within a regional context like the north-ern European case that is elaborated here. With the EU conceptualized as the main geopolitical subject of northern Europe, the nation-states of the region continue to exist, but they are best taken as constitutive parts of the construction processes of the new EU subject.

What laid the basis for the processes of which the northerners are now part was fundamental shifts ensuing from the end of the Cold War era bipolar struggle between the US and the Soviet Union that influenced the northern European set-ting significantly (see also Chapter 2), and the more recently altered postures of the US, NATO and Russia within the region.

During the new millennium, we have witnessed a steady decline in the explicit influence of the sole remaining superpower, the US, in northern Europe in the face of its more global ambitions. In the early 1990s, the US gradually became a visible supporter of the Baltic states' newly (re)gained independence vis-à-vis Russian pretensions by engaging them in bilateral and multilateral cooperation networks and programmes. The US was first instrumental in pressing for the withdrawal of the Soviet/Russian troops from the Baltic states in 1993–4, and then agreed a non-binding Baltic Charter with them in 1998. The Baltic Charter was intended to re-assure the Balts and deter Russian interest without offering the prospect of NATO membership. During the following years the US eventually played a decisive role in the Baltic states' gradual incorporation into NATO. Russia finally accepted Baltic NATO membership in 2001 after opposing it throughout the 1990s, and has itself become a partner with the organization, as it has done vis-à-vis the EU. In parallel with the Baltic NATO accession process, the US worked quietly with its North European Initiative (NEI) introduced in 1997, which derived heavily from the EU's ND policy and was in a similar manner intended to help in stabilising northern Europe after the Cold War confrontation by soft means of cooperation. During the first term of President George W. Bush, the NEI underwent a steady downgrading amid perceptions of its having largely fulfilled its task (Browning and Joenniemi 2004a: 243).[2]

With the conclusion of Baltic NATO membership and the NEI, we have seen the US fulfilling most of its self-defined post-Cold War strategic tasks in the northern European region and consequently dropping a large part of its interest there, in particular since the launching of its 'war on terrorism' in September 2001 and the consequent reorientation of priorities away from Europe. Moreover, as a result NATO has become less of a talking point in the northern European region. Despite the occasional bursts of NATO membership debates in non-aligned Finland and Sweden, NATO has become at best some sort of a last-resort guarantor of national security for the Baltic states and Poland, as well as for established NATO members like Denmark, Norway and Germany. NATO fighter planes patrol Baltic airspaces but, importantly for our purposes, NATO has conspicuously refrained from any notable ordering of the northern European political space since the joining of the Baltic states and Poland, and has instead faded into the background in a region where questions of military security are more or less settled in the middle term. The ongoing mix of partnership ties and intelligence battles between NATO and Russia that experts are witnessing in the northern European context does not really merit treating the organization as something that would occupy the day-to-day attention of northern European policy makers, or the media, in the way EU matters often do (cf. Mouritzen and Wivel 2005a: 30–1).

The relative withdrawal or fading into the background of the US and NATO, Russia's retreat regarding the Baltic and Polish EU and NATO memberships, and Russia's own partnership ties with the last two entities have laid the grounds for the strategic reorganization of northern Europe's great power structure. This has allowed for the construction of a new northern European political space where the EU is assuming more centrality and is increasingly designing developments. This structural shift is especially noticeable in the territories formerly under Soviet/Russian power like Poland and the Baltic states. It is not an exaggeration to say that, today, no major political process in the northern European region seems to proceed without the name of the Union being invoked. Resulting from the strategic reorganization and the EU-bound choices of the region's states and other agents, the EU has been invited into envisaging and practically making what can be termed its 'wider northern Europe'. The Union has also increasingly exploited the opportunity to create such a new political space (Figure 1.1).

Questions may of course arise about to what extent the EU is responsible for any project of making a wider northern Europe, and how wide such a project can ever be. Even after the breaking of the Cold War era bipolar division of the world, once also so evident in northern Europe, we continue to live in a world of boundaries and frontiers, where 'wide' always remains a relative term. In order to justify my major claim of the EU's pivotal position in creating a new political space in northern Europe, some basic points related to the character of the EU and its foreign policy towards northern Europe and other directions need to be spelled out. The following discussion will also serve the aim of locating this study into the broader literature on European integration and, in particular, EU foreign policy studies.

Away from Westphalia[3]

Notions of the EU as the main geopolitical subject of northern Europe intent on making a wider northern Europe, and displaying both the ability and the

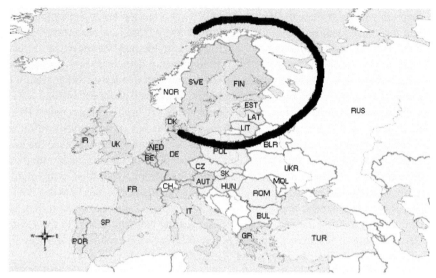

Figure 1.1   The EU's wider northern Europe. Source: European Communities, 1995–2003. The EU's wider norther Europe is marked by the circle in the figure. It corresponds to the geographical area of the Northern Dimension. Within it the countries coloured dark grey have been members since 1995 or before; countries coloured light grey have been members since 2004; and areas coloured white are associated with the EU through partnerships and cooperation programmes under the Northern Dimenson and other policy frameworks.

willingness to create and maintain order there, do not represent the mainstream of European integration studies or EU foreign policy studies.

Textbooks on European integration studies usually begin by surveying traditional international relations (IR)-inspired theories – functionalism/neofunctionalism and intergovernmentalism/liberal intergovernmentalism. These theories offer only limited value for our purposes. Neofunctionalism paves the way for the emergence of a supranational EU polity that can be compared to other already existing domestic political systems. By contrast, liberal intergovernmentalism portrays member states as continuing to exercise the biggest impact when big decisions are made on the EU's functioning. Put otherwise, these traditional theories focus on the character of *EU integration as such* and deal with the degree to which already existing member states decide to cooperate or compete. They concentrate on arguing to what extent integration has come to define European politics. In that sense, they are mostly about *internal* dynamics within the Union (Friis and Murphy 1999: 212).

By contrast, in this book attention is directed to the EU's foreign policy in the context of the processes accounting for the making of a wider northern Europe. Therefore, the theoretical focus will not primarily be on studies mapping internal developments, but on EU foreign policy studies. As already implied, contributions to EU foreign policy studies comparing the Union to Westphalian entities

– whether Westphalian nation-states or Westphalian-federal states – will be taken as unfruitful for theory development purposes insofar as they merely compare the Union to existing conventional templates. They thus fail to offer any new theoretical perspectives in a field notoriously short of genuine theory building, and which is renowned for its habit of simply replicating the EU's own clumsy structures and terminology. Simultaneously such approaches compromise our prospects of understanding in what peculiar ways the EU creates order through its foreign policy activities.

The first Westphalian claim made about EU foreign policy that should be mentioned here concerns the lack of a common European identity. Allegedly, it provides a shallow grounding for EU foreign policy. The work of the essentialist scholar Anthony Smith is fundamental to this genre of writing. Smith suggests that the shared European traditions such as Roman law, political democracy, parliamentary institutions and Judaeo-Christian ethics do not quite account for the claim of 'unity in diversity', which is often heard from EU officials and pro-European policy makers. Instead, for Smith, Europe remains at best a family of diverse nation-states, which prevents the emergence of a European identity (A.D. Smith 1992, 1993). The intergovernmentalist scholar Stanley Hoffmann, for his part, laments the lack of a common European polity, which shows up in the relative lack of interest in European Parliament elections and in the alleged lack of European public space (Hoffmann 2000: 198). Although he might consciously avoid comparisons to the low turnout in US elections and to the strongly locally oriented mass media there, he would probably concur with Christopher Hill and William Wallace's (1996: 8) assertion that the EU rests upon 'a relatively weak sense of shared history and identity'. In Jan Zielonka's analysis, the allegedly poorly developed European identity and lack of European polity are suggested as the main factors underlying what he terms the EU's foreign political 'paralysis' in the 1990s. This included the EU's slowness in differentiating among the various Copenhagen criteria, introduced in 1993, for the CEE enlargement to take place, or indeed in deciding in what order the new entrants should accede and new applicants be lined up (Zielonka 1998: 15; Chapters 3 and 4 in this book).

The second Westphalian claim concerns the member states' ability to formulate common political interests. They have agreed on the single market, currency and common tariffs, but have found it more difficult to come into agreement over politico-strategic relations with partners and competitors, and over the development of military capability to back up the adopted common positions when deemed necessary. Characterizations of the Union as an 'economic giant, political dwarf' (Medrano 1999) represent this genre of writing, as do statements about the EU being far from having a single foreign policy (K. Smith 2003: 51) or lacking the character of a 'strategic actor' (Rynning 2003). Seen as aggravating the EU's difficulty in formulating common interests are the Union's imperfect institutional structures, which have been found guilty of generating even further conflicts among the members (see, for example, Zielonka 1998: 207).

Naturally, in the eyes of these authors, it probably does not help much that in a referendum in spring 2005 the French public rejected the Constitutional Treaty for the European Union. This brought the ratification process of the treaty agreed on in 2004 to a halt possibly lasting for many years, and potentially leading to the project's subsequent revision, selective adoption or even abandonment. The treaty introduced a few improvements into the EU's ability to formulate common interests: establishment of a new post of a Union Minister for Foreign Affairs, extension of qualified majority voting (QMV) in questions pertaining to foreign policy, boosting of Union-level funding and cooperation forms for such activities, and introduction of a new solidarity clause obliging member states to assist each other by all means in their power in case one of them becomes victim of aggression; measures for developing common defence capacities were mentioned as well (Inter-Governmental Conference of the European Union 2004). Regardless of the possibility that some of these measures may enter the EU agenda even in the absence of a formal constitutional treaty, it is probably safe to assume that criticism of the Union's interest aggregation capacity will not disappear overnight.

Taken together, the theses of a lack of common identity and interests – even when conceived in a less critical light – have led to sceptical predictions as to whether the EU could ever become a 'complete power', not merely a 'civilian power'. This 'civilian power of Europe' image, which was originally suggested as the Union's strength by François Duchêne in 1972, builds on the Union's evident economic weight – presently the world's largest single economic area with around 22 per cent of world GDP – which for long has failed to transform into corresponding military–political muscle. Perhaps not even the creation of the Union's 60,000-strong rapid reaction corps during 1999–2003 and the gradual, albeit painful, development of the Common Foreign and Security Policy (CFSP) and European Security and Defence Policy (ESDP), especially since the 1999 EU Council summit in Helsinki, are likely to swiftly alter the perception of critical observers like Hoffmann. For him, without tangible military power the EU can only ever be a 'second-rate actor on the diplomatic and strategic chessboard of world affairs' (Hoffman 2000: 190).

The third Westphalian claim relates to the actual capability of the EU to conduct effective foreign policy. Hill formulated his famous 'capability–expectations gap' thesis in 1993. He was inspired by how the then European Community (EC) was 'talked up' during the process of drafting the Maastricht treaty which finally transformed the EC into the EU after its ratification in 1993. According to Hill, the Union had been unable to agree a clear strategy on its CEE enlargement and on its contribution to solving the problems ensuing from the dissolution of Yugoslavia. The gap had assumed a dangerous extent, where for example the Baltic states could take excessive risks in order to approach the EU, or the Union itself could adopt unrealistic policies towards them. To prevent such a scenario, either the Union's capabilities would have to be increased or expectations decreased (see Hill 1993: 315). By 1998, Roy Ginsberg (1998: 431–2) argued that the gap was closing. Expectations were gradually becoming lowered and capabilities increased. Since then, the emergence of the ESDP and the Union's project for a Constitutional Treaty have again raised expectations. However, the fears shown by the US and the new members of the Union, such as the Balts, of the EU possibly posing a challenge to NATO (see Chapters 5–7), seem to balance the equation. Quite simply, were there no perception of the EU capabilities slowly approaching expectations, the fears of duplicating the EU and NATO functions would not exist, especially in a context where NATO's continued relevance in day-to-day policy making is increasingly questioned.

These Westphalian claims will be contested in this book by looking at the northern European case and in particular how the EU has in a short span of time gone on to develop distinct identities and interests pertaining to ordering the region. They now show up in the form of statements, acts and policy processes where key EU figures and institutions, and substantial funds, are involved, and where a great many parties are deeply affected. It will also emerge that in northern Europe the capability–expectations gap has been closing quite rapidly. In order to see the multiple effects of the Union's ordering of northern Europe, we need to adopt a broad view of EU foreign policy going beyond the limitations of Westphalian understandings.

Towards a broad view of EU foreign policy

Despite the frequency of Westphalian critique of EU foreign policy, it is probably fair to say that the majority of studies are now taking a broad view of the subject (cf. Tonra 2000: 164). The broad view of EU foreign policy does not only include CFSP actions under the Union's 'II pillar', which was instituted by the Maastricht treaty. Also included in this broad view of EU foreign policy are 'community/I pillar' actions. Their origin dates back to the Union's early days and to how its foreign economic and trade relations were arranged then. Finally, there are the external effects of 'justice and home affairs/III pillar' issues. They include the impact of the Union's management of its border and migration policies towards neighbouring countries and regions.[4]

It has been argued that foreign policy related activities within each pillar have shown signs of convergence (Whitman 1998: 236, 240). Yet some authors continue to separate CFSP actions from the other pillars in the same manner as the Union itself does (e.g. Archer 2002: 23–4; Wessels 2000: 25). The broad view of EU foreign policy that I introduce here avoids copying the Union's own, confusing practice of simultaneously speaking of both 'foreign policy' (II pillar) and 'external relations' (some policies under the I and III pillars). This distinction is hard to sustain outside the famously clumsy 'EU-speak'. Also within the Union's own institutions there are determinate efforts to abolish the outdated pillar structure, as shown by the project of drafting the Constitutional Treaty, which would have created precisely such an effect. On this basis, the problem of having to determine whether the EU has foreign policy outside the CFSP is largely bypassed in this book. It is simply argued that *what is said and done to others under the EU flag, either by representatives of the Union institutions or by member states, and what these 'others' take as EU action, can conveniently be understood to connote EU foreign policy.*

Whether a particular activity is driven or regulated by the I, II or III pillar is here deemed a peripheral consideration. It is far more important to consider the regional policy *impact* of various EU activities: how do the affected states and regions in northern Europe respond to broadly understood EU foreign policy activities? What is the position of the Nordic countries, which were traditionally responsible for integration projects within the region? Do the Baltic states mostly approve of EU policies, or would they rather see some alternative policies carried out in their region? What type of subjectivity are they willing to grant to the Union in northern Europe? What about Russia and its northwestern regions, which have, with EU enlargements, acquired a long border with the Union and, in the process, have become increasingly affected by the existence of that new border? As a result of these processes, what sort of a Union are we witnessing in northern Europe?

The broad view of EU foreign policy as operating within different spheres and extending to several competence areas helps us to see what unique foreign policy tools the Union possesses that are normally not available for Westphalian states. Enlargement policy is a good example. It has a tremendous impact not only on new accession states, their neighbours and foreign relations elsewhere, as will be shown, but also including enlargement policy into the analysis helps us to take a note of the manner in which the Union itself has diversified as a consequence of the northern European and CEE enlargements. Many authors are now arguing that more federative arrangements will only be possible among a core group of 'old' members who are better prepared for such a course of action than the new entrants. They are still in many respects experiencing transformation problems after the collapse of the socialist system in 1989–91 (Zielonka 2001; Zielonka and Mair 2002). This view on the present, enlarged Union, and especially on its likeliest future forms, draws attention to the differences between the most integrated member states and those who are less integrated, including 'reluctant' or 'awkward' Europeans like Denmark and the United Kingdom (UK), newcomers like Baltic states, accession states like Romania at the time of writing and potential membership aspirants like Ukraine. Quite naturally, growing diversity within the Union also brings with it new identities, interests and capacities, as well as handicaps, into its foreign policy.

The broad view of EU foreign policy I suggest here maintains that the manifest geopolitical form of the EU – whether federal or something different, as I will argue – results from processes whereby variously integrated and otherwise EU-bound and EU-impacted agents assign subjectivity to the Union, or refuse to do so, and the way in which the Union correspondingly puts that subjectivity into practice by trying to create and maintain particular regional orders. This *intersubjective moment* is what in broadest terms differentiates my geopolitical subjectivity approach from previous approaches to EU foreign policy. The construction of geopolitical subjectivity is a more fundamental phenomenon, with federal and other manifest forms of political organization being more about the 'surface' of the EU entity that we are all so used to identifying. In other words, processes of constructing geopolitical subjectivity may lead to a Westphalian, Westphalian-federal or other manifest form of political organization with its peculiar consequences for foreign policy making (Chapter 3).

Although this approach can be situated close to the camps arguing for a broad view of EU foreign policy and for the prevalence of increasing diversity within the enlarging Union, in broader metatheoretical terms this study can be considered *constructivist*. This means a focus on how intersubjective actions relate to the material reality of European integration, like arguments and views put forth by the old and new members, and the EU's neighbours, of the shape of the Union's desirable geopolitical subjectivity and their own position with regard to it (see, for example, Adler 1997; Wendt 1995; cf. Glarbo 1999). Alongside discussion of what emerges from around 300 documents produced by EU institutions, new and old member states and Russia, and the exposition of views of EU officials and policy makers in the Baltic states and Russia as revealed in thirty-eight expert interviews and specifically arranged Q methodological field experiments, I will also discuss issues pertaining to material reality like trade patterns within the northern European area and other factors of international political economy, which for their part influence what sort of an EU subject is emerging and what positions various agents can take with regard to it.

On the whole, the purpose of the new theoretical approach is to increase our understanding of the various ways in which the EU impacts the political praxis of international relations in northern Europe and of how it has become part of the perceptions and calculations of other agents in the region. The focus of this book will in this sense be less on explaining the EU's activities against conventional templates, or in relation to conventional theories, and more on charting some new territory while simultaneously challenging some claims made in previous literature.

Plan of the book

The following three chapters look in more detail at how the EU has become a northern European subject, accentuating the emergence of the Union's identities and interests towards the region. Chapter 2 charts the early stages of the process until the mid-1990s. This is the EU's encounter with *Norden* – the group of the Nordic states – and the manner in which the EU in the process helped to erase a lot of the peculiarities that were still left from this unique bloc at the beginning of the post-Cold War era. Issues to be discussed include the reunification of Germany, the EU membership of Denmark, Finland and Sweden, Norway's failed accession, Iceland's failure to start an EU debate, and the manner in which the Baltic Sea and Barents Sea region-building activities launched by these northern states gradually became EU-designed and eventually renamed as 'northern *European* cooperation'.

Chapter 3 takes up the even bigger challenge for the EU – that of encountering the post-Soviet space in northern Europe – and moves the argument towards a more theoretical direction. Northern Europe represents the only instance where the Union has actually crossed the borders of the former Soviet Union. The discussion includes the impact of the accession of the Baltic states and Poland, the Union's arranging of its relations with Russia by means of the EU–Russian strategic partnership and the EU–Russian regional cooperation within the ND framework. It will be argued that by integrating parts of the post-Soviet space – the Baltic states – the Union posed itself a very demanding identity and interest project, as it in fact set out to erase some of the remaining traits of post-Soviet order in northern Europe and in the end expanded its own subjectivity. In this sense, the EU threw a clear challenge to Russia's traditional sphere of influence in the region.

As a result of all this we can identify not a Westphalian but a concentric geopolitical form emerging for the Union, with the centre consisting of EU institutions and surrounded first by closely integrated insiders, then less integrated semi-insiders and finally close outsiders/semi-outsiders like Russia and its northwestern regions. Mapping these developments gives me grounds in the concluding part of the chapter to conceptualize the EU's impact on its northern European fringes into a more detailed theoretical model outlining the geopolitical subjectivity approach. The concept of geopolitical subjectivity is broken into its identity and interest components, with the former including the *time* and *space* aspects, and the latter the aspects of *geo-policy* and *geo-strategy*.

Chapter 4 puts the theoretical model of geopolitical subjectivity into practice by analysing the EU's efforts of ordering northern Europe, discussing its identity- and interest-based drivers and the actual policy tools such as enlargement, the Schengen borders policy, the Common Strategy on Russia (CSR), the Partnership and Cooperation Agreement (PCA) with Russia, and the regional level frameworks and funding channels that started to centre around the ND towards the turn of the millennium. The main claim is that the Union is forming a strategic gaze on the northern European region as part of its overall subject-construction process. At the same time, it is clear that the whole constellation of the EU's northern European geo-policies remains double-edged, being divided into universalizing policies, intended to apply uniformly across regions, and regionalizing policies such as the ND that confront new challenges with the emergence of the Union's neighbourhood policy.

Chapters 5 to 8 push the analysis to the intersubjective direction by discussing the views held in Estonia, Latvia and Lithuania, who are termed new semi-insiders to the Union, and in close outsiders/semi-outsiders Russia and its northwestern parts, of the development of the EU's subjectivity in northern Europe. These cases are selected for closer scrutiny as they pose a particularly demanding challenge to the EU by including the problems of post-Soviet order, and thus the issue of inter-imperial rivalry between the EU and Russia. In other words, these cases are assumed to pose a severe test to the EU's subjectivity. A detailed look is presented on how the Balts' and Russians' views of the EU's subjectivity in northern Europe have evolved since the 1990s. Interviews with Baltic and Russian EU experts – policy makers, politicians, observers – will be used to illustrate the perceptions and experiences of growing EU subjectivity within Europe's northern borders.

Chapter 9 finally pulls together all this intersubjective analysis and attempts to locate the extent to which the views held by the scrutinized new semi-insiders and close outsiders/semi-outsiders in the European north are different from each other and whether they have anything in common regarding how the Union should build its subjectivity in the region. With the help of an experimental technique – Q methodology, which makes use of the subjective perceptions of a carefully selected respondent group – a thin common ground is located. However, a much more prevalent trait is divergence, and three different views are uncovered, plus a strongly eurosceptic minority perspective. One of the interesting issues arising from this analysis is that, whereas the consulted Baltic respondents express only two coherent views, the selected Kaliningradian respondents are scattered across all three views. This indicates that being a 'semi-outsider' is not necessarily a uniform experience, and that the Union's borders are indeed in this sense fuzzy, failing to follow precisely the concentric model built analytically in the previous chapters. In fact, from this perspective and on the basis of other findings of the book, it becomes clear that the circles of the concentrically formed EU subject are best conceived of as not entirely and only concentric, but mutually overlapping as well.

Overall, the research results of the book do not lend much support to any other manifest form of geopolitical subjectivity for the Union than a continued but constantly evolving concentric order with some important mutual overlaps across the circles. In this sense, the whole process of making the EU's wider northern Europe – from Denmark's accession in the early 1970s to events in the 1990s and the new millennium – is part of the overall process of making a concentric Europe with territorially and functionally overlapping borders. This is also the forecast for the upcoming decade that this book will dare to make.

2   The EU encounters *Norden*

The EU's encounter with *Norden* took full shape only in the early and mid-1990s when Denmark's EU membership was complemented by the emergence of a wider Nordic attention in the Union's direction. This wider EU–*Norden* encounter constituted the early stages of the Union's north European engagement. In the case of *Norden*, the Union encountered a historically developed, primarily socio-cultural but also partly political group consisting of Denmark, Finland, Iceland, Norway and Sweden. *Norden* represented the main regional project in northern Europe during the Cold War era. Underlying the wider EU–*Norden* encounter must be seen the broader context of post-Cold War structural changes in global and European politics, such as the end of the bipolar rivalry between the West and the Soviet Union (USSR) and the eventual collapse of the USSR. Although the effects of these changes for the EU relations of a northern country like Denmark (member of the EC since 1973) were not profoundly dramatic, for Finland in particular, and to a lesser extent for Sweden, the collapse of the Soviet Union was of importance and for its own part helped to prompt the EU membership application. And for the EU–*Norden* relationship on the whole, the post-Cold War strategic changes created an entirely new situation, erasing the geopolitical arrangement known as 'Nordic balance'.

The Nordic balance referred to the relatively low tension that prevailed in the Nordic area during the Cold War era as compared to the very direct East–West confrontation in mainland Europe, at the strict borderline between the West and East. The Nordic balance entailed that Denmark and Norway kept a low profile in NATO, not allowing the stationing of foreign troops or nuclear weapons on their mainland territories, or the arranging of military exercises in the vicinity of the Danish island of Bornholm in the Baltic Sea and the Norwegian–Russian border in the north. In return, Sweden stayed mostly neutral in its publicly presented policies, although later on the fairly close, covert military–political ties of Sweden with the West and NATO have been made public. Finland tried to maintain its independence by declaring neutrality, and the Soviet Union, for its part, abstained from invoking the military consultation paragraphs in the Finnish–Soviet Friendship, Cooperation and Mutual Assistance (FCMA) Treaty (Mouritzen 2001: 297–8; Vaahtoranta and Forsberg 2000: 8–9). In a sense, the strictly security political nature of the Nordic balance at the same time connoted a north European region mostly lacking the involvement of the EC, which at the time lacked an explicit security policy, with its overall foreign policy also being at its early stages of development (Figure 2.1).

The disappearance of the Nordic balance at the turn of the 1990s was part of the opening up of a new and wider northern European political space, and it is the process of how the EU initially became drawn into defining that space and how it simultaneously encountered *Norden* that is of interest in this chapter, as well as the consequences of these processes. In the following section, I start charting the early stages of the development of the Union's 'north Europeanness' and discuss the impact of Germany's reunification at the dawn of the post-Cold War era, and the peculiarities of the EU–Danish relationship from the Cold War era to the mid-1990s, with some references also made to Iceland's position. In the third section, a contrast will be shown regarding the effects of the Union's 1995 Nordic enlargement,[1] i.e. Finland's and Sweden's EU accession, as well as the repercussions of Norway's failed accession. Thereafter, in the fourth section I will proceed to argue how in the early and mid-1990s the relative significance of *Norden* within the geopolitical map of northern Europe was eroded in an important manner by the Baltic Sea region-building efforts initiated by Germany and Denmark as 'old' EU members and even more pronounced efforts by the then new members Finland and Sweden, and to a slightly lesser extent Norway's promotion of Barents Sea cooperation in the north. In the concluding section of the chapter, I acknowledge that some important elements of *Norden* still remain. Yet it is clear that the developments in the early and mid-1990s and thereafter led the northern European region to lose many of its exclusively Nordic characteristics. Northern Europe

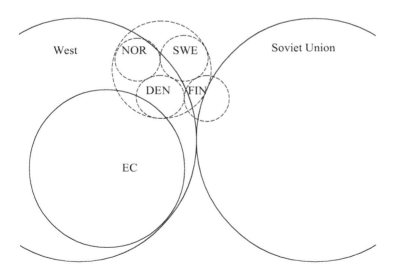

Figure 2.1 The Cold War era Nordic balance.

became a meeting ground of the European integration process and the German and Nordic sponsored region-building projects. This for its own part helped the EU to familiarize itself with Poland and what I will call the 'post-Soviet north', i.e. the Baltic states and Russia's northwest.

German reunification and the EU–Danish relationship

For the EC, which at the turn of the 1990s was debating the Maastricht Treaty and its implications for building EU foreign policy, it was important that German reunification took place in 'western European' terms. The fact that the reunified Germany became a member of the EU and NATO instead of opting for neutrality was finally blessed during the early part of 1991 in the 'two plus four' negotiations between the two German sides and the victorious allies of the Second World War who originally divided Germany and Berlin. The most important single factor was the last Soviet President Mikhail Gorbachev's acceptance of the reunification (Hubel 2004a: 351; Wæver 1996: 37). After all, until then the eastern parts of Germany had functioned as the western outpost of the Soviet army, contributing to the militarization of the Baltic Sea shores. Although the series of events preceding the 1990 German–Soviet agreement is worth a study of its own, it will suffice here to simply discuss briefly what consequences Germany's reunification had for the development of the Union's 'north Europeanness' in the early 1990s.

At the sheer geographic plane, reunification increased Germany's coastline on the Baltic Sea by 250 km eastwards. The notion of 'eastwards' is important here, as the German word denoting the Baltic Sea is *Ostsee* (Eastern Sea). Therefore, what might seem like Germany's further opening up to the Baltic Sea and towards the north does not actually have any direct implications for a strengthened northern Europe, but rather implications for a relinking of the former West and East (Schmalz 2000: 216). This is very indicative of the ambiguity of how Germany's reunification relates to the process of the Union acquiring subjectivity in northern Europe. Almost regardless of the angle from which one looks at the issue, the conclusion will hold that, since Bismarck's times and the birth of the German state in the late nineteenth century, Germany's *Mittellage* – being located literally in the centre of Europe – has made Germany very important to various parts of Europe and yet, at the same time, this location has made Germany at times ambiguous towards the various edges of Europe, be they in the west, east, north or south. The German ambiguity towards the north deserves a few specifying comments.

In the post-Cold War era, after an initial but short period of confusion, it became fairly quickly obvious that a reunified Germany would continue to be committed to the EU and NATO. However, almost immediately afterwards some fears emerged regarding possible new German assertiveness in these organizations which have a pivotal role in Europe at large (Bach and Peters 2002: 11). Yet, whatever one thinks of the relevance of such fears, Germany's mostly unambiguous commitment to transatlantic cooperation until its refusal to support the US-led war in Iraq in 2003, and especially to the promotion of European integration as an overall project for Europe's healing after the Second World War, have ensured that less energy has been channelled to promoting the EU's subjectivity in northern Europe. These priorities are coupled with the strong German interest in central Europe and Germany's special relations with Russia, which can easily be traced back to the legacy of the West German *Ostpolitik* since the late 1960s, and which later led to Germany's strong role in the launching of the Union's relations with Russia. Taking all this into account, it is clear that, in German diplomacy, northern Europe is always subordinated to these wider goals. In particular, in German eyes, Russia can never be fitted into the northern European context alone in the way that the Nordics might perceive their relationship with that country. And added to the handicaps of German diplomacy in northern Europe are also the historical pressures related to Germany's *Mittellage* location and the real-political developments associated with such a location in the past.

First, there are the sensitivities of the Balts. They were ruled for centuries by the Baltic German nobility, first from the thirteenth century on within the Swedish kingdom, and finally as German-administered parts of Tsarist Russia until 1917 and the advent of Baltic independence. Subsequently, after two decades of independence (1918–40), the Baltic states were occupied by Nazi Germany in the Second World War, before they ended up as the Soviet Union's possessions for almost half a century. Second, Poland was also occupied by Nazi Germany. During the early 1990s, some Polish worries resurfaced regarding the re-emergence of a strong Germany (Mouritzen 1996c: 276). Third, Russia's Kaliningrad region on the southeastern shores of the Baltic Sea, or Königsberg in German, has a long-running history as a German territory. It is the former northern part of East Prussia, which subsequently became a war conquest of the Soviet Union. This new status was confirmed after the Potsdam conference in 1945. The German legacy of the region, coupled with demands to return the region to Germany by right-wing parties and organizations of former East Prussians, made both Germany and Russia sensitive towards German influences in Kaliningrad. These sensitivities prevail regardless of the German recognition of its present borders in several international treaties, for example in connection with the reunification (Oldberg 1998: 17–19; for Denmark, see below; see also Chapter 8).

Under the shadow of such higher-order priorities as the EU and NATO, Central Europe and Russia, and historically grounded suspicions of the Balts and Russians, it is noteworthy that northern Europe has witnessed German region-building activities. These projects have been promoted most forcibly by the north German *Länder*, and they primarily fall into the category of 'low' politics. They have therefore admittedly failed to form very high-ranking priorities for German diplomacy on the whole (see below). Thus, overall, one must say that, concerning the development of the EU's subjectivity in northern Europe, German reunification remained a relatively inconclusive event (cf. Mouritzen 1996c: 262). It is true that with the reunification Germany became a European great power again but, in a stark contradistinction to Bismarck's era and the era between the World Wars, this took place in the mediating framework of supranational integration within the EU. The result was the strengthening of Germany's role as one of the constituent powers of peaceful European integration on the whole, and more focus on the

Union's relations with Russia, whereas the explicit northern European implications of the reunification remained structural, and in actual terms even somewhat shadowy.

The relative inconclusiveness of German reunification vis-à-vis the EU's 'north Europeanness' in a sense only followed the pattern set earlier by Denmark's accession to the EU's predecessor, the EC, in 1973, together with Britain and Ireland. Like Germany, Denmark has a history as a great power. However, Denmark lost its possessions in Schleswig-Holstein (to Germany), Norway (to Sweden) and Iceland (with Iceland achieving independence in 1944) during the nineteenth and twentieth centuries and became a small Danish nation-state. It is hence understandable that the country's EC accession did not signify a big push for European integration. Rather, for the EU, Danish accession meant a somewhat 'reluctant' new member (Miljan 1977), although not perhaps such an 'awkward' partner as the UK, as famously termed by Stephen George (1998). For the majority of Denmark's political elite and the broader public, it was clear that the image of *Norden* constituted a far more important socio-cultural and political reference group than 'Europe'.

There are several reasons for the strong position of *Norden* in the Danish mental map. *Norden* relied on a rich history, extending from the 1397–1523 Kalmar Union to the Scandinavian movement aiming to establish a unified Scandinavian polity in the 1830s, and to the establishment of institutions such as the inter-parliamentary organization the Nordic Council (1952), a common labour market (1954), common social security provision (1955), a passports union (1957) and the Nordic Council of Ministers (NCM, 1972), which has its permanent administration in Copenhagen (Joenniemi and Lehti 2003: 131–2). The extent of integration these Nordic institutions introduced in their own time far exceeded the level prevailing in Western Europe in many important respects, practically realizing free movement of workforce from one Nordic country to another. That was in practice facilitated by the inter-Nordic language ties within the Scandinavian language family, with predominantly Finno-Ugric Finland linking up with its two official languages (Finnish and Swedish) and a traditional Swedish-speaking minority. In the midst of Cold War divisions, but partly as a result of the shield of relatively low tensions provided by the Nordic balance arrangement, *Norden* was for many an exemplary integration project predating what happened only decades later on a European-wide scale.

It was therefore only natural that the bulk of the Danes preferred to take mainly an economic attitude towards European integration. In fact, at the time this was a relatively correct idea. The economy was the dominant sector of European integration. In the foreign political and socio-cultural sense, the Danes identified themselves mainly with *Norden*. And what must be kept in mind here is that, in the historical perspective, one of the claimed political interests underlying the construction of *Norden* was to delimit German influences in northern Europe, especially when keeping in mind the troubled history of German–Danish relations (Østergaard 1997: 29). In the socio-cultural or identity political sense, in the eyes of many, *Norden* functioned as a democratic, progressive, Protestant and egalitarian region distinct from Catholic, conservative and capitalistic Europe (Sørensen and Stråth 1997: 22). These long-lasting Danish perceptions helped *Norden* to remain the main regional project in northern Europe until the turn of the 1990s.

It is illustrative of Denmark's balancing act between European integration and *Norden*[2] to take a look at how both the 'yes' and 'no' camps in the 1972 Danish accession referendum accepted that *Norden* should in all conditions constitute an important element of Danish identity and interests. In the referendum and afterwards, the 'yes' side argued that *Norden* could not pose a real alternative to the promotion of Danish economic interests in 'Europe', which are particularly strong in the agricultural sector and especially towards the British Isles where a large part of Danish agricultural exports go (Hansen 2002: 62–3; cf. Ingebritsen 1998). However, the 'yes' side argued that Denmark should take the economic advantages of 'Europe' through the construction of a '*Norden* in Europe'. The 'no' side, by contrast, argued that the Danes had to make a choice between Europe and *Norden*.

In any case, from the 1970s to the time the EC was about to transform itself to the EU with the Maastricht Treaty and the subsequent referendums in 1992–3, the mainstream Danish views of 'Europe' were notably coloured by economic considerations. This led to a Danish position that the plans for a deeper integration in Europe not only in the economic but also in the security and foreign political, societal and other policy sectors were unrealistic, and something with which the Danes, representing *Norden*, need not concern themselves (Hansen 2002: 50–64). This state of affairs thwarted the plans of the Danish elite of abandoning Denmark's traditional 'reluctant' posture towards European integration at the face of the dramatic changes of the early 1990s (Mouritzen 1996c: 271) and meant that, on the whole, Denmark was ill prepared to face the deepening and widening of EU integration.

Denmark's subsequent rejection of the Maastricht Treaty in the 1993 referendum led to the Edinburgh Agreement or, when viewed from the Danish side, to the so-called 'national compromise'. Denmark was allowed to abstain from Union citizenship, common justice and police affairs, the single currency and the common defence policy (Hansen 2002: 73, 80). In this way, Denmark rapidly moved further away from the loosely defined EU centre that as a result of the Maastricht Treaty was forming around Brussels, and became a 'semi-insider' in the ever closer Union (cf. Kelstrup 2000). But the Danish opt-outs did not prevent the Union from extending its integration process to northern Europe. By the early 1990s, such prospects were no longer dependent on the Danes. Much more important here was how Finland, Sweden and Norway started reconsidering their position. Denmark's former colony Iceland, for its part, never really managed to start a proper debate on Europe. Iceland was the first country to recognize Lithuania's declaration of independence in 1990, and together with Denmark the first to establish diplomatic relations with the Baltic states during the Soviet Union's failed August 1991 *coup d'état*. Later Iceland participated in Baltic Sea and Barents Sea region-building even though it is geographically distant from both regions. But its failure to ever really build on these initial steps, coupled with its small size and reservations (related to fisheries issues) towards EU membership contributed to its remaining sidelined in the new developments (see Kristinsson 1996; Mouritzen and Wivel 2005b: 175).

Europe and *Norden* in Finland, Sweden and Norway

The manner in which Finland, Sweden and Norway became parties to the Union's 1995 enlargement process showed well how the EU integration issue was fragmenting the relative degree of political unity that had existed within the Nordic balance arrangement and *Norden*. The Norwegian government applied for membership in 1992, and in 1994 it issued a pro-'yes' recommendation to the Norwegian public after the successful conclusion of Norway's accession negotiations. However, this recommendation was defeated in the ensuing referendum on membership. Sweden's application in 1991 took Finnish policy makers by surprise, and Finland's application was submitted slightly later in 1992. Thereafter the Swedish and Finnish publics voted 'yes' and simultaneously accepted the Maastricht Treaty provisions and other EU legislation with some minor exceptions and transition periods. Combined with the Danish 'national compromise' on the Maastricht Treaty, these processes and their divergent outcomes in the building of EU–Nordic relationships created an entirely new context for the rich historical legacy of Nordic cooperation.

Norway had actually applied for EC membership two times before its 1970 application was accepted. Negotiations were concluded for the first Norwegian referendum on EU membership in 1972. The resulting first Norwegian 'no' in 1972 did not signal a death stroke for the idea of political *Norden*, although Denmark concurrently opted for membership. However, the Norwegian 1994 'no' vote contributed precisely to the demise of political *Norden*. The vote was determined by 52.2 per cent of votes against membership and 47.8 per cent in favour of it. In short, it signified the end to efforts at maintaining Nordic political cooperation in the post-Cold War era, even in the diluted sense of creating a Nordic bloc within the EU. The geographically and politically rather strictly delimited *Norden*, which never came to include such far-reaching integration projects as a single currency and common foreign and security policy, had as a political project become overrun by the more ambitious, universal and expansion-geared project of the EU.

As for explaining the Norwegian 'no' in 1994, the main lines of the scholarly opinion go between the liberal-intergovernmentalists who postulate *interests* as the decisive factor in the Nordics' EU applications, and those who instead focus on *identities*, and who could in the broadest sense be termed constructivists, or perhaps more precisely poststructuralists. For example, in her much-discussed, 'modified liberal-intergovernmentalist' book *The Nordic States and European Unity* (1998), Christine Ingebritsen claims that sectoral economic interests within Norway accounted for how the country could afford to stay outside, at least for the time being. After the discovery of considerable oil resources in the 1960s, during the following decades Norway became an oil-led economy, with the oil sector accounting for one-third of Norwegian exports. With the oil revenue, Norway developed an ability to subsidize the agricultural and fisheries sectors in a country with harsh northern climatic conditions. In Ingebritsen's liberal-intergovernmentalist explanation, these sectoral interests then made a strong case for staying outside the EU, which had developed particularly strong common policies in the agricultural and fisheries sectors. The result was a disadvantageous integration scenario for Norway (Ingebritsen 1998: 45, 119, 129–43).

However, Iver Neumann argues that the main reason was not an interest-based one as Ingebritsen claims, but rather identity-grounded. Neumann notes that in 1972 the agricultural and fisheries sectors were able to contribute to the emergence of a 'no' vote, at a time when there were not yet oil-generated subsidies for these sectors. According to Neumann, the underlying reason in both the 1972 and 1994 'no' votes was not oil, but that the peasants and fishermen were able to use the power of identity politics and portray themselves as the embodiment of the Norwegian nation in a completely different manner from the Oslo-based political elite, who were not seen as the 'real owners' of Norwegian territory. The supposed centralization emanating from Brussels would threaten to cut the prospects for maintaining a lively Norwegian countryside, and the 'real' Norwegian identity cultivated therein (Neumann 2002).

Crucially, the same division into interest- and identity-based explanations can also be found in the scholarly analyses of the Swedish and Finnish EU membership applications and the subsequent successful accessions of these two Nordic states in 1995. For example Lee Miles (1996: 63–5) argues that in both countries economic considerations predominated. In Sweden's case, the long-standing economic recession at the turn of the 1990s and the slow progress in the negotiations for the treaty on the European Economic Area (EEA) – linking the EU with the then European Free Trade Area (EFTA) members like Finland, Sweden and Norway[3] – meant that the Swedish government perceived EU membership as the only credible cure. In contrast to EEA membership, it would also give Sweden a voice in decision-making. Finland was experiencing a similar recession to Sweden's, and frustration with the slowly proceeding EEA negotiations. All of this was aggravated by the collapse of the once so lucrative Finnish–Soviet trade. In these conditions, Sweden's application pushed Finland to lodge its own application. According to Ingebritsen, it was the structure of the manufacturing sector in Sweden and Finland and the sectoral interests resulting from therein that guaranteed popular support for the idea of joining the EU, which initially was perhaps somewhat alien for these Nordic electorates. Export-led economies and dependency on EU markets meant that the most significant trade unions and interest groups were bound to recommend a 'yes' vote to their constituencies in order to save jobs (Ingebritsen 1998: 143–56).

In the other camp, Lars Trädgårdh (2002), Pertti Joenniemi (2002) and Sami Moisio (2003a), for example, hint that the structure of identities rather than the pressures emanating from sectoral economic interests helped to tilt the balance in Sweden and Finland in favour of joining. For the Swedish Social Democratic 'yes' side, EU membership was not about a Danish-style mere taking of economic benefits from EU integration while looking over the other shoulder towards the

Nordic direction and partly inwards. Rather, it was about confidently bringing *Norden* and Nordic identities to other Europeans to learn and embrace as a model. Although the Swedish Greens, the Left Party and half of the Social Democratic grassroots opposed 'going to Europe' on the grounds that it stood for a less developed modernity – submission to Catholic and formerly colonial Europe which is not a proper *Gemeinschaft* community in the sense of *Norden* – the outcome was a fairly comfortable 52.3 per cent in favour of joining (see Trädgårdh 2002: 165–72). However, support levels for the Union have since then been among the lowest within the EU.

In Finland's case, EU membership was not about accommodating the 'European' with the 'Nordic' as in Sweden or, to a lesser extent, Denmark. Rather, it was about viewing 'Europeanness' as something which could easily coexist alongside 'Nordicity' and 'Finnishness' (Joenniemi 2002: 206). Lauri Karvonen and Bengt Sundelius (1996: 255–7) argue that Finland's centralized and elite-based style of decision-making in foreign policy questions enabled such flexibility in questions of belonging. It helped to construct Finland, *Norden* and Europe as mutually compatible (see Joenniemi 2002). Sami Moisio develops the identity argumentation even further and claims that, in the Finnish EU membership campaign, in the end those who portrayed *Norden* as an old-fashioned Cold War era arrangement prevailed. During the Cold War, for the Finns, *Norden* had ensured a connection to Europe in the midst of Soviet pressure on Finland's independence, but now, with the collapse of the Soviet Union, a direct connection to Europe became available in the form of EU membership. Whereas the victorious side argued that Nordic cooperation could only maintain its relevance within the Union, and even then at best in a considerably rebuilt form, their opponents lost the battle as they portrayed 'Europe' and 'Norden' as difficult concepts to merge (Moisio 2003a: 229–34).

Apart from economic interests and identity political considerations a more popular sort of explanation as to why Finland joined the EU relates to traditional security political concerns. Especially during the final stages of the campaign for the EU membership referendum, security issues were put on the table. The rapid dissolving of Finland's former position as a partly Soviet-leaning neutral state within the Nordic balance created an opportunity and a need to rethink the country's security solutions, although Finland's reliance on territorial defence and a large, well trained army continued. On this plane the reasoning related to the soft security guarantees offered by EU membership against possible Russian revisionism. The so-called 'Zhirinovsky effect' resulting from the populist and nationalist Vladimir Zhirinovsky doing well in the December 1993 parliamentary elections in Russia boosted such perceptions (Mouritzen 1996d: 146). At that time the debate on developing the Union's own foreign and security political capacity was already in progress, and membership in the forthcoming single currency might act as a further soft guarantee – Finland's former imperial patron might simply be unwilling to risk relations with a large economic bloc with which it was in an interdependent economic relationship (Chapter 8). According to Teija Tiilikainen (2001: 97), the security argument explains well the very pro-European policies of Finland after accession and the continuously high level of popular support for membership.

On the whole, these identity/interest-coloured cases of the EU accession processes and resulting EU relationship arrangements of Norway, Sweden and Finland led to a highly differentiated *Norden*. Denmark had opted out for an uneasy 'national compromise' between the nation and Europe, and in the new situation, even for the Danes, it became very difficult to think of *Norden* as some sort of a viable alternative to anchor oneself. Norway remained outside the Union and only became a member of a diluted EEA arrangement together with Iceland. Since then, both countries have been forced to adopt EU-induced practices in various fields, for instance in the field of border controls, in order to maintain the Scandinavian Passports Union in a situation where Denmark, Finland and Sweden were implementing the EU's border regulations, as agreed on within the Union's Schengen treaty, on their own borders. In fact, both Norway and Iceland now apply the EU's Schengen borders regime and actually patrol the Union's northernmost borders, even though they are not members of the EU (!). Sweden, for its part, sought to export *Norden* to Europe, and Finland decided to redefine its European and Nordic vocations. Taken together, this all finally opened up the Nordic region to the EU's gaze in a completely different manner from ever before.

To this must be added how in the early 1990s Germany and the Nordics started to practise specific, both interest- and identity-motivated region-building politics in the context of the Baltic Sea. These region-building efforts were directed towards engaging Germany, the Nordics, the Baltic states, Poland and Russia in a new mode of cooperation after the historically built tensions between Germany/ *Norden* and the Soviet Union/Russia, and Baltic states and Russia, which in many cases were only sharpened as a result of the Cold War era experiences. With the risk of over-generalizing, it can be said that, apart from its special relations with Russia, Germany linked up with Estonia and Latvia, and adopted a somewhat cautious approach to Kaliningrad due to the historical sensitivities mentioned above. Finland directed its main attention to Estonia and to Russia's northwestern territories on its own Russian border that it brought with it to the EU. Sweden developed distinctively close relations with Latvia (but also close relations with Estonia), and Denmark with Lithuania and Kaliningrad, whereas Norway was particularly active in the very north and the Arctic on its own Russian border (cf. Tiilikainen 2003: 19; see below).

These patterns of multilateral and bilateral ties meant that to the EU's sight emerged identities and interests opening up not only to the Nordic region, but also to the wider area of northern Europe. The accession of new members with northern identities, and interests in the Baltic Sea and the wider north European region, and the new strategic context of the post-Cold War era prompted the Union to take a new look at the north after its southern or Mediterranean bias of the 1980s enlargements. In fact, the biggest change was that, whereas in the case of the Nordics' arranging of their EU relations in the early and mid-1990s it was *their* identities and interests that were at issue, now, when these identities and interests were imported into the Union context, the *EU as a whole slowly started to formulate identities and interests towards the region.* In this sense, the EU–*Norden* encounter laid the foundations for the EU acquiring subjectivity in northern Europe.

The EU and northern European region-building of the 1990s

In the early 1990s, the EU was developing its own regional approach in order to give voice to the regional level where a substantial part of Union policies were and are still implemented. Although the Union's Committee of Regions was established in 1991, in the context of the Baltic Sea region (BSR), the Union encountered a regional setting quite different from what it had encountered in connection to earlier enlargement rounds.

In the early and mid-1990s, the BSR was an area characterized by a rapidly building network of German- and Nordic-initiated regional organizations that can with good reasons claim to be unique not only in the European but also in a global context. The unique character of region-building in the BSR stemmed from the dense network initiated by self-conscious region builders promoting *both* intergovernmental and sub-state level regional organizations and activities. Many of the region builders were academics and policy makers from the Nordic countries who felt a need to find a new locus for Nordic cooperation in the changed strategic context. Analogous ideas for a new locus of cooperation were heard from the north German provinces in the form of a new *Hanse* or an *Ostseeraum* (Neumann 1994; Wæver 1997b). In scholarly literature, these region-building patterns within the BSR were taken as one case of the formation of a regionalized European order. Its *Europe of regions* version looks like a mosaic of political agents and subjectivities, where regions and cities form non-Westphalian chains extending across state borders. Another version of this geopolitical form is termed *Europe of Olympic rings*. It represents a more ordered but yet regionalized formation, where the subjectivities centre around an imagined region like the BSR instead of the EU centre. In this vision, integration among both state level and sub-state level regional actors overrides integration between them and the EU centre that here remains only loosely defined (Figure 2.2). The existence of visions and political experiments like these inspired scholars to refer to the BSR as a 'laboratory' of peaceful change in Europe (Hubel 2004b: 283).

For example, together with Denmark, Germany initiated the launching of the Council of the Baltic Sea States (CBSS) in 1992 to facilitate various forms of 'low politics' cooperation linking together all the Baltic Sea coastal states, plus Iceland and Norway, and, crucially, the European Commission as one of the founding members. After some lobbying, the Commission somewhat reluctantly agreed to join, despite the fact that its legal mandate to participate was relatively unclear (Johansson 2002: 385). The mission of the CBSS was conceived to assist in the transformation of the Baltic states, Poland and Russia so as to reduce the risks and soft security threats that they were perceived to pose to their EU neighbours in the region. In this manner, the covered policy sectors include economic development, environment and energy, nuclear safety, democracy and human rights, and also

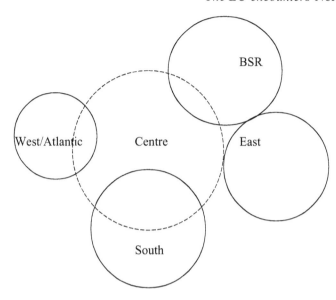

Figure 2.2 The early 1990s vision of a Europe of Olympic rings.

issues such as education. The CBSS relies on funding provided on a voluntary basis by the participating countries, and this quite understandably implies strong sponsoring by Germany, the Nordic countries and, as will be noted, increasingly also by the EU.[4]

Although the CBSS had a rather slow start to its activities, as the Baltic–Russian tensions proved persistently difficult to overcome, it is noteworthy how the European Commission's gradually emergent, more active approach served to revitalize the organization. The Commission simply acknowledged that, with the Finnish, Swedish and Norwegian membership in sight then, it had been inexorably drawn into the BSR, and thus felt a need to 'examine the future role [that] the Union [would be] called upon to play to further stability and economic development in the [area]' (European Commission 1994; cited in Johansson 2002: 379). Consequently, the Commission's own Baltic Sea Initiative in 1996 helped to streamline the working methods of the CBSS and prioritize its actions (Gänzle and Hubel 2002: 405; Johansson 2002: 379). Finally, for example in the case of the CBSS, perhaps the biggest impact of Finland's and Sweden's EU membership and the EU's more prominent involvement in the BSR was that EU programmes became available to fund the CBSS activities and, crucially, in previously unseen amounts. These programmes also introduced new, EU-designed partnership-building and implementation routines (Mariussen 2002: 225).

As for the regional cooperation initiatives coming from the Nordic states, it should first be mentioned how many of the 'old' regional cooperation programmes under the NCM – the oldest and most established regional organization in the BSR – also became affected by the EU in a similar manner to the CBSS programmes. Several new Interreg programmes of the EU, which were designed to promote cross-border cooperation, improvement of relations between public and private institutions and the setting up of institutions at the regional level, were made conditional upon the co-sponsoring of the NCM. In fact, the EU's Interreg programmes 'europeanized' the existing NCM programmes by having largely the same geographical coverage, while at the same time offering up to twenty times more funding and new EU-designed routines (ibid.: 225).

Such a 'europeanization' pattern can also be found in the environment-centred activities of the Norwegian-initiated Barents Euro-Arctic Council (BEAC), which was founded in 1993 to deal with environmental problems originating from the Kola Peninsula on the Russian side, and other northern and Arctic cooperation. As with the CBSS, one of the goals was simply to get the formerly divided parties sitting at the same table and speaking of issues other than the most divisive military security concerns. At the same time the BEAC relied on the Soviet leader Gorbachev's calls many years earlier for environmental matters within Arctic areas to become a pilot sector of East–West cooperation and stability building. Finally, for Norway the BEAC helped to get the EU involved in the very north and open up a new channel into that direction. The Union joined the BEAC as a founding member. Interestingly, with the Union's increasing involvement, some regional actors within the associated Barents Regional Council started to express fears that the europeanization of the Barents cooperation was compromising their own prospects to influence the implementation of the increasingly EU-funded programmes. In a broader sense, EU involvement started to challenge the original nature of the whole Barents endeavour in an analogous manner to the pattern established within the CBSS and NCM (see Myrjord 2003: 253–5).

As for other forms of regional cooperation in northern Europe, Jussi Jauhiainen notes in his study of two EU regions (Karelia, Helsinki–Tallinn) and the ESTRUFIN network, linking cities in Finland, Estonia and Russia, that the importance of the EU programmes and the funding they offer led to a situation where many cross-border projects were launched with the precise aim of obtaining EU funding. In this manner, although cross-border cooperation in the cases studied by Jauhiainen continued to be 'state controlled' and 'public authority driven', it concomitantly became 'European-designed'. Owing to the importance of EU co-financing, the networks had to start following EU spatial policy practices which the EU programmes were teaching them (Jauhiainen 2002). In addition to the Interreg, the well funded PHARE was launched in 1989–90 to assist with the transition in CEE. Since 1992, it also included the Baltic states. The considerably less well funded TACIS is directed to the former Soviet Union (FSU) excluding the Baltic states. As such, it indicates lucidly whom the Union was about to exclude. Indeed, it has been noted that since 1990 the Union's spatial planning policies have assumed a clearly cartographic character and that, in the context of northern Europe, evocative maps of the region have become central in the EU's activities (Scott 2002: 140, 146).

However, in conceptual terms the most ambitious coordinating role gradually taken by the EU came in the shape of the Finnish initiative for a Northern Dimension of the EU in 1997. The ND was accepted by the Union during 1997–8 in order to, among other things, introduce cohesion and bring better structure into the various region-wide activities that existed alongside the many bilateral programmes of Germany and the Nordics, targeted at institution-building and alleviation of the transition problems in the Baltic states and northwest Russia. By the time of the ND's introduction, the Baltic Sea and Barents Sea cooperation agendas were becoming understood as part of a wider conceptual framework of 'north European cooperation'. This conceptual shift in favour of the term 'Europe' accentuated the northern European region's position in becoming a more integral part of continent-wide processes instead of indigenous patterns. Before proceeding further into these issues that signalled a new era in the development of the Union's 'north Europeanness', a few concluding remarks on the EU–Nordic encounter are due.

Summary

In this chapter, I have argued that Germany's reunification and Denmark's EC membership opened up the question of the EU's relationship with northern Europe, but mainly implicitly and somewhat inconclusively. However, the decisive push for the development of the EU's 'north Europeanness' came in the form of Finnish, Swedish and, to a lesser extent, Norwegian bids for membership. The materialization of Finland's and Sweden's membership in 1995, and the resulting larger funds for the EU's gradually increasing involvement in the BSR and Barents cooperation furthered the process. As the old regional cooperation within the framework of *Norden*, which had been strictly limited in geography and identity politics, became to a large extent replaced by the wider BSR and Barents networking with the Balts, Poland and Russia, the EU's strategic gaze turned to this region. In this sense, the accession of Finland and Sweden into the Union helped to first prompt and then strengthen the EU's foreign policy towards the northern European region. Of no minor importance in this shift were emerging perceptions of the richness of Russia's northwest in terms of natural resources that are badly needed by the enlarging Union (Chapter 8).

The Polish and Baltic EU membership applications in the mid-1990s, which were prompted by the Union's introduction of the Copenhagen criteria for membership in 1993, accelerated the process considerably. Finland brought with its membership the Union's first border with Russia, a traditionally imperial state that still in the mid-1990s had hegemonic ambitions vis-à-vis the Baltic states. In this manner, Finland's inclusion facilitated the extension of the new EU–Russian border towards the Baltic direction. This prospect was perceived as both a major challenge and an opportunity within EU institutions and in the major European capitals. The Union's encounter with *Norden* for its own part thus led to an encounter with the post-Soviet north. The main characteristics and consequences of that process for EU foreign policy and the EU's geopolitical form will be discussed and conceptualized in the next chapter.

3 The EU encounters the post-Soviet north I

A new theoretical approach

The EU's participation in the region-building that was initiated by the Nordic states and Germany within the framework of the Baltic and Barents Seas in the early and mid-1990s helped the EU to develop contacts with Poland, the Baltic states and Russia, as well as with Russia's northwestern regions. These contacts strengthened the bilateral relations that were developing on the basis of the membership applications received from Poland (1994) and the Baltic states (1995), and the negotiations with Russia on the EU–Russian Partnership and Cooperation Agreement (PCA), which was finalized in 1994 and entered into force in 1997. Moreover, as noted, the Union introduced its Northern Dimension (ND) policy on Finland's initiative in 1997–8 in order to better coordinate its participation in the regional level activities and the uneven development of its bilateral ties with northern Europe's states – most of them being members or in line for membership by the mid-1990s, while Russia alone was lined up only as the EU's partner.

This all meant that in the identity political sense, during the mid and late 1990s, the Union in fact became engaged with the task of changing the identity political context of northern Europe. Effectively, the Union's actions were intended at erasing the 'post-communism' of Poland, transforming the traits of 'post-Soviet space' of the Baltic states, and helping Russia to europeanize its own post-Soviet space, in particular with regard to the northwestern parts of the country bordering the EU. In this chapter, I argue that the EU's encounter with the post-Soviet north – the Baltic states and Russia's northwestern regions – is particularly revealing from the point of view of the development of the EU's subjectivity within the northern European region. The EU's encounter with the post-Soviet north also reflects on the Union's overall geopolitical form in an illuminating manner. The purpose of this chapter is to outline in detail a new theoretical approach and a conceptual scheme opening up these issues.

Differentiating between 'post-Soviet' and 'post-communist' spaces

The difference of the EU's encounter with the post-Soviet north compared to its inclusion of the type of post-communism associated with Poland and the rest of the CEE speaks volumes about the Union's goal-orientedness. For the Union, the inclusion of post-communist states like Poland does, of course, represent a tremendous challenge of overcoming the legacy of fifty years of communist rule, with its multiple side effects in the political, economic and social sectors. As shown by the long-lasting problems Germany has had with reunifying the long separated western and eastern parts of the present German state, it is clear that the coordination and financing of these transformation processes is a very demanding task. For the period 2000–6, the EU budgeted 22 billion euros for the pre-accession preparation of the CEE countries (Smorodinskaya 2001: 67). Although Poland was among the major recipients of these funds, in economic terms alone, the most optimistic calculations predict that the country will catch up with the average EU GDP level only by 2015 (Musial 2002: 292).

But apart from the obviously challenging economic transformation problems and, no less, the concomitant economic potential and markets offered by Poland's 38 million inhabitants, the country is simultaneously widely regarded by Germans and others as enjoying a privileged position in the EU's CEE enlargement (ibid.: 289, 304). To put it in Milan Kundera's famous terms, among the CEE countries, Poland perhaps most lucidly epitomizes the idea of Central Europe politically 'kidnapped' from the West by the Soviet Union for fifty years. Culturally, Poland shares many key elements of the European legacy such as democracy, European law and morality; until the 1960s, in Catholic documents Poland was termed *antemurale Christianitas* ('the fortress of Christianity') (Medvedev 1998: 53; Mouritzen 1996c: 265). With such a cultural perception, and the long-serving, anti-communist Pope John Paul II coming from Poland, it is easy to see how Poland is in principle seen as fitting well into the EU, which during the drafting of its Constitutional Treaty in 2002–3 also debated the inclusion of a clause on the Union's Christian foundations. Finally, we have seen that, for Gorbachev and the Russian leadership since 1991, events such as the disintegration of the Warsaw Pact, and Poland's NATO membership in 1999, were not seen as similar shocks to the Baltic states' attempts to distance themselves from Russia's sphere of influence after the collapse of the Soviet Union. This shows how Poland ceased to be part of the perceived Soviet/Russian sphere of interests far earlier than the Baltic states. From the Union's point of view, in identity political terms Poland was a lot easier to include than the Baltic states. It can even be argued that, despite the huge scale of the transformation problems in Poland, its inclusion was altogether necessary in order for the whole enlargement exercise to make sense (see also Sjursen 2002: 505).

At the first sight, the challenge of overcoming the fifty years of communist rule looks admittedly very similar in the Baltic states to Poland, although in the Baltic case the scale is clearly a lot smaller, with only 7.5 million Baltic inhabitants entering the Union. They consequently constitute a much smaller economic burden for the Union, one which may not even exceed the burdens posed by the poorest members of the EU-15 (see Wiberg 1996: 51–2). Nevertheless, I argue that, by deciding to include the Baltic states and simultaneously deepen its relations with Russia, the Union embarked on a rather different sort of task from that in the case of Poland. Peter van Elsuwege (2002) claims that, by its inclusion of the Balts, the EU 'undoubtedly complicated the EU enlargement process' (p. 176). In the Baltic case, the Union crossed the 'red line' (Kasekamp 2005: 163), and started including states formerly belonging to a traditional type imperial entity, the Soviet Union, and which were still in the mid-1990s and occasionally also later regarded by Russian policy makers as belonging to Russia's sphere of interests (Aalto 2003a). The reasons for sphere-of-interest thinking are many, and include factors like great power prestige, losing air and military bases in the Baltics, as well as many of the Soviet era ports to the Baltic Sea, and losing direct land connection to Kaliningrad with Lithuania's regaining of independence and joining of the EU's Schengen treaty that regulates visa and border policies within the Union. However, without any doubt, the most important reason for Russia's interest is the presence of large Russophone minorities in Estonia and Latvia.

The citizenship and linguistic rights of these internally very heterogeneous Russian-speaking groups have been a source of controversy. In both Estonia and Latvia, the Russophones constitute roughly one-third of the population; with the regaining of independence, most of them were made non-citizens,[1] and subsequently about 100,000 people in Estonia opted for Russian citizenship. But in Lithuania the Russophone minorities have never exceeded one-tenth of the population, and practically all residents have received Lithuanian citizenship after Lithuania's regaining of independence. However, Russia's need to use Lithuanian territory as a transit corridor to Kaliningrad keeps Russia interested in Lithuanian developments, although the Russian pressure experienced by Lithuania has consistently been lesser compared to Estonia and Latvia. Finally it can be noted that, in Estonia's and Latvia's case, the Union started including states with outstanding territorial disputes with Russia (for more, see Chapters 5 and 6).

Van Elsuwege goes on to suggest that factors such as the psychological heritage of the Cold War era, and precisely the instability and nationalism that prevailed in the 1990s in Russia, and the pressure Russia put on the Baltic states persuaded the Union to include them (pp. 180, 191). Vello Pettai (2003), by contrast, suggests Russia's relative weakness in the 1990s as the main reason for the EU leaders' perception of the Baltic states' inclusion as being 'safe' (p. 6). This and the ensuing chapters will probe into these controversies and highlight how sensitive issues were in fact involved. Also it will be argued that, simultaneously with its Baltic engagement, the EU started to develop goal-oriented positions vis-à-vis Russia. As early as 1991, the Union decided to attach political conditionality to its Russian aid (see Herrberg 1998: 93).

What emerges from these short remarks is that, in starting to encounter the post-Soviet north during the 1990s, the Union in fact embarked on the task of encountering former and present parts of a potential competitor to itself in northern Europe. What actually took place was that the Union started to *change* in a fundamental manner the political context in the Baltic states and, somewhat less dramatically, in northwest Russia and Russia on the whole. In this way, the Union started erasing elements of 'post-Soviet space' from the northern European region and replacing them by supposedly more 'European' traits. True, in identity political terms, 'post-Soviet' is a label which chiefly connotes negative associations, and which neither the Balts nor the Russians want to carry, even though we often deem it a useful term to invoke. Yet, in this region, the EU set to itself the task of relieving others from this sort of an identity political baggage – the Balts by offering membership, and the Russians by offering partnership.

The Union's differentiated engagement of the Balts and Russians also tells us a lot about the geopolitical form the EU is assuming as a result of these processes, which, of course, must be understood in the context of the Union's overall development. The EU's emerging geopolitical form in northern Europe replaces the models of Nordic balance and regionalized European order that were discussed in the previous chapter, and in the present context represents an entirely new-looking configuration. As emerges from a survey of the so-called 'network governance' literature and the literature terming the EU an 'empire', it can fruitfully be termed a *concentric EU order*.

Towards a concentric EU order

Network governance and boundaries

The literature on the *network governance* practiced by the Union, and the *boundaries* forming as a consequence of this type of rule, is part of the new *multi-level governance* approach of European integration studies. This school springs up from the tradition of comparative politics rather than from traditional IR influenced European integration theories, and is widely followed for example in the US and Germany, and likely to strengthen its position within the field of European integration studies. The multi-level governance approach conceptualizes the EU's system of rule as mixing elements of foreign and domestic policy, and relying on partnerships, networks and interactive dependencies. The application of the principle of subsidiarity, or the devolvement of policy issues to the lowest possible level where they can be solved, strengthens the multiplicity of layers of rule within the EU, and brings up the role of subnational actors in prompting and implementing EU activities (DeBardeleben 2005: 12–13). The multi-level governance approach accentuates how the EU's system of rule represents a more complex form of political agency than is conventionally found in Westphalian nation-states, federations and international organizations. This observation often leads the proponents of this literature to portray the EU's policy activities as prone to incoherence due to the various levels and actors involved, which often makes the policies difficult for their target groups to grasp.

There is definitely a seed of truth in this characterization of the EU's system of rule provided by the multi-level governance literature. And the manner in which this framework is extended into the Union's foreign policy activities also helps us to take issue with the Union's northern European powerness, including its differentiated treatment of the Baltic and Russian territories. The multi-level governance literature introduces the notions of the Union's network governance and the boundaries that the Union is creating around itself in exercising such a mode of governance, in order to conceptualize the manner in which the EU approaches its borders in the various corners of Europe. In this way, the term 'network govern-ance' tells us how the EU's system of rule is not very often unidirectional, but rather a non-hierarchical and fragmented one that uses a mixture of levels and actors to influence events (see Jachtenfuchs 2001: 253–5). For example, the Eu-ropean Commission, the European Council, particular member states, organiza-tions like Council of Europe, or regional entities and organizations within a single member state or an interconnected group can simultaneously, sometimes more and sometimes less concertedly, carry out EU-supported policies with transborder effects. The effect of such a complex network governance is that it often becomes unclear for outsiders to figure out who is doing what within the EU, and where the EU's boundaries eventually reach.

As Michael Smith puts it, first, the networked EU governance establishes a *geopolitical boundary* separating the 'stabilized' insiders from outsiders, al-though, since the end of the Cold War, security interdependence at the Union's geopolitical boundary has increased drastically. Second, the EU creates an *institu-tional/legal boundary* separating the 'community of law' and its institutions from outsiders. Today, however, many of the Union's institutional and legal norms are simultaneously extended into the wider European area by voluntary association and imitation. Third, the *transactional boundary* is from the outset more fluid, with the EU trying to protect its single market and tariffs, while globalization works in the opposite direction and third parties strive to establish and main-tain access to the EU area. Fourth, the *cultural boundary* between the assumed Europeans and non-Europeans can be constructed in a gradated and open-ended form, but in practice it may also assume a geopolitical function when it is used to restrict access for those perceived as unwanted (see M. Smith 1996: 13–18). On the whole, the framework of network governance and boundaries highlights the balance struck between the perceived benefits and costs for actors broadly under the EU flag or those who otherwise participate in the implementation of EU gov-ernance, as well as the differentiated effects of the EU's handling of its boundaries on neighbouring territories through boundary construction, maintenance, blurring or transgression (Friis and Murphy 1999: 216–7).

Mette Sicard Filtenborg *et al.* (2002) apply this approach to EU foreign policy towards northern Europe. They argue that the Union is relatively effective in its efforts to solve the various post-Soviet problems that it encounters in the northern direction. The Union is effective despite the fact that its resources are scattered along different levels of governance, ranging from the Union to the member state level, and to the level of the Union's network of associate members, partners and other agents. In other words, Filtenborg *et al.* argue that by engaging in the BSR and Barents Sea region-building in the 1990s, and by subsequently starting to develop the ND policy, the EU assembled a northern European network around it – consisting of non-member countries like Norway and Iceland, and international organizations like NATO, CBSS, NCM, BEAC, the Organization for Security and Co-operation in Europe (OSCE), etc. These bodies gradually expressed their willingness to share and coordinate their resources and policies with the Union in order to work more effectively with the Balts, Poles and Russians. As a consequence, having engaged these bodies into its network, the Union governs northern Europe in increasingly EU-designed ways (see also Gänzle 2002; cf. Mariussen 2002: 225; Myrjord 2003: 247–55). The main geopolitical effect of the formation of the EU-led network, and of the EU's considerable policy export to its network partners, receiving states and regions, is the subsequent construction of fuzzy, differently constituted, partly overlapping and partly separate boundaries around the Union along geopolitical, institutional/legal, transactional and cultural divisions.

Filtenborg *et al.* assert that along the geopolitical boundary the Union has fairly successfully avoided the emergence of the so-called 'fortress Europe' scenario in the European north, with sharp borders intended in a Westphalian ideal-type fashion to form a protective wall against the external world. The Union's multi-level and multi-agent, regionalist engagement of the Baltic states and northwest Russia has according to these authors resulted in webs of decentralized cross-border and interregional cooperation, where previous tensions have been partially reduced. Along the institutional/legal boundary, familiar perceptions of the various soft security challenges seen as emanating mainly from the Baltic states and Russia, in the form of organized crime, money-laundering, and trafficking of arms, drugs and human beings, create a need for a considerable alignment of legal frameworks between the EU and its network partners. The transactional boundary, for its part, opens up a perspective on the efforts to reduce trade barriers among northern European countries. Notable advances have been made regardless of Russia's rather complex economic transition problems, and there are some signs of voluntary, though yet partial, adaptation to EU market and trade principles in Russia (Chapter 8). Finally, along the cultural boundary, for example youth and student exchange, and town twinning programmes have been targeted at spreading European social and institutional cultures into the northern European region (Filtenborg *et al.* 2002: 398–402).

In summary, the literature on network governance and boundaries draws us a picture of a Union extending well beyond its formal, so far constantly extending bounds of sovereignty. In this way, this literature challenges the traditional Westphalian notion of the concept of sovereignty, and offers a vision of a multi-perspectival, in some accounts even a postmodern European polity (cf. Caporaso 1996; Ruggie 1993). The contributing authors identify fuzziness and messiness in the Union's geopolitical form, and locate several 'grey zones' such as the post-Soviet north, where the Union and its members, on the one hand, and its network members and target territories, on the other, meet and mingle with each other.

However, regardless of these merits, I remain critical of the tendency of network governance and boundaries literature, and the multi-level governance school on the whole, to posit a model that looks to elude goal-oriented action and responsibility into the multiple layers of EU governance. For example Stefan Gänzle laments that 'foreign policy on the European level appears "crab-wise", incremental, and lacking any kind of master plan and strategic policy-making' (Gänzle 2002: 98; also Filtenborg *et al.* 2002: 392). The notion of incremental progress in EU policy making is definitely in many ways correct, but it concomitantly raises questions. For example, it can be claimed that foreign policy indeed fairly often emerges in an incremental and somewhat messy manner, as for example Gerard Toal has shown in the case of US foreign policy towards Bosnia (Toal 2002; cf. Zielonka 1998: 7). Moreover, the notion of many incremental steps taken raises the question of whether they will at some point help us to speak of something reminiscent, if not of a 'master plan', then at least of patterns of goal-oriented action emerging out of them. Merely assuming that the many, albeit incremental steps taken by the Union does not in any manner help in identity building and interest formation ends up strengthening the familiar image of the Union as a faceless network entity, where policy outcomes simply 'happen' without anyone or any institutional bodies actually being responsible. It remains unclear who within the 'network' in fact does what and for what ends.

Empire

At first sight, the picture of the Union's fuzzy borders drawn by the network governance literature is not entirely different from the depiction of the Union's geopolitical form that is offered by the literature treating the EU as a form of 'empire' rather than a Westphalian nation-state (Zielonka 2001: 509fn1). In the theoretical sense, however, the empire literature differs considerably from the network governance and boundaries literature. Whereas network governance is inspired by the multi-level governance school of comparative politics, empire literature is associated with the field of critical geopolitics (Aalto 2002a), as well as IR approaches, and among them most closely by constructivism and the English School (ES). As discussed in the introduction, constructivist metatheory is the theoretical reference point to which this book can broadly be located. The ES, for its part, has for long elaborated the concept of empire, which is historically a much more prevalent form of political organization than Westphalian nation-states (Diez and Whitman 2002: 49–51). Moreover, compared to network governance literature, the empire literature introduces the issues of *power* and *responsibility* much more explicitly into the analysis. This feature is here regarded as a strength.

The empire literature suggests historical analogies for the contemporary organization of European order by looking at pre-Westphalian world systems. Probably the most notable contributor to this literature, Ole Wæver, notes that the thesis of 'neo-medievalism', which started to appear after the end of the Cold War to depict the EU's likeliest future development, or even of 'neo-sumerianism', as in his own analysis, connotes the idea of non-sovereign, imperial centredness of the Union in opposition to the centredness of Westphalian nation-states, its constituent parts. Such imperial centredness is about complexity, overlapping authority, and a diffused nature of the distribution and exercise of power from the EU centre. This means that the power of the loosely defined EU centre gradually fades when one moves away from it, first towards the inner circles, and then towards the outer circles and the fringes of the metaphorically understood EU empire (Wæver 1997a: 61). In this way, we end up with a gradated or concentric model of European integration (cf. Mouritzen 1996e).

Thomas Christiansen *et al.* (2000) apply this concentric model to the Union's northern European fringes. They imply that by the late 1990s the concentric EU empire had developed its own sphere of interests or a 'near abroad' within the Baltic Sea region (cf. Scott 2002). Christiansen *et al.* suggest that such an EU 'near abroad' emerged through the EU's incremental northern European engagement during the 1990s, and acquired an analogous shape to Russia's own supposed 'near abroad' within the territory of the FSU. The main declared target of this policy was the approximately 24 million persons belonging to the Russophone minorities that as a legacy of the Soviet era remained within the Commonwealth of Independent States (CIS), the organization built on the ruins of the Soviet Union and which the Balts refused to join. But in the Russian debates there were references that at times led one to think of as equal targets for the 'near abroad' policy the sizable Russophone minorities of Estonia and Latvia (Aalto 2003a). However, to provide a sobering comparison of the EU and Russian empires and their competing 'near abroads', Wæver (2000) points out how the EU empire commands a striking amount of legitimacy among the Balts, Poles and others, in the sense that they voluntarily set themselves the task of joining the Union as a means of distancing themselves from Russia. To this could be added the support shown by a significant contingent of the Baltic Russophone populations towards the EU accession of their countries of residence (Chapter 5 n. 1, Chapter 6 n. 1).

With regard to the encounter of the EU empire with its Russian counterpart, Ola Tunander makes the interesting point of how the fuzziness of borders, implicated in the EU's and Russia's efforts in the 1990s to create a greater space for themselves within the Baltics, in fact opens up the prospect of dialogue, which did not exist in a similar sense in the sharply bordered Cold War era Europe (Tunander 1997: 25). However, writing before the turn of the millennium, Wæver argued that the subsequent expansion of the EU empire into the Baltics – at the expense of Russia's influence – and the manner in which the EU enlargement process was conducted overall, failed to offer Russia a particularly identifiable place in Europe. Yet not all prospects of EU–Russian cooperation were destroyed. On the whole, Wæver maintained that the EU–Russian encounter can be characterized as a 'semi-cooperative relationship' (Wæver 2000: 275).

This sort of reference to an EU empire with fuzzy borders and its northern European 'near abroad' partly acquired from the Soviet Union/Russia may of course sound unwarranted and even dangerous for the more mainstream observers of EU foreign policy, and certainly for EU policy makers. Yet it should be kept in mind that the contributors to the empire literature are themselves explicit on the fact that the EU empire that they currently identify should not, regardless of the historical analogy, be confused with the way in which pre-modern empires exercised power and viewed their legitimacy and responsibilities (e.g. Zielonka 2001: 530). Bearing in mind these qualifications, we can now map the visual characteristics of the concentric EU order and its north European reflections (Figure 3.1).

The concentric model of EU order conveys a loosely defined *centre* consisting of Brussels and other loci of EU institutions that is well bound together in terms of institutional density, and then various circles surrounding it and differentiated

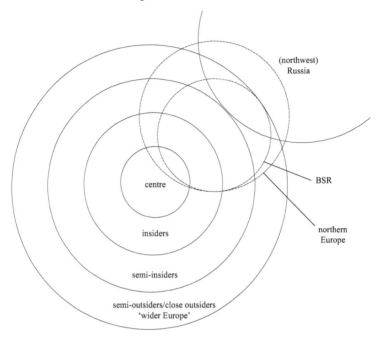

Figure 3.1 Concentric EU order with a focus on northern Europe.

according to their degree of integration with it. Thus, the centre is surrounded by a circle of well integrated *insiders* who participate in practically all sectors of common policy. Of the northern European countries, Finland and Germany can be placed in this group. The second circle consists of *semi-insiders*. Some of them have voluntarily remained outside certain sectors of common policy, as for example Denmark and Sweden have in the case of the single currency. Naturally, they could be joined by some of the current insiders who are considering the prospects of opting out, in case integration spills over too fast to new policy areas such as common defence (e.g. possibly Finland). Some others within the semi-insider circle, such as the Baltic states, Poland and the rest of the CEE, are in the midst of a process of integrating into the Union and gradually approaching its centre along some sectors of policy. But they were forced to accept transition periods before fully participating in the EU labour market (with limitations set for the free movement of workforce into most member countries), before their entry to the single currency and before receiving full financial support for agricultural production.

The circles of the concentric model are best understood as a theoretical organizing device. In practice there is movement and tension between the circles when member states take the lead or strive towards the centre in some policy sectors whilst expressing reservations in others, and when there are competing positionings vis-à-vis the centre (Chapter 9). A crucial issue at this plane is the evolution of and movement between the second and third circles. Such evolvement and tension is particularly evident in the EU's encounter with the post-Soviet north.

Another added value in looking at peripheral second and third circle positions is that they can also provide useful viewpoints for purposes of casting developments in the EU centre in a new light (Browning 2005b: 4–7; cf. Parker and Armstrong 2000: xv). Compared with the second circle semi-insiders, the third circle provides a view upon a group of *close outsiders and semi-outsiders* such as Russia and its northwestern regions, which have no EU accession perspective in sight. They thus lack prospects of rapid promotion into a semi-insider status.

Russia's position since the collapse of the Soviet Union in 1991 is on the whole best characterized as a close outsider, i.e. not 'in' in any clearly conceivable manner, but at the same time situated close enough to the EU to be affected by EU integration. This has led into important mutual ties and dependencies. Russia's northwestern regions occupy mostly a semi-outsider position by virtue of their geographical interface with the Union and their participation in the Union's ND process. This is not enough to make them insiders, but by no means are they completely outsiders either. Recently, the ND framework has been developing into a part of the Union's overall neighbourhood policy dealing with the whole 'wider Europe' area in the north, east and south. Wæver (2000: 262) has aptly termed this web of variously integrated and attached countries and regions around the EU centre as resulting from the pull of the Union's 'magnetism'. The larger the Union becomes by new enlargement rounds, the larger its market becomes and the more necessary it becomes for others to get in (see also Mouritzen 1996e: 21–2). Through time, this magnetism may work to erode the relevance of discriminating analytically between close outsider and semi-outsider positions for Russia and its northwestern regions.

In the concentric model of EU order conceived of in this manner (Figure 3.1), the BSR crosscuts all three circles because the region includes states and regions with varying degrees of EU integration. The wider northern European region – denoting also regions beyond the immediate BSR, for example the Barents region, and the Arctic part of Europe, which until recently has remained outside 'EU order', and naturally also the ND on the whole – can be conceived of as a slightly more extensive circle crosscutting more pronouncedly also the 'Russian order'.

This sort of model of concentric EU order as applied to the northern European context – with often problematic encounters with Russia at the fringes – portrays fairly fruitfully the prevailing patterns of EU engagement within the region. However, I argue that, writing back in the 1990s, the empire analysts did not fully foresee the strength of the EU in relation to Russia. Ola Tunander wrote of the Cold War era division of Europe having been replaced in the 1990s by a 'military–cultural dividing line between Friend and Foe coexisting with an economic–political hierarchy from Cosmos to Chaos', and by a competition or even a 'Cold Peace' between Europe and Russia (Tunander 1997: 38). Wæver discussed the prospects of the EU empire and Russia's empire project clashing with each other, and identified the Baltic states as a possible confrontation point (Wæver 1997: 80). Rather than partially, yet slowly and very painfully, giving in to the EU order, Russia was likely to opt for a mixture of confrontation and cooperation (Wæver 2000: 275). Whereas similar forecasts were aired by other analysts as well, I suggest that what we have seen since then is the Nordics, the Baltic states and Russia *all* actively taking part in the strengthening of the EU order in northern Europe, although in Russia's case some limits for this order are concomitantly perceived and built. In this sense, the empire models introduced in the 1990s did not entirely satisfactorily shed light on how successfully the EU empire expands as a result of intersubjective processes with its new northern members and neighbours.[2]

In other words, I acknowledge that the empire writers were correct in postulating a horizontal image of a concentric, increasingly EU-led order which Russia is also approaching slowly and painfully. However, I also suggest that, although they managed to incorporate issues of power and responsibility into their analyses much more successfully than the network governance and boundaries writers have done, they underestimated the strength and expansion potential of the EU. More precisely, I argue that the concentric model is merely the surface – the manifest geopolitical form. As such, it only reflects underlying, *intersubjective construction processes of a northern European geopolitical subject*. During the course of this book, it will become evident that the patterns we observe in these construction processes by the Union, its Nordic and Baltic members, Russia and others, are currently leading to the somewhat covert *strengthening* of the EU's concentric form.

Constructing a northern European subject

My main theoretical argument in this chapter is that, in order to understand the intersubjective construction and maintenance processes of the concentric EU order and its northern European reflections, we need to study what views the insiders, semi-insiders and semi-outsiders/close outsiders have of the EU's desirable subjectivity in the northern European region.

With regard to more conventional conceptualizations of the EU, the import of the concept of *subjectivity* that I introduce here is that it does not presuppose any problematic Westphalian notions, nor imply any inherently passive, apolitical, or messy references to multi-level governance, where no one seems to be directly responsible for policy outcomes. Moreover, this conceptualization gives us a clearer idea of the *construction* of the EU's concentric form than is available in the empire literature. The concept of subject directs our attention to the *intersubjective processes* of recognizing and building subjects. It is an umbrella concept embracing both 'internal' and 'external' aspects of intersubjective processes, i.e. the EU's own actions and policies, and its neighbours' views of these. Further, the concept of subjectivity includes only an *analytical* internal/external distinction. In that way it is also suited for elucidating the construction of a concentric EU order with no pre-set limits to where the Union's various circles begin and end and where its 'wider Europe' eventually lies. In this fashion, the concept of subjectivity allows us to maintain a broad view of EU foreign policy and a highly differentiated image of its impact on the Union's borders and its neighbours.

With this sort of a conceptualization of the EU in terms of subjectivity, why do we need the word 'geopolitical'? In brief, the term 'geopolitics', accounting for a '*geopolitical* subject', is employed here in order to accentuate the spatial–territo-rial dimension of the EU's ordering efforts in northern Europe that is of interest here, as opposed to a functional or sectoral dimension, for example in the field of economic and budgetary policy, or mere legal competence. On the whole, the strongly intersubjective character of geopolitical subjectivity is reflected in its definition as *goal-oriented ordering of territories and political spaces, extend-ing from one's own sphere of sovereign rule to broader regional contexts* (Aalto 2002a: 148–51). That this type of ordering is always goal-oriented means that it is always directed at creating a certain pattern of social and material relations with a teleology that is desired for a given territory or political space. In other words, this pattern should be prone to develop or change only in a desired manner (Rengger 2000: 18–19).

To act as a geopolitical subject – i.e. to order its own space and its environs – the Union must be capable of promoting its own *identity* and *interest projects* with tangible effects regarding the construction of the EU order and its (fuzzy) borders. Because identities and interests represent highly political and constructed categories and are subject to change not only in major political upheavals but also in day-to-day political skirmishes, I opt to speak of them in the constructivist sense as 'projects' (Aalto 2002a: 157). The Union's identity and interest projects can thus be contested both by member states or other actors located in any of the concentric circles around the Union. Moreover, in many ways, identity and inter-est projects represent two sides of the same coin. In the conceptual sense, no iden-tity project exists without the involvement of goal-oriented instrumental factors. This is because thinking of what one 'is' in relation to others is also about thinking of what one 'wants' to be and what goals one has in relation to others (Neumann 1997). In the empirical sense, identity and interest projects are not easily sepa-rated from each other, because agents often appeal to both of them simultaneously in political struggles. It follows that neither concept has any essentialist content. The precise relationship between them is a matter of case-specific empirical study (Marcussen *et al.* 1999: 617).

Despite the fact that identity and interest projects are very much intertwined in political practice, for operational purposes I make an analytical distinction and divide each of them into two sub-aspects. This is necessary in order to develop a more concise conceptual scheme of the Union's ordering that would be amenable for detailed empirical research. As for identity projects, I argue that they always contain an idea of *time* and *space*. In this way, identity projects are about the his-toric struggles for constructing political spaces and their boundaries. This makes identity a relational concept that represents the relationship between the 'self' and 'other' in time and space. As for the goal-oriented interest projects, I argue that they always involve considerations of *geo-policy* and *geo-strategy*. Geo-policy refers to purposeful, goal-oriented action in a particular sector or issue area with territorial or spatial consequences, especially as regards boundary construction and, in rarer cases, boundary-breaking. Geo-policy also gives instructions on how to use the resources *within* each sector or issue area. By contrast, geo-strategy is a broader concept. It refers to the overall constellation of geo-policies and the underlying discourses across different sectors or issue areas. Geo-strategy gives instructions on how to allocate resources *between* different sectors or issue areas. For example, the EU's geo-strategy in northern Europe is the 'sum' of the EU's geo-policies towards different sectors or issue areas such as the enlargement, and the arranging of its relations with Kaliningrad and the rest of northwest Russia (Table 3.1; cf. Aalto 2002a: 157–8).

The breakdown into identity and interest projects and their sub-aspects is necessary in order to develop a detailed conceptual scheme enabling systematic comparisons of how views expressed by EU institutions of the Union's ordering in northern Europe (Chapter 4) compare to views within second circle countries Estonia, Latvia and Lithuania (Chapters 5–7) and third circle actors such as Russia and its northwestern regions (Chapter 8). Furthermore, it will be of interest to see what sort of a common ground exists among the Balts and Russians as to the EU's ordering efforts in northern Europe (Chapter 9).

Summary

In this chapter, I have argued that the EU's encounter with the post-Soviet north since the mid-1990s represents a more demanding challenge than the inclusion of the type of 'post-communism' seen in the case of Poland and the rest of the CEE. The post-Soviet north thus represents an interesting test case of the EU's goal-oriented ordering efforts of territories coming within its own sphere of rule and of territories set to remain more outside than inside. Some of these tensions and important aspects of the manner in which the EU copes with them were found to be usefully grasped by the literature on network governance and boundaries. This

Table 3.1 Theoretical model: construction of geopolitical subjectivity

Component of ordering	Sub-aspect	Explanation
Identity projects	Time	Temporal considerations in the construction of geopolitical subjectivity (e.g. assessment of the development and present state of integration within the Union)
	Space	Spatial considerations in the construction of geopolitical subjectivity (e.g. assessment of the desirable spatial organization, geographical extent and regional operating environment of the EU)
Interest projects	Geo-policy	Assessment of the degree and desirability of purposeful, goal-oriented action by a geopolitical subject in a particular sector or issue area (e.g. the EU's enlargement policy in northern Europe)
	Geo-strategy	Assessment of the overall constellation of policies by a geopolitical subject across sectors or issue areas (e.g. the EU's overall goals in northern Europe)

Source: adapted from Aalto (2004a).

literature fails, however, to attribute a sufficient degree of goal-oriented action and responsibility to the Union. The empire literature manages to open up these aspects better, but at the same time remains too vague on the construction processes of the EU order and too pessimistic about its prospects of expansion. For this reason a new theoretical approach and a conceptual scheme were proposed in this chapter, focusing on the Union's ability to function as the main geopolitical subject of northern Europe.

In the next chapter I will first examine some issues of international political economy and security problems in the EU's encounter with the post-Soviet north, and then put the developed model of the construction of geopolitical subjectivity into use in order to outline in more detail what views EU institutions express of the Union's ordering of northern Europe. Particular attention will be paid to the ordering of post-Soviet space in the second and third circles in this region, i.e. the Baltic states and Russia.

4 The EU encounters the post-Soviet north II

EU views

This chapter discusses the EU's ordering efforts and the processes by which it is constructing geopolitical subjectivity vis-à-vis the post-Soviet north. The fairly short history of the EU's encounter with the post-Soviet north that was conceptualized in the previous chapter must at the same time be understood as part of the development of Union-wide processes since the 1990s. The Baltic members were welcomed as part of the 2004 'big bang' enlargement after difficult but ultimately successfully conducted negotiations between them and the member states. The negotiations were initiated on the basis of the European Commission's draft negotiating positions, and the negotiation process was chaired by the presidency of the European Council. The final accession decision was approved by the European Parliament and ratified in all member states of the EU-15. The EU's Russian relations were built with the involvement of the European Commission, the rotating EU presidency and in many cases intergovernmental decision-making and bargaining, plus the more or less regular intervention of individual member states and the European Parliament in the capacity of a moral watchdog and budget controller, often much to Russia's dismay.

The multi-party and multi-level involvement of the EU in developing its relations with the post-Soviet north tells us that a large part of the Union's machinery participates in the process. In other words, when an entity of the Union's character, size and weight engages the post-Soviet north, more generic features of EU integration and EU foreign policy making are necessarily involved and must be taken up in the analysis. But tailor-made EU ordering efforts and specific challenges are discernible in this geographical direction as well. I will start examining this mixture of the general and particular features by taking a quick glance at some of the economic and security issues underlying the EU's relations with the post-Soviet north. Whilst the more case-specific features of the economic and security issues are left for a more detailed discussion in the subsequent chapters, the remainder of this chapter concentrates on outlining the views within the EU about how to order this region.

Issues of political economy in the EU's encounter with the post-Soviet north

In order to review the economic dimension of the EU's encounter with the post-Soviet north it is necessary first to situate the region in the wider context of northern Europe and the overall European area. A good starting point is the 1990s image of northern European region-building that was discussed in Chapter 2, and which, if fully realised in the economic sphere, would have implied indigenous northern European trade ties and interdependence surpassing the region's ties with the whole EU area. But, as hinted, such a degree of regionalized order was proved unattainable in northern Europe by the end of the decade. To this contributed the waves of EU accession, the deepening EU–Russian partnership and strengthening of the EU's 'magnetism'. The general limitations of a strictly regionalist perspective also come up when considering patterns of political economy.

The liberal-intergovernmentalist claim of how the Nordic countries are economically bound up with large EU members and the EU area as a whole (Chapter 2) gives us a good focus point to strike a balance between regional and European-wide patterns. As for the regional patterns, the Nordic countries trade intensively with each other but also with Germany. Germany is also the dominant trade partner for Poland within the northern European context. For Russia, Germany is a long-standing and important trade partner, not least in the context of Russia's substantial energy deliveries to increasingly energy resources poor Germany. The Baltic states' economies are tied up with Germany and the Nordics, but also to a degree with Russia. However, because of the small size of their economies, their foreign trade patterns are relatively unimportant to their neighbours (Figure 4.1; Chapters 5–8).

Notable regional interdependencies within the trade sector prevail in northern Europe. With the exception of Russia and, to a slightly lesser extent, Norway, the countries of the region have from half to two-thirds of their EU-bound trade with other northerners (Köll 2003). Germany occupies a central role in these regional patterns. But the fact that Germany was in Chapter 2 deemed a not-so-pronouncedly northern European country, thanks to its *Mittellage* position and the consequent identities and interests, may in fact be read as implying a linkage between the northerners and European-wide economic patterns. And on top of those European-wide linkages which Germany's centrality within the European economic area unavoidably raises must be added the northern European countries' extra-EU trade, for example with the US and Asia. Hence, on the economic plane, despite the very strong regional biases especially towards Germany, northern Europe, and the post-Soviet north with it, is best understood as a European sub-region. Despite notable degrees of regionality, it is clear that economically northern Europe does not stand alone, and even less does the post-Soviet north with its vulnerable small Baltic economies and export-geared natural resources industries of Russia.

A bolder manner of putting the same argument is conceiving of the post-Soviet north only as a small piece in a larger geo-economic jigsaw puzzle. The building blocks for such a view can be taken for example from the scenario put forth by the

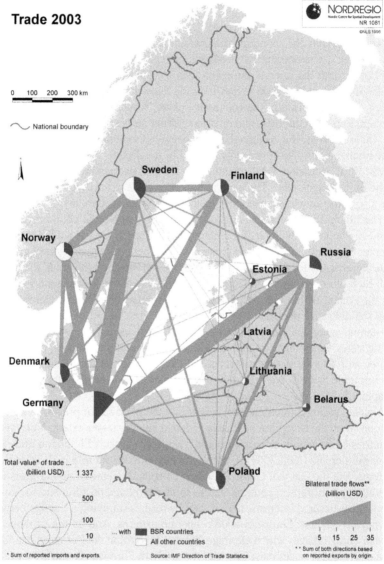

Figure 4.1 Germany's role in northern European trade flows. Source: Nordregio at www. nordregio.se

American geopolitician Saul Cohen as early as 1991. Cohen recast the traditional geopolitical role of the CEE lands located between Germany and Russia by proposing that this region should free itself from its long-standing buffer zone function. Instead, it should become a gateway region linking the formerly antagonistic western and eastern parts of the Eurasian landmass. Cohen argued that the then EEC and Soviet Union would find competing over the region counterproductive and in fact would be inclined to see new, lasting prospects of achieving balance with the help of this economic interface. This would mean geo-economics taking over from old-fashioned geopolitics within the wider European area (see A. Smith 2002: 648–50).

The development of the EU's subjectivity and integration processes witnessed within the region since then seem to support Cohen's interpretation of the lands in between functioning as a gateway for European capital on its way elsewhere. As will become evident in the subsequent chapters, for example the Baltic states function as a pivotal transit area for Russian and other energy resources, as well as other natural resources that are contained within Russia's northwest and elsewhere within the CIS. This role represents practically the only way in which the Baltic states can be seen to occupy any economic significance of note to the whole Union (Chapters 5–8). One indication of such a geo-economic gateway function for the Balts and CEE within the broader picture might be how the EU's 2004 enlargement cannot be well explained solely by means of the supposed economic benefits that the opening up of a bigger market is set to bring to the Union.

The projected economic gains to the EU area resulting from the 2004 enlargement include expanding the EU's single market into the CEE, with its relatively cheap primary and labour resources and higher growth than is found in the older member states, as well as the added incentive of promoting trade between the old and new members. However, as most studies have concluded, the economic costs of the enlargement will outweigh benefits in the short and medium term. The costs include pouring 22 billion euro of pre-accession funds to the accession states during 2000–6 in the form of programmes like PHARE, pre-accession structural funds like ISPA for improving environmental and transport infrastructure, and SAPARD for adjusting the agricultural sector and for supporting rural areas.[1] At the same time, the CEE countries, with the exception of Slovenia, will mostly continue to be net receivers from the EU budget at least for a decade or two. And, as noted by an EU policy maker in an interview, the combined economic strength of the associated states was in 1995 the size of the Netherlands (interview). Although the CEE economies have since then considerably strengthened, the underlying balance of economic potential between the former West and East has not significantly altered.

The emerging picture is that cold numbers speak strongly against a liberal-intergovernmentalist economic interest explanation for the EU's launching and promotion of enlargement, as opposed to individual countries' decision to apply for membership. Purely on grounds of economic interest, in the medium term enlargement does not seem to make sense to the Union as a whole. But here it is of note how the staunchest supporters of the CEE enlargement have been the northern European EU members. The net contributors to the EU budget among them, Germany and Sweden, will probably benefit from the 2004 enlargement. Finland, by contrast, will most likely lose some of its EU financial support and strengthen its position as a net payer, a status that the country assumed already before the enlargement. Many Finnish regions cease to be among the poorest ones within the enlarged Union and thus will lose some of their existing support. But, of course, at the same time there are relatively strong economic interests in Finland vis-à-vis the EU accession of Estonia, with which many Finnish companies have intense trade and other business relations; but again, the Finnish fears of intensified competition work to balance off the Finnish interest for Estonia's EU membership (Chapter 5). For Denmark's promotion of enlargement, economic interests are not really in evidence (see Sjursen 2002: 497–8).

It transpires that whereas, according to liberal intergovernmentalists, economic issues explain well the Nordic countries' EU accession – and of course their claim is staunchly disputed by the constructivists or poststructuralists holding identity as the key – they remain unable to account for why EU institutions remained committed to expanding the Union's northern European contingent. Remarkably, this situation only changes when the actual and potential gateway function of the Baltic states and the CEE is introduced, as their territories provide access to and transit potential for taking the substantial natural resources in Russia and the CIS into EU use (see below; also Chapter 8). In the end, the indecisiveness of the economic factors gives us strong reasons to consider what role security issues play in the Union's efforts of making a wider northern Europe by engaging the post-Soviet north.

Security issues in the EU's encounter with the post-Soviet north

The projected security gain is another issue often mentioned as underlying the EU's enlargement policy. The 1989–91 transformations in CEE are said to have unleashed social forces that could topple their democratic achievements in the absence of EU enlargement, which, in this way, could be conceived as the EU's exercise in risk management within its own sphere of ordering (Cecchini *et al.* 2001: 155–9). In this connection can also be mentioned the transformation problems experienced by the CEE states, such as the spread of organized crime, corruption, communicable diseases, environmental threats and other soft security challenges with a cross-border character that have proliferated after the collapse of the old regimes in 1989–91. Indeed, in an interview, as regards the Balts, a European Commission policy maker expressed very clearly this message of the need to spread stability. His Finnish colleague corroborated the same argument concerning Estonia's inclusion:

> If you look specifically at the Baltic states, then from the EU perspective I think the main aim will be to stabilize the region . . . as long as there is a grey zone between northern Europe and Russia, this will always lead to friction. But once the Baltic states are really in the EU, then Russia will simply be the neighbour, and then everything will presumably become much easier.
>
> (EU policy maker, May 2002)

> I think the motivation consists of two issues. There is the peace project that was started after the Second World War, and which must be pursued to its logical conclusion. Thus the question is not only about one singular country

[Estonia], but also of the broader issue of stabilizing the countries that belonged to the sphere of interests of the Soviet Union, so that peace and stability would continue to prevail. Therefore, their membership must be accepted. And secondly, there is the market thinking.

(Finnish policy maker, February 2003)

The security issues within the EU's involvement and enlargement into the Baltic states hence indicate a soft security function to the Union by means of stabilizing its environs and future markets and transit areas. The desire to minimize security risks related to transformation problems, and avoid situations of the type that emerged in the Balkans after the collapse of Yugoslavia, applies to the Union's development of relations with Russia, whose own even more pressing transformation problems are opening up more forcefully to the EU's sight with an extended EU–Russian border. The conclusion follows that, on this plane, the Baltic states' accession only worked out to highlight and amplify security questions related to the Union's new neighbourhood. But here one can find another dimension to the security issues in the form of questions related to securing EU access to Russia's energy resources. This is pivotal for the Union's continued economic development – or, put another way, for the prevention of a possible energy crisis within the Union and the related prospect of economic depression. This security character of the energy supply question springs from the fear of Russia turning out to be uncooperative, which would cause a direct security threat to the EU (Browning and Joenniemi 2004a: 249n11).

However, as existential as it may sound, this latter energy security issue can be reformulated as well. First, Russia has been a very dependable energy supplier to the EU, and the energy trade relations constitute the key integrative force in the strongly interdependent EU–Russian relations (Chapter 8). Second, with the development of the Union's energy relations with Russia emerges the question of the Union's energy relations with the CIS states that traditionally are within Russia's sphere of interests. Not only do they have their own transformation problems but many of them also possess energy resources of their own and are partly interlinked with Russia's energy provision system. This interlinked chain of dependencies and vulnerabilities means that, at the end of the day, there is no quick or easy way out of the energy security problems by means of enlargements and establishment of new partnership relations, although alleviation of some problems definitely may ensue in each instance. As a result, the security issues provide important views into the EU's Baltic and Russian openings, but leave equally important questions imperfectly answered.

The ultimately not entirely satisfying analysis of the economic and security issues within the EU's engagement of northern Europe and the post-Soviet north leaves us with a need to delve more deeply into the Union's own views of its geopolitical subjectivity within the northern European region and the post-Soviet north. Why in fact did the Union become involved in northern Europe? Why did it resort to the highly differentiated engagement of the CEE and Baltic states on one hand

and Russia on the other? What policies has the Union employed for attaining these ends, and what is the ultimate strategy underlying the Union's activities? These questions are answered by making use of the sizeable previous literature and by illustrating the argument by references to key EU documents and speeches of EU leaders picked from a large bulk of empirical material. The systematic empirical analysis relies on the model of the construction of geopolitical subjectivity introduced in the previous chapter, with its division into the Union's identity and interest projects and their sub-aspects: time and space, and geo-policy and geo-strategy.[2]

The EU's identity projects in northern Europe

Time

It is often noted how the Union, as a peace project, wishes to overcome Europe's conflict-ridden past that includes the experiences of authoritarianism, fascism, World Wars I and II and the resulting economic hardship. As it is well known, smoothly functioning political democracy and market economy regulated by the rule of law, as well as a largely civic conception of the nation, are now an integral part of EU time. In this light, the Commission has engaged on a conscious task of erasing the remnants of 'post-Soviet time' in the Baltic states and also, to a lesser extent, transforming such features in Russia. The EU Commissioner responsible for enlargement, Günter Verheugen, and the president of the European Commission, Romano Prodi, make the time aspects very clear with regard to the Baltic states' inclusion in the EU order:

> With the disappearance of the Iron Curtain we have the opportunity and the duty to go forward with integration and heal the wounds inflicted by the division of our continent. This project is about peace first and foremost and enlargement second.
>
> (Verheugen 2002)

> Integration is the only instrument we have to overcome the past and build up a peaceful, stable and prosperous future in Europe.
>
> (Verheugen 2001)

> Enlargement is also Europe's historic duty. Enlargement – in other words, the unification of this continent – closes one chapter in Europe's history and lays the basis for building the future.
>
> (Prodi 2001)

The statements by Verheugen and Prodi reflect the official view of EU institutions that the problems of 'post-Soviet time' in the Baltic states and the 'post-communist time' of the other CEE entrants can be overcome, and that in the longer run they will not affect the future development of the Union negatively. These countries are seen to possess a link to the tradition from which the contemporary 'EU time' has evolved, in the form of their short-lived experience of political democracy following the end of the First World War; in Estonia and Latvia this lasted until 1934, and in Lithuania until 1926.[3] That they subsequently remained behind the Iron Curtain evoked a perception of a European 'moral' debt for them. There is also scholarly support for the assumed proximity to 'EU time' of democracy and rule of law between the established EU members and the 2004 entrants. Dieter Fuchs and Hans-Dieter Klingemann (2001) analyse the histori-cally developed characteristics of groups of European states and their citizens' responses to the 1995–9 *World Values Survey*. They find a difference in values pertaining to democratic community between, on the one hand, more established EU members like the Nordics, the western part of Germany and Spain and, on the other, new CEE entrants, in particular the Baltic states. However, at the same time Fuchs and Klingemann assert that the differences are not very pronounced and, much more than a clear dichotomy, they form a continuum from 'Western Europe' and the Nordics to Central Europe, and then to the Baltic states, of whom Estonia stands closest to the rest of the CEE. In the Russian case, by contrast, the distance to 'Western Europe' grows disturbingly large. According to these authors, no solid foundation was perceivable for a democratic community in the historical develop-ment of the Russian society and state, nor in the uncovered attitudes and values of Russian citizens (Fuchs and Klingemann 2001: 38, 50–2).

Along these lines, the attitude taken by EU bodies towards Russia's efforts in overcoming its transformation problems after the Soviet era is relatively critical. This is evident in the Commission's first proper document on the Kaliningrad question, and Russia's prospective transit access there. The document was pub-lished when the region was becoming a topic of intense EU–Russian diplomatic wrestling early in the new millennium (see below; also Chapter 8). It expresses an aim to promote Kaliningrad's democratic development so that the Union would avoid confronting the disorder of its own past in a region where it is expanding. The document also included an offer of ties with the EU that is conditional upon the Kaliningrad region overcoming many of its serious transformation problems:

> Kaliningrad's own development and its future involvement in the wider region depends on the strengthening of the rule of law, and the broad im-plementation of good governance principles, particularly through promoting institution building and civil society development.
>
> (European Commission 2001)

Space

The incorporation of the Baltic states into a semi-insider group, and Russia into 'wider Europe', which was well conceivable along the time aspect, becomes only sharper when the space aspect in the EU's identity politics is examined explicitly. As a whole branch of literature on the spatial construction of post-Cold War Eu-rope has made plain, since the introduction of its 1993 Copenhagen criteria for membership the Union has perceived the CEE states, including the Balts, as coun-tries on their way to EU membership. And, as is also evident in the model of con-centric EU order, Russia and the rest of the post-Soviet states are relegated to the status of 'partners', and thereby firmly refused treatment as potential members of the Union. The president of the Commission, Romano Prodi, in fact commented that he himself had already in 2000 told the Russian president, Vladimir Putin, that Russia would never succeed in becoming an EU member (*Helsingin Sanomat* 27 November 2002). Indeed, in EU documents Russia is regularly referred to as the Union's 'eastern partner', or as part of 'eastern Europe'. This pattern is unlikely to alter swiftly, save for the low probability situation of a severe EU–Russian conflict where Russia would outright lose or give up its partner status. Thus, what 'East' meant during the Cold War era – the territories east from the Iron Curtain – has in this manner been simply moved eastwards, to refer to Russia and the other CIS states. Nonetheless, the spatial marker 'east' itself has stayed as a pivotal ingredi-ent in the EU's identity projects (e.g. Moisio 2002; Neumann 1998).

Some authors have expressed fears of such spatial identity politics leading to a sharply bordered 'fortress Europe' (see, for example, Batt 1999; Bort 2000; Fairley and Sergounin 2001; Grabbe 2000; Moisio 2003b). This scenario also in a very unfortunate manner excludes territories that are completely surrounded by the EU, as Kaliningrad is since May 2004 (!). However, as I will argue in the next section, for various reasons such a closure of Europe mainly concerns specific aspects of geo-policy like the Schengen borders regime promoted by the EU. A tightly bordered EU along all possible policy sectors is not in sight. This is what the network governance and boundaries literature and the empire writers have been so keen to point out. Also, by implication, it follows that the mixed Westphalian and federalist ideas for the geopolitical form of the EU, as proposed for example by the German foreign minister Joschka Fischer at the turn of the millennium, are not very realistic.

In his widely quoted and analysed remarks that relaunched the federalist EU debate, Fischer noted that the aim of building a federal EU state presupposes the existence of a 'centre of gravity'. In actual terms this translates into an EU core. In order to succeed, the federal project needs to be pushed forward by a core group of determined and powerful member states (see, for example, Joerges, Mény and Weiler 2000). This condemns the CEE countries to a peripheral and less integrated status in the enlarged Union. Regardless of the large EU funds, they cannot catch up with the core in the medium term. During their first decade within the Union, with the exception of Slovenia, and some specific policy sectors, they will be far behind all 'old' members in terms of their overall integration capacity. And if as this sort of 'laggards' they cannot participate in the Union's policies in the same way as the core members, fixed boundaries around the Union simply will not follow.[4] Instead, in the northern European context the boundaries will represent variable geometry.

However, of note here is the emergence of the BSR cooperation in the early 1990s under the supposedly unifying spatial marker of the Baltic Sea, as well as the Barents Sea cooperation, and the subsequent transformation of these cooperative arrangements into the even more inclusive 'northern European cooperation' where the Nordic, post-Soviet, post-communist and European elements meet. These spatial shifts are introducing some additional fuzziness into the concentric EU order, which is marginalizing Russia into the EU's 'eastern partner' or, at best, into a 'wider Europe' country. For the Nordic EU members, 'northernness' is a natural identity political marker which is easy to accept, whereas for the EU as a whole it is a relatively new designation; at the same time it logically complements the southern dimension of the EU that emerged with the Mediterranean enlargement of the 1980s. Some scholars have suggested that the northern marker carries considerable potential for embracing Russia in an alternative manner. For example, there have been alternative, northern proto-Russian states: medieval Novgorod (1136–1478) and Pskov (1348–1510), reaching to the arctic waters of the White Sea and to the North Urals. Likewise, the Pomor trade of northern Russia linked it to the Hanseatic League in the fourteenth and fifteenth centuries. Entertaining this legacy could help Russia to overcome the psychological conflicts of the Cold War era, the 'East/West' division and the strongly disciplining projects of Russian imperialism, Soviet communism, Atlanticism and Europeanism (Medvedev 2001: 96–9). Also, it has been argued that northernness is one part of a wider range of Russian characteristics and that it has also played a role, albeit not always a very central one, in Russia's definition of itself (e.g. Joenniemi and Sergounin 2003: 105–10). To this could be added how the collapse of the Soviet Union disconnected important southern (Ukraine) and western (the Baltic states) territories from 'Russia', and so moved it a long way towards the north (Aalto *et al.* 2003: 8).

The EU's interest projects in northern Europe

Geo-policy

The Union's enlargement policy is its most influential ordering device in northern Europe, with seven new members from the BSR included during 1995–2004. The enlargement policy is based on the Union's 1993 Copenhagen criteria for enlargement. The fulfilment of these criteria by the CEE states was monitored annually within the Agenda 2000 process. The overall organizing assumption of the policy is the Union's character as an association consisting of 'European' states. The specific criteria for membership candidate status that the Balts and those currently in line for membership have to satisfy include in political terms the stability of institutions guaranteeing democracy, the rule of law, human rights and respect for and the protection of minorities. In economic terms, they include the existence of a functioning market economy capable of coping with competitive pressures and market forces within the Union. Finally, the Union expects candidates to be able to take on the Union's legislation, the *acquis*, in its totality of 80,000-odd pages, and other obligations of membership, including the goals of political, economic and monetary union. Of the northern European candidates, Estonia was invited to start the accession negotiations in 1997 together with Poland, whereas Latvia and

Lithuania were invited only in the second wave in late 1999. All accession negotiations with the CEE countries were finalized by December 2003.

The economic and security issues underlying the 2004 EU enlargement that
also reached to the Baltic sates were discussed above as meriting some serious
attention but ultimately failing to conclusively answer all questions on why the
Union decided to include the Balts. From this realisation springs the suggestion
that *moral* arguments and considerations should also be counted, and perhaps as
among the most decisive drivers of the EU's enlargement policy. According to
these arguments, the Cold War era separation of the CEE countries and the Balts
from Western Europe is seen as artificial, and something that must be overcome.
This would supposedly allow for a truer European configuration to (re-)emerge.
This sort of moral argumentation, pertaining not only to easily calculable economic facts or identifiable security risks, but to the very *idea* of Europe and Europe-making, was not only used conspicuously often by representatives of the
CEE countries themselves, but was also heard in statements made by representatives of EU institutions. The CEE enlargement was in this fashion constructed as
a due occasion for 'Europe' to welcome back the countries that had a moral right
to be part of it and who had a moral mission to contribute to its building process
(e.g. Moisio 2002; Schimmelfennig 2003: 171–3; Sjursen 2002: 498–9). Hence,
only when the economic, security and moral issues are considered together does
the EU's enlargement process become a more intelligible policy tool alongside the
multitude of EU policy instruments.

With the enlargement and the adoption of the *acquis* by the Balts, Poland and
others came also the extension of the Union's Schengen borders regime eastwards.
This geo-policy lifts the Union's internal border controls, but concomitantly introduces tighter visa and other control procedures in the external borders in order
to tame the 'soft' security threats seen as emanating into the Union from the post-
Soviet space. In fact, the Union's ordering efforts on this plane became evident
in the requirement for the accession states to start applying Schengen-compatible
border crossing practices on their eastern borders already before their EU accession. In practice, this translated to the EU requiring the unilateral abolishment of
the simplified border crossing practices from the Estonian–Russian and Lithuanian–Kaliningradian borders that were in place during the 1990s.

On the Estonian–Russian border, the simplified regime was in place for those
in need of frequent border crossing for work, family and other social reasons,
many of which dated back to the relatively free movement of people of the Soviet era across the border between the then Estonian Soviet Socialist Republic
(ESSR) and the rest of the Soviet Union. The simplified regime was in place until
September 2000 and applied to about 17,000–20,000 people on the Estonian and
3,000 on the Russian side. The procedure was replaced by a system of simply
issuing free multiple entry visas for 4,000 people on both sides (see Berg 2002).
On the Lithuanian–Kaliningradian border, the simplified regime meant visa-free
travel for the Kaliningraders for trips to Lithuania of up to thirty days, and the
same for the Lithuanians. The old Soviet internal passports, the only documents
that many Kaliningraders possessed, were accepted. Moreover, a bilateral Lithua-

nian–Russian agreement regulated Russia's military and other transit to and from Kaliningrad. The Commission was initially ready to negotiate with Russia only over minor details on the Schengen issue. As stated by the European Council:

> Developing efficient and secure borders with neighbouring countries after enlargement should build on the EU acquis on border management (Schengen) while also learning from the experiences gained at the Fenno-Russian and the German–Polish borders.
>
> (European Council 2000)

In Kaliningrad's case, the prospect of full application of the Schengen regime led to the opening of a whole array of problems and tensions in EU–Russian relations that are outlined in more detail in Chapters 7 and 8. Suffice it to say here that these Schengen-induced cases reflect well on the EU's considerable ordering interests and on its policies of inclusion and exclusion. Such interests can also be observed in the Union's 1999 Common Strategy on Russia (CSR) and the EU–Russian Partnership and Cooperation Agreement (PCA). These documents laid the basis for the declaration of the Union's strategic partnership with Russia at the turn of the millennium. They manifest very clearly the Union's goal of trying to teach its own order to Russia, yet at the same time being somewhat indecisive as to just how firmly this should count as the Union's interest. The CSR and the PCA depart from the notion of 'common values' and aim to support the development of Russia's political democracy, rule of law and market economy. They envisage the creation of a common EU–Russian socio-economic space and a free market area, but decline to present any timetable or practical means for the attainment of these goals.

The CSR was introduced in order to bring coherence and direction to the EU's and member states' Russian policies. It declares as the EU's goals a stable, open and pluralistic democracy in Russia, market economy and rule of law. These aims do not in fact fall far from the Union's Copenhagen criteria (!). Moreover, it is asserted that the Union aims at 'maintaining European stability, promoting global security and responding to the common challenges of the continent through intensified cooperation with Russia' (European Council 1999). However, some analysts have claimed that the adoption of the 'common strategies' concept towards the EU's new neighbours was in part motivated by an effort to 'smuggle' the otherwise controversial QMV into the CFSP, which so far had operated on a largely intergovernmental basis (Haukkala 2001a). However, the CSR document and its practical implementation came to receive considerable criticism; for example, the document was seen as too general and imprecise regarding the actual means of EU–Russian cooperation (e.g. Haukkala 2003a: 14). Moreover, its implementation was often seen as suffering from large member states' own Russian policies and from a lack of funds.[5] The CSR gradually lost its significance in the face of more technical EU documents specifying the Union's financial and other project commitments with fewer declarations on issues like common values and democracy. The PCA, for its part, has since its introduction remained the main institutional channel for EU–Russian interaction. It includes the establishment of bodies such as the EU–Russian summit twice a year, the Cooperation Council with meetings once a year, and the Cooperation Committee at the senior official level with meetings whenever necessary.

The Schengen borders regime, the CSR and also partly the PCA represent EU geo-policies with a disciplining and *universalizing* tone familiar from the EU's enlargement policy, but lacking some of its ordering determination. This is also to be seen in the lack of funds of which the realization of these policies suffers in the Russian direction. The mere 300–360 million euros reserved for Russia's TACIS and the 30 million euros reserved for Russia's Cross-Border Cooperation (CBC) funding for 2000–3, implies that, at the outset, the Union has considerably less positive and persuasive power towards Russia than it has towards the much more generously funded CEE countries (Haukkala 2001b: 21–3). For a long time, before the EU–Russian clash over the Kaliningrad transit issue early in the new millennium, Kaliningrad's share of Russia's TACIS funding was a mere 3–3.5 million euros a year (Smorodinskaya 2001: 67; see Chapter 8). The relative scarcity of resources was also among the main reasons why the Union's *regionalizing* Russian policy, the ND, took off quite slowly and was thus largely unable to fulfil all the early promises of a new opening to the enlarging EU's relations with Russia.

The ND was formally put forth by the Finnish prime minister, Paavo Lipponen, in 1997 in Rovaniemi, northern Finland. It was first recognized EU-wide by European governments at the Luxembourg European Council of December the same year. The EU's first Action Plan for the ND (2000–3), which was adopted by the Feira European Council in June 2000, covered cooperation and policy areas such as the environment, energy, human and scientific resources, health, fight against crime, trade and investment and the special problems of Kaliningrad. It is surely worth noting how, in the ordering of northern European affairs, the first Action Plan relegated the CBSS, BEAC and Arctic Council to a subsidiary role, asserting that they '*may* assume a significant role in consultation with the Council of the EU in identifying common interests of the Northern Dimension Region'. The NCM, the Baltic Council of Ministers and the Barents Regional Council '*may* be consulted *in accordance with EU internal rules and procedures* when implementing the Action Plan' (European Council 2000; emphasis added). The second Action Plan (2004–6) formalizes this subsidiary function. It does assign an important role for many regional organizations in specific policy sectors but, importantly, it also reserves the right of the EU to define the overall order of regional cooperation in northern Europe on the whole (see European Commission 2003b). Finally, with the second Action Plan and the materialization of Baltic EU membership, the focus of the ND started to turn increasingly towards Russia's resources-rich northwest, with the Arctic also mentioned as a possible locus (Browning and Joenniemi 2004a: 244–5).

For those scholars who take an *optimistic* or *positive view* of the ND, it created a new and fruitful opening to the EU's engagement in the northern European region. As opposed to the old East/West division, it (re-)introduced the notion of the 'north', which, as noted, might represent a promise of new prospects for Russia's inclusion and engagement. Moreover, the ND also boosted the efforts towards a broad conception of EU foreign policy. Its successful implementation presupposes the aim of the EU's Constitutional Treaty of at least gradually breaking the Union's Maastricht-treaty-induced, compartmentalized pillar organization which goes with relatively little communication across policy sectors and competencies. Overall, according to the optimists, the ND is geared towards a more open-minded 'dialogue' compared with the 'negotiations' on a pre-set agenda that is peculiar to the EU's universalizing Russian policies (Aalto 2002a).

However, those taking a *critical view* of the ND have deemed that, in terms of material outcomes, results have been much more meagre than some of the wildest expectations of a new style of EU policy suggested in the late 1990s. The critics do not share the optimistic expectations that the regionalizing and relatively inclusionist ND alone can do very much to change realities on the ground. For them, mere talk and the promotion of northernness will not change regional realities; only more concrete actions and the use of financial resources instead of mere words will suffice. Well implemented policies, measurable outcomes and effective allocation of funds, preferably in the form of its own funds, which for a long time the ND did not have, would represent more significant progress. Yet the introduction of the ND environmental partnership (NDEP) in 2002, with its own earmarked funds of 100 million euros committed initially, and set to rise eventually to 2 billion euros, the ND partnership in public health and social well-being, launched in 2002 with specially committed country contributions, go some way towards correcting the financial problems.

The limitations in the status of the ND became also partially addressed by its gradual inclusion in the EU's neighbourhood policy since 2003. This new EU policy merges all the different EU regional cooperation instruments into one Neighbourhood Instrument during 2004–7, in order to provide a coherent framework for all the existing neighbourhood policies of the Union across the northern, eastern and southern directions, in the same coordinating manner as was initially attempted with the ND in the northern direction. In this context, according to the Commission, the ND might function as some sort of a model for the development of a regionalizing EU foreign policy towards its new neighbours. The Commission issued a communication document on the 'wider Europe' to the EU Council in March 2003, which sets out a clearly declared *responsibility* for the Union towards its new neighbours:

> The EU has a duty, not only towards its citizens and those of the new member states, but also towards its present and future neighbours to ensure continuing social cohesion and economic dynamism. The EU must act to promote the regional and sub-regional cooperation and integration that are preconditions for political stability, economic development and the reduction of poverty and social divisions in our shared environment.
>
> (European Commission 2003c)

The neighbourhood policy aims at providing a strategic gaze at the Union's new borders in order to 'develop a zone of prosperity and a friendly neighbourhood – "ring of friends" – with whom the EU enjoys close, peaceful and co-operative relations' (ibid.). In practice, this means spreading the EU's own order as far as possible towards its new neighbours without offering the prospect of membership or replacing existing treaties and partnerships. Potentially, this could also mean other dimensions to be introduced alongside the ND, such as Poland's proposal for an Eastern Dimension of the EU, bearing on Belarus, Moldova and Ukraine, besides Russia. It is not totally impossible that Poland's proposal may in some form end up in the neighbourhood policy umbrella, as its target areas include some of the same post-Soviet countries as mentioned in the Union's neighbourhood policy documents. However, in referring to Russia, it problematically lumps it together with its post-Soviet sphere of influence, and also overlaps with the focus of the ND policy (Browning and Joenniemi 2003).

Finally, with all the talk about the Union's increasing fuzziness of borders, concentricness or 'dimensionalism' (Haukkala 2003b), it is clear how crucial the debates about making the Union's foreign policy more effective have become. As noted in Chapter 1, the EU's project for a constitutional treaty proposes upgrading the status of the EU's foreign policy representative (since 1999, Javier Solana) to that of a Union Minister for Foreign Affairs, extension of the applicability of QMV into questions relevant to foreign policy, improvements in funding and support for forms of cooperation in foreign policy, and the introduction of a solidarity clause, as well as building up defence capabilities. And, as said above, some of these reforms may very well go on also without the treaty entering into force. Although they would undoubtedly boost the EU's capacity to formulate and implement its geo-policies in the northern European direction and elsewhere, it should be clear by now that the Union's toolkit is not by any means dependent on them.

Geo-strategy

The Union's historically developed overall strategic goals are well summarized in the Constitutional Treaty, which states that the Union will promote peace, the well-being of its peoples and its values, defined as respect for human dignity, freedom, democracy, equality, the rule of law and human rights, including the rights of persons belonging to minorities. The Union also declares to pursue an area of freedom, security and justice, and vis-à-vis its neighbourhood and the wider world it claims to promote its values and interests, and contribute to:

> peace, security, the sustainable development of the Earth, solidarity and mutual respect among peoples, free and fair trade, eradication of poverty and the protection of human rights, in particular the rights of the child, as well as to the strict observance and the development of international law, including respect for the principles of the United Nations Charter.
>
> (Inter-Governmental Conference of the European Union 2004)

These goals represent long-lasting aims of the EU's international involvement and are not likely to disappear with the difficulties of ratifying the Constitutional Treaty. The same goals are also clearly visible in the Union's northern European engagement. As discussed above, this engagement ranges from the enlargement policy, with its Copenhagen criteria, to establishing the Schengen borders regime around the enlarged Union and thereby supposedly protecting the area of freedom, security and justice, and finally to the treaties and documents pertaining to the Union's strategic partnership with Russia and its regional cooperation with the northwestern parts of the country within the framework of the ND and neighbourhood policies. In addition, it can be said that the Union is trying to take a more elaborate look at the human and natural resources on its northern borders, especially in relation to the rich but largely untapped oil and gas resources of Russia's northwest.

These strategic goals and the EU's northern European geo-policies, which were discussed above, make it clear that the Union is forming a strategic outlook on the northern European region as part of its overall subject-construction process. At the same time, it is clear that the whole constellation of the EU's northern European geo-policies remains double-edged. This manifests the complex intersubjective processes in which the Union is engaged. The enlargement policy, the Schengen borders regime, the CSR and the PCA are all universalizing policies that do not pay much particular attention to the identity and interests projects of their target areas, i.e., in the northern European context, the Baltic states, Poland and Russia. In simply and sometimes rather crudely outlining relatively narrowly conceived EU interests, they are geared at changing the prevailing regional contexts and patterns of regional interaction, as well as to erasing the remaining traits of 'postcommunism' and 'post-Soviet space' in the region. Simultaneously they ignore for example Estonia's, Lithuania's and Poland's bilateral experiences of cooperation and conflict with Russia and other 'wider Europe' countries like Belarus and Ukraine. Such a disregard for the accession countries' resources and experiences represents rather short-sighted waste. Moreover, as will be seen in Chapter 8, in Russian eyes the EU geo-policies have long failed to pay sufficient attention to most of Russia's views and proposals. In short, despite their apparently strong formulation and manifestation of specific EU interests, I will argue that these EU policies do not always help the Union to strengthen its subjectivity within the 'wider Europe' as hoped for. The main reason for this shortcoming is the EU's hesitancy to listen to and learn from those who have first-hand experiences of the post-Soviet problems the EU has set out to solve.

By contrast, the ND and neighbourhood policies boast a somewhat different, more regionalizing aim which naturally remains far from being ideal, but is certainly considerably more context sensitive. Paradoxically, as will be seen in the case study chapters that follow, such a more innovative, more responsibility-geared and multilateral policy such as the ND does not always automatically receive a standing ovation from its target areas. Of the Balts, Estonia in particular was relatively slow to embrace this type of policy, and Russia became frustrated with the ND after its initial enthusiasm, much to the disappointment of the country's northwestern regions, which have an even more pressing need for a constructive dialogue with the EU than Russia's federal centre does. Overall, the ND and neighbourhood policies manage to bring more balance into the EU's northern European engagement, although they simultaneously make the Union's overall strategy more complex to read to observers and to the EU's new members and neighbours.

On the whole, in the northern European context it turns out that the Union's concentric form displays strategic aims typical of a *civilian power* (Duchêne 1973) or *normative power* (Manners 2002). Here it can be recalled that most northern European EU members are also NATO members (Denmark, Germany, Poland, the Baltic states), while some are carefully and painfully weighing options for military alignment either in the EU or NATO context (Finland, Sweden). Russia is partly integrated into NATO, and its cooperation with the EU's ESDP is at its

Table 4.1 The construction of the EU's geopolitical subjectivity in northern Europe: the EU view

Component of ordering	Sub-aspect	Summary
Identity projects	Time	Overcome the European past. Erase threats to 'EU time'. These include the remaining traits of 'post-Soviet time' within the CEE, including the Baltics. Strive to reduce such elements from the enlarging EU's neighbouring regions such as Kaliningrad, northwest Russia and Russia on the whole where the difference remains much more notable
	Space	Emplotment of the Baltic states into the semi-insider group whilst taking Russia as the Union's 'eastern partner', or at best, a 'wider Europe' country. Tension between, on the one hand, claims of a sharply bordered 'fortress Europe' and the unrealistic idea of a Westphalian-federal Europe, and on the other, the more inclusive north European cooperation as an alternative means of engaging Russia
Interest projects	Geo-policy	Enlargement policy understood not only through economic and security benefits but also as a moral exercise in Europe-making and healing. Yet contradiction between universalizing EU geo-policies such as enlargement, Schengen borders regime, CSR and PCA, and regionalizing geo-policies such as ND and neighbourhood policy. Also efforts to strengthen the CFSP and ESDP, which do have some reflections for EU foreign policy towards northern Europe
	Geo-strategy	Ensure the prevalence of peace, security and other EU goals and values – i.e. EU order – within 'wider Europe'. Some tension between the mutually contradictory geo-policies intended for the realization of this overall goal.

planning and early implementation stages. But regardless of these differentiated patterns of military security orientation, it can be deemed that in the new millennium it is the EU, not NATO, that has grown to be the primary geopolitical subject in northern Europe. The EU is the entity towards which most of the diplomatic talk and action is directed in this region, and thus the one whose geo-strategy counts for the most. Further, it is the EU's civilian side, not its slowly forming military side, that currently and in the conceivable future is likely to form northern Europe's geopolitical point of gravity.

Summary

The discussion in this chapter of the two components of the EU's ordering efforts in northern Europe – its identity and interests projects – is summarized in Table 4.1.

The aspects outlined reflect the construction of the Union's geopolitical subjectivity as seen from the Union's point of view, and how the Baltic states and Poland are treated differently from Russia as a result of perceptions of time and space and the consequent character of the Europe-making project. In the next four chapters, some of the more detailed economic and security challenges ensuing from the Union's engagement with the post-Soviet north are touched upon. Also the region's input vis-à-vis the idea of Europe as embodied within the Union's northern European subject-construction process, i.e. the official views of the EU within the three Baltic states and Russia, including its Kaliningrad region, is spelled out together with its evolution since the 1990s. This analysis of their argumentation on what type of relations the enlarged EU should develop with themselves and its neighbours will help us to approach the less often examined side of the intersubjective construction processes of the EU's subjectivity in the northern European region. In other words, the case-specific challenges and the response the EU receives from the post-Soviet north become the issue of interest.

5   New semi-insiders I

Estonia

This chapter discusses the issue of what it means for the EU's subjectivity in northern Europe that Estonia joined the Union as a new 'semi-insider' in May 2004, after 67 per cent of the eligible voters said 'yes' in the referendum held in September 2003. With about one-sixth of Estonian residents ineligible for the referendum on grounds of their lack of Estonian citizenship – including mainly Russophone people – the end result was much more comfortable for the Estonian government and the pro-EU campaigners than was feared in a country which allegedly was the 'most eurosceptic and anti-integrationist' among the CEE candidates (Raik 2003a: 177; Tafel and Raik 2002: 34).[1] This gives us a good reason to ask what will Estonia bring to the Union, and how will it contribute to its 'north Europeanness'?

The first point of note is the even shorter history of the whole question than the Finnish and Swedish memberships and the accession process of the other CEE countries outside the Baltics. Estonia's relations with the EU did not constitute a real issue before the mid-1990s. Estonia restored its independence after half a decade of Soviet rule, in the aftermath of the Soviet Union's unsuccessful *coup d'etat* effort during early autumn 1991. The term 'restoration' refers to the independent Estonian Republic of 1918–40. This short-lived state emerged in a somewhat contingent manner from the ruins of the Tsarist Russian empire, in the midst of the chaos resulting from Russia's collapse and socialist revolution and Germany's defeat in the First World War. These two powers had dominated the geopolitical neighbourhood of Estonian territory after the demise of Swedish, Danish and Polish power. The connections of the 'first republic' of Estonia to the Nordic, European and western direction in general remained embryonic. In all honesty, even in the eyes of the Estonian political elite of the time, they left a lot to be desired. This was attested by the relative lack of interest from other powers in Estonia's fate of ending up as part of the Soviet Union after the Soviet–German duel on its territory during the Second World War.

And to make things worse from the Estonian point of view, during the early 1990s, the country's foreign policy makers were forced to commit their primary efforts to strengthening Estonia's sovereignty by ousting the remaining Soviet/ Russian troops from the country. This foreign policy issue was closely tied to the

Estonian–Russian controversy over the treatment of the approximately 10,000 Soviet military pensioners residing in Estonia, and the general treatment of Estonia's Russian-speaking population, a group making up approximately one-third of Estonia's population of 1.35 million, despite the emigration of about 110,000 Russophones mainly in the early 1990s (see Hallik 2002: 69). With pressure from European and US governments, and in particular with the US Congress's explicit threat to cut all of its financial assistance to Russia, the Soviet/Russian troops finally left after protracted negotiations by the end of August 1994. Formal Estonian sovereignty in foreign relations was then restored to the finest detail. Some technical decommissioning work of the Soviet-built nuclear reactors was allowed to continue at the Paldiski naval base, near the Estonian capital, Tallinn, until August 1995. Thereafter, attention quickly turned to the EU and NATO in the same manner as had happened in the CEE countries slightly earlier.

Estonia's free trade agreement with the EU was signed in July 1994. It came into force in January 1995 without any transition period of the type granted to Latvia and Lithuania. This constituted a propaganda victory of sorts for the Estonian elite responsible for EU integration, who prided themselves on a rapid transformation from the central planning of the Soviet era to a liberal market economy. At that stage, the EU largely constituted an undifferentiated image for the Estonian policy makers, let alone the broader public.

However, there was always a small northern European component involved in Estonia's integration project. The two-times Estonian prime minister, Mart Laar, suggested in 1995 that Baltic cooperation was hindering Estonia's development and should be replaced by a clearer Nordic orientation (D. Smith 2002: 170). Laar's comment was connected to the materialization of Finland's EU membership in January 1995. But it definitely was not about arguing for a unified northern Europe in the EU context, but rather about dissociating Estonia from the other two Baltic states in the heavily competitive rush to EU membership, where the Baltic solidarity shown during the 1987–91 Baltic independence movements weighed little (Väyrynen 1999). Laar's idea of playing with the Finnish connection did not come out of the blue: the Estonian language is fairly closely related to Finnish, and this, coupled with the geographical proximity to Finland and the strong interests of Finnish capital in the Estonian markets and cheap workforce, helped Estonia to reorient its trade away from the former Soviet Union a lot quicker than Latvia or Lithuania (Table 5.1). At the same time, as noted in Chapter 2, Finland and Germany especially were vocal supporters of Estonia's EU membership bid. This support was neither totally unselfish nor unreserved, but importantly it was seconded by Denmark, Sweden and other northern EU members.

Estonia's EU membership application was lodged in November 1995, and in 1997 Estonia was invited into EU accession negotiations alongside Poland, Hungary, the Czech Republic and Slovenia, and, crucially, ahead of Latvia and Lithuania. The European Commission's decision was initially somewhat perplexing to the Latvians and Lithuanians, albeit not totally unexpected. They implied that, in comparison to themselves, Estonia had a good image but did not offer anything completely unrivalled in economic terms, while at the same time, in the

Table 5.1 Estonia's foreign trade with the EU-15 and CIS, 1993–2003 (% of value)

	1993	1994	1995	1996	1997	1998	1999	2000	2001	2002	2003
Imports/ EU	23.3	23.9	66.0	64.6	59.2	67.8	65.3	62.6	56.5	57.9	76.5[a]
Exports/ EU	17.8	19.0	54.0	51.0	48.5	66.7	72.5	76.5	69.5	68.0	82.4[a]
Imports/ CIS	21.6	20.4	18.8	17.0	17.4	14.2	17.0	9.8	10.0	9.5	13.4
Exports/ CIS	30.4	30.3	25.1	25.1	26.4	20.8	13.4	4.0	5.1	5.4	6.0

Sources: 1998–2002 figures for the EU: European Commission (2003d); figures for the CIS 2000–3: Statistical Office of Estonia (2004); rest of the figures: Köll (2002: 349–50).

Note
a   These figures relate to the EU-25; see Estonian Statistical Office (2004).

Union's eyes, Estonia surely constituted as severe a security challenge as they themselves. I will next review some details of these issues of political economy and security, and then proceed to an in-depth analysis of Estonia's input into the construction of the EU's subjectivity in northern Europe and the realization of the idea of Europe there.

Issues of political economy in Estonia's EU accession

The rapid reorientation and subsequent good performance of the Estonian economy are often cited as the chief reason for its early invitation into EU accession negotiations. Foundations for this were laid already during the Soviet era. In the early 1980s, the Estonian workers were striking in solidarity with the Polish workers' movement led by Lech Walesa. The Estonians' knowledge of the Russian language was weaker than that of the other native Balts, and they expressed a keen interest in learning the Finnish language. At the time of the Soviet Union's collapse, they already had some experience of economic reforms, having made good use of the opportunities afforded by Gorbachev's perestroika policies late in the Soviet era. In addition, compared to Latvia and Lithuania, independent Estonia inherited a smaller share of heavy industries dependent on eastern sales, and thus a lesser degree of vested economic and social interests connected to industries rapidly becoming obsolete. Finally, Estonia's energy sector was half based on locally produced oil shale, which provided some freedom from Russian supplies. This Soviet legacy helped the Estonian governments of the early 1990s to quickly introduce Estonia's own currency, the *kroon*, tied to the German mark, in 1992, liberalize prices, reduce subsidies and implement other liberal style economic reforms (Panagiotou 2001).

Against these obvious economic advantages, and Estonia's resultant competitive edge vis-à-vis the other Baltic EU membership candidates, must be weighed the fact that, for the EU, the Estonian economy offered only relatively little, and this in the context of the CEE enlargement on the whole which is difficult to justify by references to economic gains in the short to medium term (Chapter 4). By 2002, Estonia's GDP per capita was only 42 per cent of the average EU level, and income disparities among the population were much higher than within the EU-15 countries, or even in Latvia and Lithuania (D. Smith 2002: 141; European Commission 2003d). EU aid to Estonia stood at 83 million euros during 2002 through PHARE, SAPARD and ISPA (European Commission 2002a). By 2001, the volume both for Estonian imports and exports with the EU-15 reached 3 billion euros, a figure which still remains of negligible importance to the Union side (European Commission 2004a).[2] Finland had surpassed Russia's place as Estonia's number one imports country already in 1993, well before the materialization of its own EU membership. Upon Finland's joining in 1995, it became Estonia's number one export partner. Finland, Sweden and Germany have thereafter provided the main pull for the strong reorientation of Estonia's trade in the direction of the EU and away from the Russian-led CIS (Table 5.1).

But in line with the idea of a CEE gateway introduced in the previous chapter, Estonia's potential as a transit country for goods on their way from Russia into the EU area is of some importance. In 1990, the Baltic republics handled almost a quarter of the Soviet Union's total freight shipments, and in 1993 they continued to handle a similar share of Russia's foreign trade shipments. During the next five years Estonia's transit cargo almost doubled. In comparison to Finland, which has similar potential as a transit country, Estonia offers lower transit fees and overall prices (D. Smith 2002: 123). During 1995–9, on average 56 per cent of Estonia's total transports were Russian transit, and by 1999 oil had assumed 70 per cent of these. Underlying the growth of transit trade were Estonia's improvements on railway transports and logistics, the expansion of the Muuga oil terminal near Tallinn and the good cooperation between the Estonian Pakterminal oil shipment company and the Russian oil giant LUKoil. These factors helped Estonia to grab 9 per cent of the value of Russia's westbound transit by 1999 (10 per cent of the volume) (Laurila 2003: 44–8). The LUKoil investment in Muuga might help to keep some of the Russian supplies coming through Estonia in the future as well, although Russia's port-building projects around St Petersburg since the turn of the new millennium are set to double Russia's own transport capacity and, by 2010, reduce the Baltic transit by 75 per cent (D. Smith 2002: 124; see also Chapter 8 below).

Estonia's transit potential may thus be under medium- or long-term threat, although the projected increase in Russia's export volumes into the EU may work to offset these threats. However, Estonia has another asset in the rapid adoption of information technology into administration, education and society at large, in a similar manner to neighbouring Finland. But during Estonia's membership negotiations the economic potential never rose to prominence as it did in Poland's case. The economic issues were overshadowed by concerns for technical issues such as the weakness of the judicial system, the small country's administrative capacity to cope with the relatively large structural and other funds set to flow increasingly from the EU coffers, and more political issues like the security concerns associated with Estonia's Russophone population (Raik 2003b: 48–56). At the background also lurked more profound questions of Estonia's problems in its relations with Russia.

Security issues in Estonia's EU accession

Apart from the soft security challenges encountered by the Union in an almost identical manner throughout the CEE and the post-Soviet space (Chapters 3 and 4), the security issues peculiar to Estonia's accession are tied to the controversies around Estonia's Russophone minority. Some of them belong to the 80,000-strong traditional Russophone minority dating back to the Russian-speaking contingent of the Estonian state of the interwar era. The majority, close to 400,000 people, are Soviet era immigrants or their descendants. In 1991, the latter suddenly found themselves as non-citizens with Soviet passports in a restored state of Estonia, in a situation where their knowledge of the Estonian state's historical origins was dim and where Estonian was made the only state language. On the basis of the 1992 citizenship law and its 1995 revised version, they were required to pass relatively stringent tests on the Estonian language, culture and constitution in order to become naturalized. At the time, only about 15 per cent of them were fluent in the Estonian language. About 100,000 opted to become Russian citizens in 1995–6. During Estonia's EU accession process, the European Commission expressed repeated concerns at the slow progress in naturalization, until a significant legislative change was made in 1999. The new regulations allowed the children of the close to 250,000 stateless persons in Estonia in the late 1990s – those former Soviet citizens who had not opted for either Russian or Estonian citizenship – to become citizens upon application. These young people will also receive systematic language instruction at school (Aalto 2003b: 28–9; 143–4; Hallik 2002: 69–77).

To the ethnically coloured legislation on the citizenship issue were tied other legislation inspired by the principle of restoration of Estonia's statehood. The application of the principle of restoration was set to 'estonize' the country after the russification tendencies of the Soviet era, when the number of Russian-speakers rose to nearly 40 per cent from the around 10 per cent of the interwar era. Through the 1989 and 1995 language laws, the Estonians introduced relatively strict regulations intended to making the Estonian language the only one in use in the public sphere. The elections law of 1998 required knowledge of the state language from the candidates, and there were provisions for civil servants to possess or apply for Estonian citizenship. Suffice it to say here that, as an effective precondition for Estonia's EU accession, all legislative changes required by the EU to ease the language and citizenship regulation were eventually made by successive Estonian governments, regardless of the unpopularity of these changes among large sections of society. This speaks of the Union's notable power in its enlargement policy. In several instances the Union used its 'network governance' and demanded that Estonia conform to the standards and requirements of the OSCE, which had an ethnic relations monitoring office in Estonia until 2001. Socialization into the EU's prevailing discourses on inter-ethnic matters was expected to keep the momentum going in Estonia's national integration project. Although exclusionist attitudes towards the Russophones persist among roughly half of the ethnic Estonians, it is clear that since the late 1990s the integrationist voices have become better empowered in Estonia. The majority of the older generations of Russophones, in particular those without Estonian citizenship and language proficiency, and who largely reside in Russian-speaking areas of eastern Estonia and Russian-speaking suburbs of Tallinn, are unlikely to participate in this integration project. The focus of the current integration policies is clearly on the younger generations. The state integration strategy was adopted in February 1998 and the integration programme in March 2000. Support measures for Estonian language tuition and other activities have been funded by the Estonian government, the Nordics, the UK and the EU, as well as international organizations (Aalto 2003a: 588–9; 2003b: ch. 2, 5, 6).

The Estonian government was initially reluctant to bow to the EU requirements on the inter-ethnic issues. The reason for such hesitancy can be found in the perceptions of the remaining connections of the Russophones to the Russian Federation. These perceptions were made only stronger by Russia's 'near abroad' policy. Regardless of the debatable justification of such fears, this means assuming the possibility of Russia using these people as a tool of its foreign policy, in order to press Estonia in a time of crisis (Aalto 1997; also Chapter 3). From the EU viewpoint, such a prospect of open conflict between the Estonians, Estonia's Russophone population and Russia is certainly not an appealing one. In fact, the Union has done its best to minimize it by encouraging and insisting on the necessity of national integration in Estonia, in order not to acquire new members with pockets of ethnically mobilized and politically Russia-bound Russian-speakers, some of whom are Russian citizens. In this way, the Union has tried to avoid compromising its Russian relations in connection to the CEE big bang enlargement of 2004. For the Estonian side, EU accession has soft security functions too, as it involves the Union more closely with the previously hugely asymmetrical Estonia–Russia dispute over the Russophones' rights.

The Estonian–Russian border dispute was an instance in which the Union's leaders were very relieved to see a technical agreement reached in 1996–7. The background to the emergence of the whole issue can be seen in the Estonians' adoption of a restorationist state-building model. Apart from the effort to restore the position of the Estonian language and ethnic Estonian citizenry by means of citizenship and language laws, this also presupposed restoring the land borders of interwar Estonia. However, during the Soviet era, the Soviet leader Stalin had changed the borders of the then ESSR by cutting around 5 per cent of its territory. This included the city of Ivangorod (Jaanilinn) with its surroundings east to the current Estonian–Russian border, and the Pechory (Petserimaa) area bordering current southeastern Estonia. The declared restoration of interwar borders was partly an unfortunate artefact of the overall restorationist state-building policy, and partly a result of nostalgia for these once Estonian territories (1918–40). As for nostalgia, particularly important was the Pechory area's settlement of the Setu people, who are ethnically and linguistically close to the Estonians. But worryingly from the EU point of view, a membership candidate country was engaged in a border dispute with the Union's great power partner and neighbour. Estonia dropped its territorial claims in 1996, but the technically agreed border treaty still awaits signatures (Aalto 2003b: ch. 2, 6).[3]

The other Estonian–Russian conflict issues were derivative of the larger conflict over Estonia's state-building model and the post-Soviet relationship between Estonia and Russia, and were mostly resolved during the course of Estonia's EU accession. At the turn of the new millennium the Constantinople-bound Estonian Apostolic Orthodox Church and the Estonian Russian Orthodox Church of the Moscow Patriarchate finally agreed on the dispute over the division of the Orthodox Church premises in Estonia, after protracted pressure from the Russian state and continuous refusal by the Estonian political elite to make the issue a subject of interstate negotiations. Russia, for its part, finally gave up its double tariffs for Estonian export goods with the materialization of Estonia's EU membership. Yet in the build-up Russia tried to prevent the automatic extension of the EU–Russia PCA agreement – which specifies the tariffs for EU–Russian trade – to the new member countries such as Estonia. This was to a degree a symbolic effort on Russia's part to maintain some of its power over the former members of the Soviet Union and to press for the same sort of privileges previously enjoyed in bilateral relations with some of the CEE states. But the resolve shown by the Union in this issue indicated a determination to include Estonia and other accession states, and merely led to a joint EU–Russian communiqué on addressing Russia's concerns related to EU enlargement, and the continuation of the EU–Russian dialogue towards creating common spaces ('Joint statement on EU enlargement and EU–Russia relations' 2004).[4]

What results from this brief discussion of economic and security issues is an image of the Union acquiring a small and in economic terms relatively insignificant new member, which during 2004–7 has only four votes out of a total 345 (1.2 per cent) in the EU's intergovernmental decision-making body the Council of Ministers, and six seats of the European Parliament's total of 732 (0.9 per cent). However, Estonia admittedly possesses some assets vis-à-vis the Union's broader aims of strengthening its northern European subjectivity. Estonia offers first-hand experience of relations with Russia, but at the same time a large part of this experience is negatively loaded and perceived. This constitutes a burden which is evident in the uneasy history of Estonian–Russian relations. How is this all reflected in Estonia's input into the Union's northern European expansion? What sort of views does Estonia bring into the Union and its Europe-making projects? These questions are answered by examining a large body of empirical material dealing with the officially sanctioned Estonian views on the EU's subjectivity in northern Europe.[5] The systematic empirical analysis relies on the model of geopolitical subjectivity introduced in Chapter 3.[6] In place of analysing the views expressed by the Union's institutions on this issue, the focus now turns to the Estonian responses regarding this project and Estonia's part in it.

But before proceeding to the Estonian views, a few remarks are appropriate.

Obviously Estonia's EU accession process consumed a lot of the energy of the Estonian political elite during 1997–2004. This focus upon fulfilling largely technical EU accession criteria for a considerable period lessened their interest in presenting any particularly innovative visions of the Union's subjectivity in northern Europe. Also, one should keep in mind that the accession countries were not encouraged to take strongly reform-oriented positions at the Convention for the Future of Europe where revealing opinions on these aspects were expressed. They merely had a right to voice their opinion, not to participate in any voting. Consequently, they might prefer to take initiatives once they are firmly inside the Union (see also Mouritzen and Wivel 2005a: 34–5). Finally, it is worth noting that the officially sanctioned Estonian views of EU's subjectivity in northern Europe are primarily pro-EU views, which are rather widely shared among EU experts in the country. Their views on details are not always universally shared by the broader public, which is not too well informed of all of the Union's activities in northern Europe. And it must be added that, during the build-up to Estonia's EU membership, politically active EU sceptics and outright opponents concentrated their efforts on criticizing or opposing Estonia's membership of the Union on grounds of national gain or loss, and thus largely refrained from envisioning the details of its northern European subjectivity (Aalto 2004a: 14–15; for more, see Chapter 9).

Estonian views of the EU's identity projects in northern Europe

Time

From the beginning of its formation in the early and mid-1990s, the Estonian view of the EU was strongly inspired by the often quoted 'return to Europe' discourse that was so characteristic of central and eastern Europe as a whole (Lagerspetz 1999). The idea of having been kidnapped for half a century by the 'East' and then finally returning to the true 'cultural and political home of Europe' is a well-known time construct (see, for example, Lauristin *et al.* 1997). It represents an attempt to escape the 'Soviet time' and enter a 'European time' in which the long-standing Soviet/Russian pressure on Estonia is supposedly overcome (Aalto and Berg 2002). Instead of repeating these arguments and the reasons for their emergence here, we will benefit from examining their persistence by taking a look at the contribution by the Estonian representative at the European Convention, Henrik Hololei, to the discussion of the so-called withdrawal article in the drafting of the Union's new Constitutional Treaty:

> Like all of you, I hope that this clause will never be used. But it is important to have an option like this in the Treaty. And not only because such a clause formally existed even in the Soviet and Yugoslav constitutions and [because] I do not want to answer my people when they ask if SU and Yugoslavia, on

paper, were more democratic than EU. Not having this article makes it difficult to defend the new Constitutional Treaty in my country.

(Hololei 2003a)

This comment, which stresses that the Constitutional Treaty of the EU should be at least 'as good' as the formal treaties in the Soviet Union, reflects the historical experience against which the EU's subjectivity is measured in Estonia. Similarly, the Estonian government's document, 'Positions of the Estonian Government on the Future of Europe', clearly states that Estonia is cautious of the proposal including any references to a 'federal basis' in the new Treaty (Government of Estonia 2003). A reference like this would again evoke negative memories of the formal federalism of the Soviet era, which in practice translated into very little local autonomy within the ESSR and should be left firmly behind by now. The Estonian view of federalism being out of place was clearly expressed in all the expert interviews conducted for this book in Estonia:

To me, as an Estonian, my preference in this question is for intergovernmental cooperation. I mean that, to an Estonian, the term 'federation' sounds somewhat . . . , well, not threatening, but . . .

(Estonian EU observer, December 2002)

The drawing of comparisons between the EU and the experience of the Soviet era bears some resemblance to the Finnish claims during the 1990s of the country becoming westernized and europeanized through its membership of the EU. In these discourses, the legacy of Finland's 'finlandization' during the Cold War – its partial loss of external sovereignty in the face of what was perceived as Soviet pressure – was more than obvious (Browning 2002: 65). As discussed in Chapter 2, Finland's EU membership application was strongly conditioned by the Soviet Union's collapse and the wish to henceforth avoid a similar pressure from the East. Thus, while Finland's EU integration must be understood in the context of 'finlandization', the current Estonian accent on the need to have a withdrawal article in the new treaty and to avoid any references to a 'federation' must be read as something peculiar to a post-Soviet country. In fact, Estonian EU experts readily accept that the legacy of the Soviet era experience still prevails in Estonia and that therefore any talk of entering another 'federation' without a withdrawal option has uncomfortable connotations. Even though there are opponents to federalism in Finland and Sweden as well, similar Soviet-influenced connotations of the term 'federalism' have not been an issue. Rather, we have seen efforts to simply guard national sovereignty that derive from other national experiences.

In other words, although it remains true that hardly anyone wants to be labelled 'post-Soviet' in identity terms (!) – i.e., to still be defined by the Soviet era experience – it is evident that such an identity label tells us something about the Estonian view of 'EU time'. As seen in the 1996 Top Decision-Makers Survey, national level policy makers and opinion leaders in the EU-15 for the most part support federal-type arrangements and increased sovereignty-sharing in several policy sectors (Hallstrom 2003: 70). By contrast, in the light of the rather extensive material surveyed here, their Estonian counterparts are far more reserved in their attitudes towards increasing federalism. They think that 'EU time', with its topical issue of federalism, represents a somewhat distant goal for Estonia, where the population is still to a large extent living in 'post-Soviet' time. This is the case, regardless of the Estonians' sincere efforts to 'europeanize', and in spite of the EU's efforts to erase the 'post-Soviet' elements in Estonia by 'socializing' them by means of the accession process and 'carrots' such as the pre-accession structural funds.

In short, with respect to the time aspect, the claims made by the Estonians since the mid-1990s about the similarity between themselves and those in the Union – about them having entered the same post-Cold War European time – have been gradually transformed into an awareness of slight but important differences between the insider group of 'old' EU members and Europe's 'post-Soviet north'. We have therefore witnessed the Estonian Minister of Foreign Affairs Kristiina Ojuland (2003a) calling for the Union to resist any pressure from groups favouring the 'development of a club-like system', which would differentiate between old, intermediate and new members.

Space

One of the most characteristic features of Estonia's European policy in the mid-1990s was the vocal preference for security issues to be dealt with on the all-European or Euro-Atlantic level. This was a direct reference to the combined role of the EU and NATO, in which the EU, in a commonplace fashion, was seen as providing 'welfare' and NATO for its part 'security'. Hence the two together guaranteed 'stability' (Aalto 1997: 21). The main goal at that time was to obtain membership in both organizations in order to avoid the prospect of a typical small-state tragedy, i.e. being left to stand alone during a crisis, as had happened during the Second World War. Thus, until the late 1990s, the Estonian view of the European space largely resembled what might be termed 'Western European pan-Europeanism'. Acts of singling out specific European regions, such as Prime Minister Laar's already mentioned recommendation for a Nordic orientation, were rare. Consequently, a major foreign policy goal was the relatively undifferentiated one of simply becoming included in the Union's space.

Another aspect of Estonia's EU membership bid is that it was introduced in an attempt to escape Russia's influence within the territory of the former Soviet Union. Therefore Estonia's attempt to escape 'post-Soviet time' and enter 'EU time' was accompanied by an exclusionist view vis-à-vis Russian–European relations. This exclusionism has not entirely disappeared, though Estonian views acquired more balanced tones during Estonia's accession period when the nation was undergoing a socialization process into EU views. In the 1990s, the often repeated message was that Russia was not a proper 'European' nation because of the imperfect character of its democracy and, no less, because of its 'near abroad' policy. In an expert interview in late 2002, reservations towards Russian–European relations continue to surface, although now in a more amenable form. During the interview, the expert was asked to comment on one of the claims that have been made frequently during the general debates on EU enlargement and the future of Europe: 'The Union should be open to all countries that want to belong to the Community, if they satisfy the membership criteria and are able to assume and implement obligations.'

> I would say 'yes' as far as all *European* countries are concerned; but as it is the *European* Union, let it remain a union of *European* countries . . . But if some different sort of union is being created, then such a union might extend further than it should.
>
> . . .
>
> If our aim is to create a different sort of a union . . . then one might actually consider the possibility of the EU extending as far as to Japan. But then it will become a *Eurasian* power, would no longer be a *European* Union . . .
>
> (Estonian policy maker, December 2002; emphasis added)

It must be granted that these Estonian views on the prospect of Russia's inclusion in the EU do not substantially differ from what one would commonly hear in almost any other EU member country. The statement of the Finnish Minister of Foreign Trade, Paula Lehtomäki, that the possibility of a Russian membership of EU should not be rejected if Russia were to fulfil the Union's criteria (*Suomen Kuvalehti* 25/2003), is very much an isolated comment, as is Italian prime minister Silvio Berlusconi's positive statement about how Russia's EU membership could contribute significantly to the Union's efforts to build a European military capacity (*Helsingin Sanomat* 25 March 2003). Still, the Estonian view of the deepening Russian–European cooperation, and of what direction this cooperation should take in the near future, differs notably from that of Finland and Sweden (Chapter 2).

In this context, the fact that a small group of Estonian policy makers, towards the turn of the millennium, started to portray Estonia as a Nordic country is significant. In October 1998, the then Estonian Foreign Minister, Toomas Hendrik Ilves, termed Estonia a 'post-communist Nordic country' (Ozolina 1999: 15). He subsequently, in December 1999, gave a speech in Stockholm, which was entitled 'Estonia as a Nordic Country'. His main argument was that Estonia, the Nordic nations and Britain together form *Yuleland*. This concept covers countries with a relatively similar tradition for celebrating Christmas, countries with identities that have many characteristics in common. His speech is often interpreted as an effort to dissociate Estonia from the negatively conceived Baltic group, just as Prime Minister Laar had tried to do already earlier. Laar, for his part, later claimed that a similar historical and cultural background unites Estonia and the Nordic nations. He called attention to such examples as the Protestant religion and the long tradition of education of the masses and of literacy. In a more contemporary context, the use of IT equipment and similar family formation patterns link Estonia to the Nordic nations (Niemeläinen 2002: 61–77).

If Ilves's and Laar's efforts to get Estonia labelled as a 'Nordic' country were to bear fruit, they would need the recognition of the Nordic countries. In Finland, however, their efforts were mostly received with reservation (Moisio 2003b: 72–3; Niemeläinen 2002: 57–8). The fact that *Norden* remained an exclusive enclave – regardless of its becoming partly overrun by EU integration – became all too evident in this context (Joenniemi and Lehti 2003: 133–6). According to one close observer and participant, Finland covertly but shamelessly pursued its own interests during Estonia's accession negotiations, while it publicly continued to tout strong support for Estonia's membership. Such a double-track strategy was adopted in order to reduce the possible negative consequences that Estonia's membership might have on Finland's economy. Finnish EU representatives strove to introduce a transition period for the free movement of the Estonian workforce, fearing that an influx of cheap Estonian labour might destabilize the Finnish job market. Similar efforts were witnessed in such areas as income taxation and taxation of tobacco and alcohol, areas in which the Estonian regulations were perceived as a threat to Finland's tax revenues because they might lead to a possible reorientation of the flow of people, goods and businesses (Estonian policy maker, May 2002).

Although the Nordic nations take it for granted that Estonia is part of the wider region of northern Europe, they still perceive a distinct difference between Estonia and the Nordic nations. These nations make a clear distinction between *Norden* and northern Europe and between the geographical areas these terms commonly refer to, a distinction that Estonian policy makers do not always make (Ruutsoo 2001). Nonetheless, the Estonian EU elite does embrace identification with the broader northern European region:

> The European Union consists of member states and there are different ways of thinking in each member state. I'm not saying that Estonia should very clearly compartmentalize itself into any particular group of countries, but the idea of Estonia as a Nordic country . . . is of course rather obvious . . . the region that we can discern from, let us say, Ireland to Finland. And in terms of its basic characteristics, it forms a rather clear counterweight to southern Europe. These are countries that much more easily comprehend our goals.
> (Estonian policy maker, May 2002)

> In reality we want to belong to the north [northern Europe], in the sense that we cannot belong to Central Europe. But one has to belong somewhere, and [Estonia's geographical position] will strengthen the co-operation in the north or within the Northern Dimension.
> (Estonian politician, February 2003)

The distinction that the two quoted Estonian experts make between northern and southern members, and their perception of Estonia's 'natural' place in the northern group, is a result of their growing socialization within the EU context. Accordingly, EU experts from Estonian political parties almost exclusively name northern European countries as the most likely partners or models for Estonia in the enlarged EU (Tafel and Raik 2002: 27). Estonian delegates' activities during the Convention also made such a 'natural northernness' evident. Here most of the Estonian small-group consultations and bilateral meetings were with north European members or accession countries (Veebel 2003: 157).

However, in order to maintain the proper perspective, it is crucial to stress that all this emerging north Europeanness is adopted within the framework of national identity, sovereignty and the idea of a Union consisting of individual member states. These are the key words appearing in the most important speeches made by the Estonian President, the Foreign Minister, the Prime Minister and the Estonian representatives at the Convention. In fact, the Estonian government advocated that the EU's new Constitutional Treaty include a clause stipulating 'that the Union shall respect the national identities of its member states' (Government of Estonia 2003). The Estonian representative Henrik Hololei also made the following comment during the preparation of the Treaty: 'it is slightly worrying that neither the first nor the second set of articles contain a reference to the official languages of the Union' (Hololei 2003b). Moreover, the Estonian government asserts that 'Estonia has reservations about the idea of granting the parliaments and regions of the Member States a right to refer to the European Court of Justice on grounds of non-compliance with the principle of subsidiarity' (Government of Estonia 2003). Whereas the insistence on the importance of national languages dates back to Estonia's struggle for sovereignty, when the language issue was used for gathering popular support, the wish to delimit regional rights can be related to memories of the struggle for 'autonomy' in the largely Russian-speaking Ida-Virumaa region of northeastern Estonia in 1993. Although the 1993 conflict is best understood as an effort to attract Tallinn's attention to the multitude of problems faced by the impoverished region, rather than as an example of separatism (D. Smith 1998: 11–14), its very emergence has made the Estonian government wary of losing its grip on sovereignty within EU integration.

The several references made by various representatives of official Estonia to the desirability of a 'Union of member states' do not, however, show any clear understanding of what this notion actually entails. In an interview, Foreign Minister Ojuland claims that the EU remains 'for an individual member state a question of foreign policy' (*Eesti Ekspress* 1 July 2003). In May 2003, the Estonian Prime Minister Juhan Parts, for his part, asserted that after Estonia's EU accession pure domestic policy will cease to exist in nearly all policy sectors, with EU integration blurring the internal/external distinction (Parts 2003a). Still, one month later he stated that European policy will 'from now on be mostly about domestic policy' (Parts 2003b). Such divergent understandings of the newly emerging internal/external distinction reflect how the Estonian EU elite tries to balance the imperatives of EU integration with the need for national sovereignty (cf. Kuus 2002a: 102). This situation is, of course, not fundamentally different from the one faced by their Danish, Finnish and Swedish counterparts.

Estonian views of the EU's interest projects in northern Europe

Geo-policy

The Union's enlargement mostly has a predetermined agenda, with no opt-outs given to the accession states as was done at the time of the Finnish and Swedish accession. This feature was instrumental in making Estonia view the Union as a given – a package which you can either choose or reject, but not modify – at least not until you have achieved membership. The answer given by one Estonian policy maker, who was asked to comment on the statement 'the EU can hardly be my most preferred choice for organizing the European political space', illustrates this. His answer indicates that one did not see too many alternatives to the EU, or alternative ways of organizing the European political space:

> Whilst speaking of options, and especially of real life options that we can choose between; among these, the EU is indisputably the best choice. You cannot make choices that are not available.
>
> (Estonian policy maker, December 2002)

This take-it-or-leave-it view of the EU and its enlargement policy is related to the treatment of the whole process in security terms – as helping Estonia to gradually leave behind its 'post-Soviet time' and the negatively conceived association with the post-Soviet space and Russia as its hegemon.[7] Because the enlargement of EU provides Europe and its various constituent states with a new historical situation and a new model for building stability, the Estonian president, Lennart Meri, would speak of the enlargement as 'the objective of Europe', as a case in which 'the process is indeed the aim, because there will never be a completed Europe' (Meri 2000a), and would refer to the enlargement as 'the motive force that sets the wheels of Europe in motion' (Meri 2000b). Foreign Minister Ilves, for his part, has stated that 'the acquis represents a detailed codification of more general principles of the enlightenment programme: respect for individual liberty, rules for the behaviour and responsibility of states, a level of rigour for laws as well as their implementation' (Ilves 1999).

This Estonian rhetoric was aimed at ensuring that the enlargement was not delayed. For the same reason the Estonian government was also quick to fulfil the EU's Schengen requirements on its Russian border well ahead of the materialization of the membership, by abolishing the simplified border-crossing scheme in September 2000 (Chapter 4). The government's decision never raised any hot debate in Estonia. Underlying such a take-it-or-leave-it view of the EU requirements is a perception of Estonia's relatively weak bargaining position. The interviewed Estonian EU experts perceived Estonia as a small country negotiating with a community that possesses well formulated interests. And certainly Estonian policy makers have become well aware of the interests of the northern member states. As mentioned above, for example, Finland has tried to limit the threat of increased competition from Estonia in the enlarged Union by arguing for lengthy transition periods for many sectors, transition periods that hinder Estonia's full integration into the Union.

Even if one keeps these factors in mind, it is clear that the Estonian take-it-or-leave-it perception differs from what was in evidence in connection with Finland's and Sweden's accession (Chapter 2). And Finland's initiative for the Northern Dimension of the EU is a well-known example of small state power in European integration (Arter 2000). Finland, Denmark and Sweden all adopted an activist approach to the ND policy and organized conferences on the ND during their EU presidencies.

Initially, the Estonians had some fears that the ND was a Finnish effort to patronize Estonia (Raik 1999: 157–8). Subsequently, Estonia went on to organize an ND business forum in April 2001. Such actions led some observers to portray Estonia as an active participant in regional cooperation around the Baltic Sea (Kuus 2002b: 297). The new Estonian president, Arnold Rüütel, also claimed that the Estonians have 'positive experiences of cross-border cooperation with Russia in the framework of the Northern Dimension' (Rüütel 2002). Yet it is clear that for a long time Estonia failed to lend consistent support to the ND. Until the drafting of the second Action Plan, Estonian policy makers preferred to view the ND as something coming from Brussels – not Tallinn, Helsinki or Stockholm:

> Estonia's position in relation to the Northern Dimension programme has always been that those priorities and programmes that provide the widest possible effects should be considered the primary ones. There is no point in promoting some sort of a small-scale and local programme, as such pro-grammes do not yield any great benefits or effects.
>
> (Estonian policy maker, December 2002)

> The Northern Dimension is not often mentioned in Estonia ... Lithuania has very effectively linked together the Kaliningrad and Northern Dimension questions ... the Latvians opted for a very active approach in relations with Moscow or the Russians; the Latvian Foreign Ministry has founded a special Northern Dimension work group ... in the web page of the Estonian Min-istry for Foreign Affairs, neither Russia nor Finland is mentioned; rather the Northern Dimension has been presented as a common policy of the Union, simply promoting cooperation in northern Europe.
>
> (Estonian EU observer, December 2002)

A speech made by the Estonian foreign minister, Toomas Hendrik Ilves, at the 2001 ND business forum clearly illustrated this fairly passive stance. Ilves was happy to simply quote Chris Patten, the EU commissioner for external relations, whilst singling out priority activities for the ND: 'working with Russia to tackle nuclear waste, and addressing cases of environmental pollution throughout the Baltic region, striving to combat organized crime' (Ilves 2001). In October 2002,

Ilves's successor, Kristiina Ojuland, quoted this same statement in her speech in Brussels – without mentioning the original source (Ojuland 2002a).

In connection with the drafting of the ND's new parent policy, the EU's new neighbourhood policy, the Estonian reactions also displayed open suspicions. Ojuland finds that the EU 'should formulate an effective engagement policy for its "new neighbours"' (Ojuland 2003b). However, the underlying reservations towards neighbourhood policies were expressed clearly in the comments made by the Estonian representative at the Convention during a debate under the special title 'The Union and its immediate neighbourhood': 'to some, this may bring back memories of a similarly sounding term employed by a neighbour of the Union in a very different context' (Hololei 2002a). Obviously the negative experience here referred to is Russia's 'near abroad' policy, which is conceived an unsuitable model for the Union's relations with its immediate neighbours.

Yet, by 2003, there were some indications that the Estonian views of the ND were becoming markedly more positive and activist. In its own contribution to the second ND Action Plan, submitted to the EU in February 2003, Estonia identified as its priority areas such items as infrastructure networks, maritime safety and sustainable development. Of these, the issue of maritime safety resonated particularly with the Finnish concerns about potential environmental catastrophes resulting from Russia's increased oil shipments in the Baltic Sea from its new ports around St Petersburg (Chapter 8). There was particular concern about catastrophes happening in the wintertime, when there were harsh ice conditions for which the old carrier ships were not built. Moreover, Estonia's contribution included a special section on the enhancement of bilateral cooperation with the Russian Federation. During autumn 2003, Foreign Minister Ojuland also signalled her emphatic approval of the ND and the neighbourhood policy (Ojuland 2003c; 2003d).

How should we interpret this change of attitude towards the ND and the neighbourhood policy? It can be pointed out that Estonian conceptions of time and space, which connote reservations in relation to Russia, were underlying Estonia's relative hesitancy with respect to contributing to the ND policy. And after all, as implied in Chapter 4, it must be granted that, after the turn of the new millennium, the ND was turning into a regionalizing policy of the Union directed towards Russia's northwest and the Arctic at the expense of a more encompassing Baltic Sea focus. In connection with the discussion of any kind of Russia-oriented policies, the Estonians have been quick to point out the familiar problems in dealing with both Moscow and Russian authorities on a regional level. As an Estonian policy maker stated when she was asked to comment on a statement claiming that the economic opportunities in the immediate neighbourhood of the new enlarged Union should be better exploited and be used as a foundation for a broader cooperation:

[statement to be commented on] The incredible economic potential that exists on the eastern rim of the European Union warrants absolute priority to be given to the Union's policies towards its future neighbours in Eastern Europe:

Russia, Ukraine, Belarus, Moldova. The concept of a wider Europe has to grow into a comprehensive policy backed by firm political will and adequate resources.

[comment] Well, surely we must also think of the fundamental principles upon which such cooperation can be based. But if it [the Union's policies towards the future neighbours] really can assume absolute priority I am not sure. It is important, but I am not sure whether it is of overriding importance . . .

(Estonian policy maker, December 2002)

What is notable here is that both the enlargement policy and, for a long time, the ND, failed to spark a strong political reaction from the Estonian side – be that in the shape of 'vital' demands or of new proposals. First, this gives grounds for suggesting that the Estonians are not set to block the Nordics' and the Union's existing policies in the north. But at the same time, the passive attitudes vis-à-vis enlargement policies and Estonia's reservations towards the ND do raise some questions about whether Estonia is likely to contribute significantly to the Union's policies towards northern Europe.

The debates concerning the Union's new decision-making rules in the field of foreign policy also speak for a cautious view on the future development of Estonia's views on the EU's northern European policies. Estonia's reservations on this point will not help the Union assume stronger subjectivity in the region. Estonia is strongly in favour of maintaining the unanimity principle, so that other members could not impose, for example, their preferred Russian policies on Estonia. As the Estonian representative at the Convention stated with regard to his government's position: 'foreign policy is an area that inherently belongs to the core of the national sovereignty' (Hololei 2003c). Yet the Estonian view allows for some flexibility in the enlarged Union: '. . . one should allow for enhanced co-operation also in the field of foreign policy where a "coalition of the willing" may pursue actions in the name of the whole Union' (Hololei 2002b). Yet again, to maintain perspective, Sweden's cautiousness with respect to this issue should be noted. Finland, however, has shown itself more ready to take steps leading towards the adoption of supranational foreign policies (Istituto Affari Internazionali 2003: 29–32).

Finally, in the field of ESDP, a policy sector which might in the future have some repercussions for the ordering of northern Europe, Estonia has displayed a rather reserved view, in particular towards suggestions for developing a European military force capable of operating independently of NATO. The Estonian government asserts that 'the emerging European security and defence policy should be regarded in the framework of broader trans-Atlantic relations. EU actions in the field of defence should focus on complementing the activities of NATO, especially on fulfilling the Petersberg tasks, where the Union would certainly be able to contribute' (Government of Estonia 2003). Estonia is, of course, not alone in having these reservations. Its preference for limiting the ESDP to the crisis management and peacekeeping-oriented Petersberg tasks, reminds one of the Finnish and Swedish cautiousness in the sector of military integration, whereas the insistence on maintaining a strong role for NATO is consistent with the Danish position.

Geo-strategy

Estonia has come to accept the Union's existing policies towards northern Europe in a somewhat passive manner. It has not always displayed great willingness to take initiatives. Estonia has shown considerable reservation towards several contemporary policy topics that were perceived as threatening national identity and sovereignty or suggesting nationally unpleasant policy labels, such as the neighbourhood policy. At the same time, it is true that, since Estonia's EU application in the mid-1990s, Estonian EU experts have developed more detailed views not only of the Union as a whole but also of the desired characteristics of its subjectivity in the northern European region, views that are increasingly in line with the Union's *contemporary position* as a northern European power. At the same time, the Estonian EU experts have, with respect to several issues, preferred to leave the EU with the subjectivity it already possesses in northern Europe. Such relative conservatism and passivity compared to Finland and Sweden may be caused by factors like Estonia's lack of any formal power vis-à-vis the Union prior to obtaining membership. The words of the Estonian representative at the Convention aptly sum up the Estonian views of EU policies: '. . . in principle it is correct that the deepening of integration can no more be a purpose in itself. In the case where it is commonly held that the integration has reached an optimal level, it would be reasonable to stop' (Hololei 2002c).

This overall assessment does not mean that the Estonians are unwilling to develop the EU's strategic posture. Already in November 1998, the Estonian foreign minister, Raul Mälk, insisted that Estonia is interested in joining a Union 'that is effective both internally and on the international stage' (Mälk 1998). In May 1999, Mälk's successor Ilves called for 'efficient decision-making, a strong Euro, and an undivided international voice' (Ilves 1999). And in November 2002, Foreign Minister Ojuland expressed Estonia's desire 'to belong to a body, which has clearly defined goals, and is capable of dealing with international issues' (Ojuland 2002b). Yet, these comments are somewhat puzzling in the light of the rather conservative Estonian views regarding proposals for the future development of EU policies in northern Europe – proposals that might be seen as, on the whole, strengthening the Union.

Such internal contradictions in the Estonian views become more comprehensible once one considers the idea provocatively put forth by the US secretary of defence, Donald Rumsfeld, of a 'new Europe' that consists of new NATO members such as Estonia and which is more closely attached to the US than 'old Europe' supposedly is. Even though this statement was made in the context of the European divisions with regard to the US-led War on Iraq in 2003, it does suggest that Estonia, among many other EU accession states, wishes to see the

US retain a strong international subjectivity. By extension, the EU is expected to continue to function mainly as a civilian power. In Estonian eyes this means that the EU in its present form could come nowhere close to being recognized as the one and only leading power in northern Europe. After all, the Union and its strategy in northern Europe are a relatively new issue for the Estonians. To them, the US interests, which date back to the Cold War, are more readily comprehensible. The US containment strategy towards the Soviet Union is well-known; as is its non-recognition policy with regard to the annexation of the Baltic states and its support of Estonia when it came to expelling the remaining Soviet/Russian troops from the country. In a word, for the moment the new forms of projecting power and exercising subjectivity that the EU stands for fall short of attracting the wholehearted commitment of the Estonians.

Summary

In this chapter, I have argued that, for the Union as a whole, Estonia represents a small and in economic terms a relatively insignificant new semi-insider. Yet, during Estonia's accession process and thereafter, the Union undoubtedly has learned some new traits related to its emerging 'north Europeanness', such as what type of policy challenges may ensue from its widening interface with Russia and the consequent encounters with Russian-speaking populations along the Union's outer circles.

At the same time, Estonia's own views of the Union have evolved considerably from the very general statements that were made in the mid-1990s about EU's role in guarding 'European' values of democracy, freedom and rule of law. During the Estonians' interaction with EU institutions, a more comprehensive and detailed view of the EU has been formed. This view of the EU as a whole has gradually led to the Estonians acquiring an idea of the desirability of EU gaining subjectivity in northern Europe. The identity and interest politics that inform Estonian views of EU's geopolitical subjectivity in northern Europe are summarized in Table 5.2.

In Raik's (2003a: 177) opinion, there is a real prospect of Estonia becoming a UK-style 'awkward' EU partner in relation to the Union's foreign policies as a whole, due to factors such as the Estonian EU elite's reservations regarding federalist tendencies in the EU, the development of the CFSP and ESDP, and their general attachment to the US and NATO. However, the analysis in this chapter suggests that Estonia will not necessarily become an 'awkward' partner for the Nordic regionalizers and EU institutions in northern Europe. At the same time, it must be noted that the Estonian views have included several reservations towards many currently debated policy initiatives that might help strengthen the Union's subjectivity. Admittedly, many of these reservations are shared by some other member states in the region, and some of the reservations have shown signs of erosion. But, in connection with the Union's deepening strategic partnership with Russia, the Estonian reservations stand out when compared to prevailing views of many of the more established members, such as Finland and Sweden, or compared to the views held by representatives of EU institutions, or even Latvia

Table 5.2 The construction of the EU's geopolitical subjectivity in northern Europe: Estonian views

Component of ordering	Sub-aspect	Summary
Identity projects	Time	Perceptions of slight but important differences between EU time – the stage of integration at the core of the Union – and Estonia's post-Soviet time
	Space	Relatively strong identification with the Nordic or northern group of EU members; however, less enthusiasm for engaging Russia than shown by many of the northerners; somewhat more accent on national identity and sovereignty than in, for example, Finland
Interest projects	Geo-policy	Cooperative attitude towards the Union's existing geo-policies in northern Europe but, until 2003, little signs of own activism. Reserved views on the planned bolstering of CFSP, ESDP and supranationalism in decision-making procedures
	Geo-strategy	Support for the Union maintaining its existing subjectivity in the region, but stronger subjectivity on the whole not supported at a concrete policy level because of interests in the parallel strength of the US and NATO

Source: adapted from Aalto (2004a).

and Lithuania, as will become evident in the next two chapters. Importantly, it should be noted that, even if such reservations were to prevail, they would not make Estonia an 'awkward' partner in the European north. But they may possibly make it a 'reluctant' partner, in a similar sense as Denmark has shown reluctance towards developing the Union on the whole.

6   New semi-insiders II
Latvia

This chapter deals with the effects for the EU's subjectivity in northern Europe that ensued from Latvia's accession as a new semi-insider into the Union in May 2004. Alongside Estonia and Poland, Latvia's EU referendum was initially expected to be one of the tightest. And in the same fashion as in Estonia, a large part of the country's Russophones were not allowed to vote because they lacked Latvian citizenship. But the comfortable end result of 69 per cent 'yes' votes gives us a good reason to look in more detail at what Latvia will bring into the Union and its 'north Europeanness'.[1]

The history of Latvia's EU relations is as short as Estonia's. Latvia also regained its independence after more than fifty years of Soviet rule in August 1991. This signified the restoration of the short-lived Latvian Republic that emerged in 1918 from the collapse of the Tsarist Russian empire, only to be incorporated into the Soviet Union in 1940. During the brief interwar era of independence, despite some frantic diplomatic efforts, Latvia never managed to build any strong enough links with the Nordic countries, Europe or the 'West' in general that would have prevented its ending up as part of the Soviet Union. Consequently, with independence regained, the foreign policy issue that came to dominate the Latvian agenda during the early 1990s was the withdrawal of the remaining Soviet/Russian troops from the country. This issue was tied to the Latvian–Russian conflict over the treatment of the 55,000 Soviet/Russian military pensioners residing in Latvia, and Latvia's very substantial Russophone population as a whole, which continues to constitute over one-third of the country's population of 2.3 million people. In 1991, the Soviet/Russian troops in Latvia numbered 51,000 and the headquarters of the Baltic Military District were stationed in the country's capital, Riga. The Latvian negotiators refused Russia's demands to keep for seven years an intelligence-gathering station near the port of Ventspils, a radar station at Skrunda and a naval harbour at Liepaja. The Soviet/Russian troops finally left in 1994, at the same time as from Estonia, with some minor activities continuing at Skrunda until 1999 (Pabriks and Purs 2002: 123). The fact that Russia tried to bargain for maintaining more numerous strategic privileges in relation to Latvia than it did vis-à-vis Estonia hints at the way in which the 'Russian issue' continued to interfere with Latvia's new priorities for EU and NATO integration slightly more than it did in Estonia's case.

Latvia's free trade agreement with the EU entered into force in January 1995, with a four-year transition period allowed for the abolition of trade barriers on the Latvian side. Latvia subsequently missed out on a similar early invitation into EU accession negotiations to the one that Estonia received in 1997, with the European Commission expressing doubts regarding Latvia's ability to respond to competitive pressures within the Union (European Commission 1997a). This led the Latvian prime minister, Andris Šķēle, to declare that the Commission was deliberately breaking up Baltic unity (Ozoliņa 2003: 212). The Latvian prime minister clang firmly to the idea of Baltic cooperation at the same time as for example the former Estonian prime minister, Mart Laar, was suggesting that Estonia distance itself from the other two Baltic states in favour of a Nordic orientation. A strong accent on Baltic and regional cooperation is indeed a lasting trait of Latvian foreign policy, and to an extent it dissociates the country from Estonia also in the context of EU enlargement.

After initially lagging behind Estonia, during 1998 Latvia started catching up in EU accession preparations. The catch-up was aided by Estonia entering a short period of declining growth rates and simultaneously experiencing a slowdown in the process of easing its interethnic policies towards the Russophones as required by the EU. Simultaneously Latvia itself progressed well in fulfilling the European Commission's very explicit requirements in national integration activities (ibid.). The result was an invitation into EU accession negotiations in 1999, together with Lithuania and Slovakia, with Malta also starting its negotiations in the second wave in February 2000.

The next two sections will take a look at the issues of political economy and security in the Union's enlargement into Latvia. Thereafter Latvia's input into the construction of the EU's subjectivity and Europe-making in northern Europe will be analysed by studying the views of the Latvian EU elite during membership negotiations and the debates on the EU's Constitutional Treaty, or the 'future of Europe' debate.

Issues of political economy in Latvia's EU accession

Latvia's starting point in reorienting its economy to suit the purposes of EU integration was not even nearly as good as Estonia's. Latvia lacks a natural foreign connection like Estonia's culturally and geographically close ties with Finland, regardless of the facts that Latvia's EU membership bid was supported by close political ties with Sweden and other Nordics, and that Germany contributed a lot in cultural and economic assistance. The period of secession from the Soviet Union during the Latvian independence movement in 1987–91 also failed to produce notable economic reforms. The previously small role of republic-level planning increased, but was unable to provide Latvia with a kick-start such as that from which Estonia benefited as a result of its perestroika era experience of economic reforms. Another problem factor was Latvia's total dependence on Russian energy supplies (Pabriks and Purs 2002: 91, 133). However, by 1999 Marja Nissinen reported that Latvia's transition to a market economy was complete, and the same year the EU also confirmed Latvia's status as a 'functioning market economy' which 'should be able to cope with competitive pressures within the Union'. The EU expressed this positive opinion after having had some doubts in its 1998 progress report on Latvia's EU accession (Nissinen 1999; European Commission 1999).

Latvia's economy offers slightly more potential to the Union than Estonia's due to the country's larger population and thus, potentially at least, a somewhat larger market. However, in 2002 Latvia's GDP per capita was only 35 per cent of the average within the EU-15, and thus well below Estonia's level of 42 per cent. EU aid to Latvia was around 100 million euros a year during the pre-accession period (European Commission 2004c). By 2001, the volume of Latvia's imports from the EU was a mere 2.09 billion euros, and exports to the EU only 1.37 billion euros (European Commission 2003e, 2004c). Again, these figures were negligible to the Union, and well below even Estonia's (Chapter 5). The comparatively low volumes also indicate how foreign direct investment from the EU area and elsewhere was initially slow in finding its way into Latvia, owing to factors such as relatively slow progress in privatization, nationalist opposition to opening up of the Latvian real estate market to foreigners, and excessive bureaucracy in operating businesses (Pabriks and Purs 2002: 101–2). But by 1995 Latvia's trade was reoriented away from the CIS area and towards the EU, in terms of both import and export volumes. Especially development of trade ties with Germany, the UK and Sweden helped in this (Table 6.1).

Latvia also offers more transit trade potential to the EU than Estonia does. The port of Ventspils is the only one in the Baltic states with a direct oil pipeline connection from Russia. In addition, there is a railway connection. Ventspils and the other Latvian ports, Liepaja and Riga, managed to grab almost 30 per cent of the total Baltic Sea cargo in 1999. In the same year, Latvia's share of the value of Russia's westbound transit was a notable 26 per cent. Although figures for the importance of the transit trade for the Latvian economy vary according to sources, careful economic calculations taking into account balance of payment information on gross revenues from transport services and all supplementary statistical information suggest that in 1998 transit accounted for 8–10 per cent of Latvia's GDP (Laurila 2003: 40–8). Against this background, it was significant

Table 6.1 Latvia's foreign trade with the EU-15 and CIS, 1993–2003 (% of value)

	1993	1994	1995	1996	1997	1998	1999	2000	2001	2002	2003
Imports/ EU	27.4	40.6	49.9	49.3	53.2	55.3	54.5	52.4	52.6	53.0	50.1
Exports/ EU	33.4	39.2	44.0	44.7	48.9	56.6	62.5	64.6	61.2	60.4	61.9
Imports/ CIS	38.2	30.5	28.2	25.5	19.7	16.0	15.0	16.9	14.8	13.1	14.5
Exports/ CIS	47.6	42.7	38.3	35.8	29.5	19.0	12.0	8.7	10.3	10.0	9.8

Sources: 2003 figures for EU and 2000–3 figures for the CIS: Central Statistical Bureau of Latvia (2004); 1998–2002 figures for the EU: European Commission (2003e); rest of figures: J. Köll (2002: 356–7).

that Latvia's problems in relation to Russia – after the troop withdrawal, mainly over the treatment of the Russophone minority – led to a total cut of oil pipeline supplies to Ventspils early in the new millennium.

The heart of the Ventspils episode is political, but technically speaking at issue is a controversy over the development and ownership of the Ventspils oil terminal. The Russian state-owned oil pipeline monopoly company Transneft controls the pipeline to Ventspils. On the one hand, Transneft represents a clear interest of the Russian state in politically pressing Latvia on the inter-ethnic question. On the other hand, there is an economic interest in smoothing Russian investment in the terminal, in order to lower the amount of profits paid to the Latvian owners since the dissolution of the Soviet Union. Ultimately these profits have ended up into the Latvian economy and the state budget. During spring 2003, Transneft announced a complete halt of supplies to Ventspils and offered to invest 143 million US dollars in the terminal in exchange for a stake in it. The majority of the Ventspils Nafta terminal is owned by the Latvian state (38.6 per cent) and a group of private investors represented by the company Latvijs Naftas Transit (47.9 per cent), who allegedly sponsor nationalist-leaning Latvian political parties (Moshes 1999: 59). The Latvian Foreign Ministry insisted that substantial investments in the terminal and its capacity had already been made and that Transneft's decision violated the 1993 Latvian–Russian agreement on the use of the pipeline. However, in March a stake was offered to Transneft, which refused it. The intent was seemingly to bankrupt the terminal, in order to buy it cheaper later, with the shares depreciating as a result of the terminal functioning on railway supplies only and well below its capacity. In late 2003, the Russian–British TNK-BP and the Kazakh oil company KazakhOil were mentioned as possible buyers (Rosbalt 2003a–f), until the Latvian government announced plans to sell its own stake via the stock market in late 2005.

The result of the whole episode has been a reorientation of the oil pipeline traffic to the expensively built Russian port of Primorsk, as well as a major decline in transit through Latvia and in revenues to the state budget. And, as Laurila notes, there are good grounds to ask if early investments into the Ventspils terminal and the feeding pipelines would have been much less expensive to the Russian side than new port developments made on largely traditional geopolitical grounds, provided that ownership questions had been settled satisfactorily in Ventspils (Laurila 2003: 46). Ironically, at the micro level, one group of sufferers are the workers of the oil terminal, many of whom are Russian-speakers. However, despite its potential significance for Latvia's EU membership, the Ventspils issue never rose into prominence in Latvia's accession negotiations or in EU–Russian talks. The mayor of Ventspils, Aivar Lembergs, consequently expressed the feelings of many in Latvia when terming the EU's acceptance of Russia's entry into the World Trade Organization (WTO) in May 2004 a 'cowardly betrayal of Latvia's interests' (Rosbalt 2004a). But the Ventspils issue works to show how questions of political economy are tied to complex, case-specific security issues that should also be noted when evaluating Latvia's input into the EU. These security issues complement the list of overall soft security challenges encountered by the Union in relation to the CEE, and range from the state of Latvian–Russian relations to the feeling of security and loyalty among Latvia's Russophone population.

Security issues in Latvia's EU accession

Another Latvian–Russian conflict episode not entirely dissimilar to Ventspils was witnessed during the 1998 Latvian–Russian crisis. Oil transit issues come up here too as one interpretation of the grounds of the conflict. The chain of events started when in March 1998 the Latvian police force violently broke up a peaceful but illegal demonstration of mostly elderly and Russian-speaking people over rising communal bills. This provoked a furious reaction from Russia. More fuel was added by a well publicized march of around 500 veterans of the Latvian Waffen-SS, who fought alongside Nazi Germany against Soviet forces on Latvian territory during the Second World War. High-ranking Latvian military figures were also present on the march. To oversimplify, from the Latvian perspective the veterans were former freedom fighters against Soviet communism, but from the Russian perspective they were fascists and now seemingly supported by the Latvian state. With diplomatic tensions escalating, a Jewish memorial site was vandalized in the port of Liepaja, and a bomb explosion occurred just outside the Russian embassy in Riga. This all resulted in increased Russian demands to improve the Russophones' situation in Latvia, and a spontaneous boycott on Latvian export goods propagated by the Moscow mayor Iuri Luzhkov. The 'oil theory' suggests that underlying these events were increased transit fees imposed by the Ventspils terminal in January 1998. This coincided with lower world market prices for Russia's oil products and with the ongoing discussions between Russian companies and the Ventspils oil terminal over the possible acquisition of a stake in it, as well as Russian debates to develop new ports around St Petersburg. For the port projects state support for the companies was needed, and in this manner the oil companies and the state presumably had a common interest in pressing Latvia (Morozov 2003: 224–6).

The economic effects of the 1998 Latvian–Russian crisis remained modest and short-lived. Economic relations were largely restored by May/June 1998. Transit fees were correspondingly lowered. But the security political effects were notable with regard to Latvian–Russian relations and Latvia's inter-ethnic policies, which were mostly designed as a security guarantee to the Latvian language and nation, and at the same time deemed by both Russia and the EU too exclusionist towards the Russophones (see Moshes 1999: 65). Late in the Soviet era, Latvia's Russophone minority had threatened to outnumber the ethnic Latvians, as a result of Soviet policies of industrializing Latvia and bringing in immigrant workers from other parts of the Soviet state. The Latvian citizenship and language laws of the early 1990s were designed to halt the russification of the country that evidently was well in progress.

From the perspective of the EU, the annual quotas in Latvia's naturalization policies in particular were not too well in tune with the requirements of national integration and social cohesion necessary for an EU accession state. Latvia had initiated a similar restorationist state-building model to Estonia's as early as 1991. But only in 1994 was a citizenship law passed regulating the naturalization of the 600,000 Soviet era Russophone immigrants and their children who were left without any valid citizenship. What is worse, the 1994 law introduced annual quotas or 'application windows' for those willing to apply for citizenship and capable of passing the related, rather demanding language tests. With such quotas, and in a situation where only 22.3 per cent of Latvia's ethnic Russians, 9.8 per cent of Ukrainians and 18 per cent Belarusians claimed proficiency in Latvian in the 1989 Soviet census, it was clear that naturalization was bound to remain unsatisfactorily slow from the EU's viewpoint, not to mention the Russian concerns (Moshes 1999: 36–41). In 1997, the EU instructed Latvia to look into the OSCE requirements on abolishing the quota system in naturalization, on allowing the naturalization of children of stateless parents, and on simplification of the citizenship tests in particular for elderly people. The 1998 Latvian–Russian crisis provided additional political pressure for finally easing the legislation to the EU's satisfaction in late 1998 (European Commission 1998). However, language policies continued to stipulate the Latvian language as the primary language in the public sphere, and the EU continued to note problems in the treatment of the Russophones.

To address these concerns, Latvia's national integration programme was prepared during the course of 1998 and finally passed through parliament in 2000. It represented a direct response to the calls by the EU for a greater degree of national integration and more effective language tuition for the Russian-speakers, in order to avoid creating potential instability in the enlarging Union and scenarios in which part of the population of an accession country could be vulnerable to a possible outside provocation. This latter prospect clearly constituted a non-negligible issue in the eyes of Latvian policy makers, who had been used to hearing Russian accusations of violations of the human rights of Russophones (Vesa and Möller 2003: 52–5). For them, EU accession thus became a soft security countermeasure. Apart from facilitating the attainment of this goal, the overall effects of the naturalization programme include an erosion of the importance of the inter-ethnic issue in Latvia, together with only a modest increase in applications for naturalization, reflecting a relative lack of interest and marginalization of a large part of older generations of Russian-speakers. In 1998, 4,439 persons were naturalized, in 1999 12,427, and in 2000 14,900. But upon the conclusion of Latvia's EU accession negotiations in 2002, altogether 523,000 persons remained stateless in Latvia (Pabriks and Purs 2002: 78–9; Vesa and Möller 2003: 57–8).

On balance, Latvia's relative progress in national integration has not eliminated the 'Russian issue' from Latvian politics completely, as can be seen from the complete stoppage of oil shipments to Ventspils in 2003. Similarly, signing the Latvian–Russian border treaty was delayed until May 2005. Resulting from the declared restoration of the interwar Latvia, with its borders based on the 1920 Riga treaty between Soviet Russia and Latvia, Latvia went on to raise claims to the Pytalovo (Abrene) region that was cut off from the Latvian territory during the Soviet era. But, as the claims were subsequently dropped in 1997, the border issue never became a big issue in Latvia's EU membership bid in a similar manner as the inter-ethnic questions did.

This all seems to speak of a small new 'semi-insider' entering the Union, with only four votes in the EU's Council of Ministers (1.2 per cent) and nine seats among the European Parliament's total of 732 (1.1 per cent), which is set to rise to 786 for the term 2007–9, eating into Latvia's voting power even further. Moreover, Latvia has damaged prospects of providing some sort of a bridge or gateway function for the deepening and widening EU–Russian relations, in particular because of the Latvian–Russian controversies that have persisted regardless of Latvia's substantial progress in national integration policies and also, somewhat surprisingly, regardless of Latvia's attainment of EU membership. Such an assessment would leave a big task for the Latvian elite's ideational discourse to provide a positive input into the Union's project of making a wider northern Europe as part of Europe-making. And an examination of a large body of empirical material reflects that the Latvian EU elite is slightly more prepared than their Estonian counterparts to see a strengthening EU subject in the northern European region, thus compensating for their relative structural disadvantages and helping to smoothen the Union's agenda.[2] The systematic empirical analysis relies on the model of geopolitical subjectivity introduced in Chapter 3.[3]

Latvian views of the EU's identity projects in northern Europe

Time

A similar 'return to Europe' discourse to that in Estonia became also characteristic of Latvia during the protracted pull-out of the Soviet/Russian troops from the country in 1993–4 (Ozolina 1998: 141–2). This discourse included the familiar references to the Latvians' position as one of the 'captive nations' during the Soviet era, whom 'Europe' was morally obliged to welcome 'back' after the fifty years of Soviet rule and the forcible cutting of the organic connection with Europe that the Latvians claimed to have had during the interwar period. But, as emerges from almost any historical account, Latvia's foreign policy during the interwar era mostly manifested a desperate search for alliance ties with both northern and western European countries, rather than Latvia's self-evident belonging to the group of European or northern European states. Moreover, Latvia ended up as a Soviet–German battlefield in the Second World War, with little help coming from supposed friends (e.g. Lehti 2004: 12; Pabriks and Purs 2002: 22–3; Sčerbinskis 2003: 158–64). Against this backdrop, it should be clear to almost any observer that, as Latvia had been one of the Soviet republics for fifty years, a whole new encounter and learning process was in fact at issue in what the Latvian prime minister, Andris Bērziņš, terms the country's continued reorientation to the EU (A. Bērziņš 2002).

As in the Estonian case, the ills of the forced unity of 'Soviet time' are also persistently denounced in Latvia. For example, Sandra Kalniete, the Latvian minister of foreign affairs and Latvia's representative in the EU's Convention, expressed her support for a withdrawal clause in the EU's draft for a Constitutional Treaty enabling member states to voluntarily withdraw from the Union (Kalniete 2003a). Already after the mid-1990s, warnings started to emerge in Latvia against joining the EU almost immediately after seceding from another union, the Soviet Union, which according to these allegations only differed from the EU on its ideological principles (Ozolina 1998: 150). The legacy of 'Soviet time' and the burdensome prevalence of 'post-Soviet time' is a similarly experienced temporal factor in both Estonia and Latvia. This can be seen in a quote from a speech by Prime Minister Bērziņš and in an interview with a Latvian official responsible for EU integration affairs:

> Ten years of renewed statehood may not sound like much. Especially when you take into account the 50 years of damage done to Latvia by the Soviets. Extensive Russification, forced collectivism and a centrally planned (but totally mismanaged) [state/economy] are the legacy we have inherited as we rebuild our country.
>
> (A. Bērziņš 2002)

> And then again these emotions from the [era of the] Soviet Union – time goes very fast, what is ten years? Nothing . . . these legacies and everything. I think this [EU integration] is a very difficult question.
>
> (Latvian policy maker, December 2002)

The burden of post-Soviet time means that European integration seems to arrive too quickly for Latvia, with the country and society still being somewhat unprepared. Yet the EU concomitantly offers Latvia a very tempting and historic opportunity to modernize itself, become part of a prosperous EU environment, and look to the future (Repše 2003a,b; Vīķe-Freiberga 2000a,b, 2003a). But in Latvia there is a clearly felt and acknowledged gap between now and 'EU time', and in the present interval considerable pressures exist for adopting far-reaching, apparently federalist decisions before the CEE states are given full rights to participate in EU decision-making:

> We believe that certain aspects of the EU's reform should be decided upon at a later stage. This would provide an opportunity for acceding member states to participate in shaping the future of the European Union.
>
> (Vīķe-Freiberga 2000b).

> Sometimes it seems to me that the enlargement process in some way re-oriented the way in which the responsible politicians think of EU integration – and they are pushing it too far, and they are pushing too fast. And it's not really about cost–benefit calculations any more.
>
> (Latvian EU observer, December 2002)

Compared with the post-Soviet time manifested by the Estonian EU elite, the Latvian president, Vaira Vīķe-Freiberga, shows a more marked tendency to publicly recognize the Latvians' own share in Europe's traumatic past, just as top EU officials are often quick to acknowledge the Union's responsibility in alleviating the member states' wrongdoings in the Second World War (Chapter 4). Vīķe-Freiberga wants to assure the European audience of how Latvia participates in the common European healing exercise:

> Latvia is also determined to come to terms with the tragic events that have ever occurred on its soil during Nazi German and Soviet Russian occupations, starting, the holocaust, but also including the mass deportations and other crimes of the Stalin period. We have established a History Commission of international scholars who are conducting extensive research on the painful episodes in our history. We are determined to remember these events and to educate our children, so that atrocities and repressions never occur again on Latvian soil.
>
> (Vīķe-Freiberga 2001)

Furthermore, elsewhere, Vīķe-Freiberga wants to point out how Latvia's political tradition boasts similar great healers to Aristide Briand and Robert Schuman, who helped to build a new Europe after the divisions of the Second World War. Vīķe-Freiberga invokes the name of Zigfrieds Anna Meierovics, the first Latvian minister of foreign affairs, who assumed her post in 1918 (Vīķe-Freiberga 2002a). However, the Latvian foreign minister, Sandra Kalniete, for her part, calls Russia to participate in the common healing exercise by evaluating its own part in Europe's tragic past: 'Russia must repay its moral debt to Europe – it must reassess, in a civilized and democratic way, its role in the tragic history of the last century' (Kalniete 2004). That Russia has not yet even started such a task is evident in the Putin-induced decision to re-adopt the Soviet era national anthem, albeit with new words, as Russia's new post-Soviet identity label (Latvian EU policy maker, December 2002).

It may be concluded that the attempt of the Latvian president Vīķe-Freiberga to relate Latvia to the history of the ongoing construction processes of a European subject manages to introduce some new flavour to the otherwise similar patterns found in the Estonian case. Vīķe-Freiberga's remarks are also rather well in tune with the statements assessing Europe's past that are often heard from the contemporary EU elite. Yet Foreign Minister Kalniete's disapproving comments about Russia's relationship to its part in Europe's history again relate Latvia closely to Estonia. On balance, it is correct to say that the Latvian EU elite manifests a relatively similar contrast between post-Soviet time and EU time to their Estonian counterparts. For instance, the Estonians' and Latvians' fears of the formation of asymmetric clubs dividing old and new members in the enlarged Union are almost identical (for Latvia, see, for example, I. Bērziņš 2000a, 2001a; Vīķe-Freiberga 2002b, 2003b).

Space

The slight differences in Latvian, compared to Estonian, identity politics that were detected in relation to time become more pronounced when examined in relation to space. In the statements of the Estonian EU elite, an undifferentiated 'Western European paneuropeanism' mostly prevailed until the late 1990s, despite some overtures towards a Nordic orientation. But in Latvia, more differentiated and regionalized views of European space have enjoyed a strong position throughout the post-Soviet era. Atis Lejinš even argues that Latvia's geographical location – being sandwiched between Estonia and Lithuania – has induced Latvia to favour regional cooperation (Lejinš 2002: 260; Ozolina 1998: 153). Ojars Kalnis, the former Latvian ambassador to the US, suggested the idea of the 'Amber Gate-way', which postulates Latvia's identity as lying within the BSR. It proposes to increase cooperation along the Baltic–Nordic, Baltic–Baltic, EU–Russian and US–Nordic vectors, possibly also drawing Germany into greater involvement as well, in order to promote regional interdependence and soft security (Pabriks and Purs 2002: 131). Whilst this idea has failed to attract attention from Latvian, Lithuanian and Estonian politicians alike, the overall thrust attached to region-building is such that the Latvian foreign minister, Indulis Bērziņš, once remarked that irrespective of whether Latvia joined the EU, the Baltic and Nordic states would together go on to establish an 'economic region' possibly also embracing Russia (Broks 2001: 197).

The Latvian document 'Strategy for the Integration into the European Union' asserts under the CFSP title that Latvia supports international activities directed at the consolidation of stability and security 'in the entire continent'; however, in the same breath, the document asserts that Latvia must contribute to regional stability as well, and that this is best accomplished by participating in BSR coop-eration (Republic of Latvia 2000). The Latvian National Security Concept notes that Latvia's foreign policy is a 'policy of European unity aimed at full-fledged membership in the EU and NATO', but then goes on to elaborate the importance of drawing the leading NATO power, the US, also into BSR cooperation. It also declares that economic and political cooperation with the countries of northern Europe will help Latvia to apply the Nordic states' experiences of European inte-gration, which in turn will strengthen Latvia's EU membership bid (Republic of Latvia 2002).

The Latvian stress on region-building comes up nicely in the comments of Foreign Minister Bērziņš at a fitting occasion, the eighth Baltic Council meeting:

> I have always stressed that it is easy to develop good relations with Chile, New Zealand and Australia, because those countries are far from Latvia. The development and maintenance of good, active neighbourly relations takes a lot of efforts in terms of work and energy, but the task is made easier by mutual understanding.
>
> (I. Bērziņš 2002)

The Latvian enthusiasm for region-building takes forms that are peculiar in the Baltic context and the broader context of EU enlargement. During the EU and NATO enlargement processes, out of the Baltic countries, Estonian politicians and, as will be seen in the next chapter, right-wingers in Lithuania played excessively upon the supposed dichotomy between the East and West. This was part of the broader effort of many CEE countries and EU institutions to move the Cold War era East–West border further eastwards and in the process exclude Russia and the CIS into the eastern part of a wider Europe and consequently out of the inner circles of EU order. Against this background, it is highly interesting that the Latvian foreign policy makers feel comfortable with putting forth phrases like 'EU's centre of gravity shifts *east*ward' to depict the new opportunities offered by EU enlargement (Vīķe-Freiberga 2003c; emphasis added), 'in Riga West meets East' as a description of Latvia's capital (A. Bērziņš 2000), and terms like 'northeast' to denote Latvia's own regional context (I. Bērziņš 2001b). The Latvian policy makers want to erode the commonplace efforts to strictly discriminate between East and West in Europe:

> . . . [T]he great schism, split the Christian church and European civilisation into two separate camps. It was to Europe's great misfortune that nations on both sides of the divide forgot what they had in common. Even today some scholars argue that Europe ends geographically where western Christianity ends and where Islam and Orthodoxy begin . . . The juxtaposition of the so-called western Christian culture against the eastern Orthodox culture is erroneous, counterproductive, and contributes to the fragmentation of Europe's creative potential.
>
> (Vīķe-Freiberga 2002c)

> Although enlargement of the EU itself will set new institutional borders of the Union, the process of European integration need not be seen as something that has a pre-defined final result as long as geographical borders are concerned . . . Latvia clearly acts with an understanding that our border for a foreseeable future will be part of the Eastern border of the Union. I would characterize this border as a *border of opportunities* that extends its outreach to everyone willing to make use of the chances provided – be it the travel of people, economic initiatives or duties in the framework of the EU third pillar.
>
> (Riekstins 2001; emphasis added)

In relation to Russia, it is asserted that dialogue, cooperation and engagement are imperative. Latvia's continuous, relatively open-minded identity politics towards the enlarged Europe's borders is striking compared to what was heard from Estonian foreign policy makers before the launching of the neighbourhood policy. Such peculiar openness of Latvia must be understood in the context of the country's lack of both strong and friendly immediate neighbours and the consequent attachment to region-building as a substitute for the good bilateral cooperation that Estonia has enjoyed with Finland, and Lithuania with Poland since settling their historically induced differences towards the mid-1990s (Chapters 5 and 7).

The adoption of the idea of 'northernness' as a spatial identity marker supports the Latvian region-building and provides a well-fitting framework for it. In Estonia, the 'northernness' discourse surfaced briefly during the early 1990s, and re-emerged only in the late 1990s, whereas in Latvia it has been present throughout since the regaining of independence, alongside other priorities such as EU and NATO integration, regional cooperation and good relations with Russia. In 2000, a group of prominent scientists and politicians issued a conceptual framework for Latvia's long-term development. They suggested that Latvia's full integration into the Nordic community should assume high importance in the overall process of Latvia's European integration. For them, Latvia was already by then a northern European country. Yet their more subtle policy recommendation seemed to be for a complete integration with the Nordic states (Sčerbinskis 2003: 165, 167–8).

The suggested northern European vocation of Latvia undeniably includes some instrumental aspects regarding Latvia's broader aims of EU integration. However, it is notable that while speaking of the new Latvian foreign policy concept, at a time when the country's EU and NATO membership was already sealed, the Latvian foreign minister, Sandra Kalniete, continues to mention the BSR as Latvia's fourth priority after EU policy, the economic dimension of foreign policy, and NATO and US relations. Kalniete comments that 'from a cultural-historical perspective Latvia belongs to northern Europe, just as Denmark, Finland or northern Germany'. According to Kalniete, the Nordic countries represent identities that Latvia wants to embrace and see firmly embedded in Europe: a liberal but socially responsible economy, with a low level of corruption, transparent democracy, equal opportunities for men and women, and modern and environmentally friendly industries. Moreover, Kalniete introduces the term 'Nordic eight', which definitely raises some eyebrows within the traditionally exclusive 'Nordic five'. She also advocates cooperation in the fields of development and environment. Responding to Finnish concerns, she mentions the safety of shipping in the Baltic Sea (Kalniete 2004). Elsewhere, however, Vīķe-Freiberga manifests a slightly more limited spatial identity politics. She argues that Finland, the Baltic states and Poland have a shared historical experience of aggression from both the west and east (Vīķe-Freiberga 2002d).

One of the Latvian EU observers interviewed for this study is sceptical of Latvia's region-building aims and its declared 'northernness'. He doubts whether Latvia has anything special to offer as a transit point or meeting ground for the northerners, including Russians, and other Europeans from the east and west, especially since the level of proficiency in the Russian language is declining among the young people. In particular, he is sceptical about whether Latvia has anything with which to respond to Estonia's well developed identity label as a young, dynamic country with a clear strategy as to how to move on (Latvian EU observer, December 2002).

Despite the region-building and northern European accent, Latvia's vision of European space as a whole does not differ much from Estonia. There is the same reluctance to include a notion of the Union's 'federal basis' in the Constitutional Treaty (Kalniete 2003a; 2003b). Although the Latvians acknowledge very frankly that the Union already includes some federal elements (e.g. Kalniete 2003c; cf. Vīķe-Freiberga 2002d), theirs is a fairly similar vision of the EU as an intergovernmental union of sovereign nation-states, where the interests of small member states are also guaranteed (e.g. I. Bērziņš 2001c; A. Bērziņš 2002; Vīķe-Freiberga 2002c, d, 2003c). But it must be kept in mind that Latvian foreign policy makers operate under conditions of heavy pressure from intellectuals and the broader society to accentuate the role of Latvian culture, language and national sovereignty as the basis of all foreign engagement, including Latvia's place within the EU (Goloubeva and Ieleja 2004).

Latvian views of the EU's interest projects in northern Europe

Geo-policy

The overriding importance of the EU's enlargement policy out of all Union policies towards Latvia was well expressed in the country's first National Security Concept, adopted in 1995. The document asserts that Latvia cannot guarantee its survival on its own, and therefore it needs EU and NATO membership (!). This type of explicit securitization of integration can be criticized as compromising the claim for the existence of the Latvian state. Although small states like Latvia are commonly assumed to actively seek alliance arrangements, an explicit construction of the Latvian state as being incapable of protecting itself only serves to make the public more threatened, whilst concomitantly inviting other powers to destabilize the country (cf. Jæger 1997). The EU, moreover, only wants to include states with no serious national security threats. In this way, the Union guarantees a controlled spreading of EU order and the stability it is assumed to bring, without compromising the achievements of integration (cf. Wæver 1994).

Since the mid-1990s, the Latvian EU elite has gone on to develop more balanced conceptions of EU enlargement better in tune with the EU's official views. The Latvian foreign minister, Indulis Bērziņš, puts aptly Latvia's socialization process in the context of EU accession: 'Earlier we used to emphasize that it was in the national interests of Latvia to become a member of the EU. Now it is in the national interests of Latvia to learn to utilize the resources of the European Union for our national development and to contribute to harmonious development of the EU' (I. Bērziņš 2001d). Now the standard comment is better in line with the Union's own official views: 'Enlargement will certainly pour new energy into the project of building a new Europe, united, free, and secure' (I. Bērziņš 2000b). The extreme securitizing voices are gone, particularly after Latvia's invitation to NATO in the Prague summit in November 2002. This has meant a more prominent place for economic arguments to legitimize Latvia's EU membership bid to the domestic public. When speaking to the Latvian parliament *Saeima* in the new conditions, the Latvian prime minister, Einars Repše, who replaced Andris Bērziņš in November 2002, simply refers to Norway's alleged need to pay more than 100 million euros for its small and medium-sized enterprises so that they would be able to operate freely in the common market. According to Repše, Norway had to assign these subsidies regardless of the country's EEA membership (Repše 2003b). However, the enlargement of the Union into Latvia among other CEE countries is still seen to warrant big efforts on Latvia's part, in the same way as in the case of Estonia:

> Question: Does the EU listen at all to these [CEE] countries, or is it mainly a one-way relationship?
>
> Answer: I would say that (with the EU) it's mainly a one-way relationship. It's the same, just imagine a situation on a street: there is a person who is frozen, and because it's cold outside, and this person tries to get into any kind of building just to get into the warmth, and for such reasons this person, really, will be ready to do everything, just to get in the warmth . . . We need to satisfy our basic needs, and for this reason we are ready to make such sacrifices.
>
> (Latvian EU observer, December 2002)

In other words, although it is not as often mentioned by the Latvian EU elite, the one-way-street or take-it-or-leave-it character of the EU accession process is mostly very similarly perceived to how it was found to be in the case of Estonia. This also concerns the adoption of the Union's Schengen borders regime. Yet, here, Latvian policy makers often suggest burden-sharing for funding the border infrastructure changes induced by the Schengen regulations. At times these demands appear unconvincing, when they are put forth simultaneously with claims that Latvia already largely conforms to the requirements with its unified visa information system (A. Bērziņš 2000; Riekstins 2000). According to the Latvians, the Union's plans for a visa-free regime with Russia should be properly considered only once all crossing points and procedures are significantly improved, and once Russia has ratified its border treaties with all of its EU neighbours (Kalniete 2003d).

But, in contrast to the EU's universalizing enlargement and Schengen policies, the Latvian views of the Union's regionalizing policy, the ND, were more activist than in Estonia almost from the beginning. Although the early Latvian reactions displayed fears of Finnish efforts to monopolize their still lucrative Russian transit trade (Raik 1999: 159), Latvia's accent on region-building has subsequently ensured a positive assessment and a genuine contribution to the ND.

Like Estonia, Latvia organized an ND business forum that took place in May 2001 in Riga. Prior to the meeting, Latvia declared its interests within the ND policy to be reliable supply of energy on the regional and European levels, development of transportation and logistics, trade and cross-border cooperation with Russia's Pskov, Leningrad and Kaliningrad regions, environmental protection, and facilitation of e-business and e-government and promotion of an advanced information society. These interests very clearly reflect Latvia's own strategic location and its consequent needs, although the Latvian foreign minister argued that they also serve broader regional needs (I. Bērziņš 2001b). In this light, the

decisions of the Russian government to rapidly start materializing its port building projects around St Petersburg early in the new millennium and the cutting
of supplies to the Latvian port Ventspils influenced Latvia's views of the ND
considerably.

The Latvian foreign minister, Sandra Kalniete, argued that the Russian decisions are motivated by political considerations, not by sound economic reasoning.
They have a bearing not only on Latvia, but also on the wider region and the
EU. To solve the problems, the EU should get more involved. The EU–Russian
energy dialogue would be an ideal forum for such discussions (Kalniete 2003e).
These concerns were also repeated in Latvia's contribution to the drafting of the
second ND Action Plan in early 2003. Russia's use of energy transit corridors was
deemed irrational, when a technologically and ecologically safe route exists to
the ice-free port of Ventspils. The possibility of starting to make use of Latvia's
own 'unique' geological conditions for creating natural gas depositories was
mentioned. If taken into full use, the total capacity of the depositories would cor-
respond to the currently used depositories within the whole Union. This resource
was offered as a seasonal regulator of natural gas flows into European markets.
The construction of new pipelines from Russia through Latvia to the wider EU
area was proposed too. Finally, on the plane of energy transit, Latvia drew attention to the Finnish concerns about maritime safety, referring to the necessity
to ensure that appropriate classes of tankers are used for oil transport within the
Baltic Sea. On the whole, Latvia advocated a more tangible institutionalization
of the ND. A coordination unit could be set up within the Commission. The new
funding models introduced within the NDEP were also approved of (Government
of Latvia 2003).

To maintain perspective, it is fair to say that, regardless of the apparent Latvian
activism on the ND issue, none of the interviewed Latvian officials dealing with
the EU or Russia was very well aware of the ND initiative. As for the broader
public, the interviewed officials responsible for informing the public and business
circles about EU issues reported that no one had ever asked them about the ND
policy (!).

The introduction of the neighbourhood policy, for its part, seems to strike a
chord among the Latvian EU elite in the same way as was the case with Estonia.
In addition to the knowledge and practical experience the Latvians claim to have
of ties with Russia, the inclusion of Ukraine was particularly welcome. Latvia
has good relations with the country and claims to be sharing its integration experiences with the Ukrainians (A. Bērziņš 2000). Moreover, the Latvians have
expressed hopes that the new policy would draw Latvia's neighbour Belarus into
the EU's orbit; student exchanges with Belarus were suggested as one possible
means to that end (Kalniete 2004). In an interview, attention was also drawn to
the Euregio projects that Latvia has with Belarus and Lithuania, called the Land of
Lakes (Latvian policy maker, December 2002). The initiation of closer relations
between the enlarged Union and these countries is seen as a good counterbalance
to the EU's Russian relations, although EU expansion in this direction should
not be seen as a goal before existing agreements are fully implemented (Vīķe-
Freiberga 2003d). Latvia welcomes the EU's 'constructive' approach through the

CSR towards Russia (Vīķe-Freiberga 2000b), but the evolving EU–Russian partnership is seen at least partly in an instrumental manner. It offers Latvia a good structure to come in, in order to improve its own Russian relations (e.g. Kalniete 2004; Repše 2003b). The deepening EU–Russian cooperation must, according to Latvia's new foreign policy concept, be based on the values of democracy and human rights, and EU accepted norms (Kalniete 2004).

As to the more general EU policies with an indirect bearing on the Union's northernness, contrary to the Estonians, the Latvian EU elite has consistently favoured the extension of QMV voting in order to strive for one voice to the Union in the fields of CFSP and ESDP (e.g. A. Bērziņš 2000; Kalniete 2003c) However, in the Convention, Latvia staunchly resisted terming the EU's new foreign policy representative a 'foreign minister', and opposed the so-called structural cooperation or closed military cooperation among a core group of EU countries (Kalniete 2003f–i; Vīķe-Freiberga 2003a). Although Latvia claimed to be ready to contribute to the ESDP, this EU policy should not compromise the position of NATO (e.g. I. Bērziņš 2000b; Vīķe-Freiberga 2000b).

Geo-strategy

Latvia displays a stronger degree of willingness than Estonia to assign policy tools to the EU enabling it to increase its subjectivity in the northern European region. On the whole, Latvia wants to assign a stronger role for the Union not only in northern Europe and Europe as a whole, but also in ensuring global peace and security (e.g. Repše 2003b; Vīķe-Freiberga 2000c, 2003b). Even phrases such as an economic and political superpower of Europe are not always shied away from, although the Latvian views in this regard are not entirely consistent (e.g. I. Bērziņš 2001e; Vīķe-Freiberga 2002a). In particular, enlargement is seen as one of the crucial policy tools by which to make the Union stronger in global geopolitics (e.g. I. Bērziņš 2001a; Kalniete 2003c; Vīķe-Freiberga 2000a). Compared to the Estonian EU elite, who express suspicions regarding the EU's role as *the* leading power in Europe, the Latvians are happy to see the EU and NATO/US sharing this responsibility equally. Sometimes the EU's role in crisis management is accentuated, sometimes reference is made to developing its military side on the whole (e.g. I. Bērziņš 2000b; Riekstins 2001; Vīķe-Freiberga 2001; 2003a; Republic of Latvia 2002).

Summary

In this chapter, I have argued that, for the Union, Latvia represents in many senses a similarly small and in economic terms relatively insignificant new semi-insider member to Estonia. Although Latvia potentially has somewhat more to offer to the Union, especially in terms of transit prospects for the EU–Russian energy and other trade, most of this potential is compromised by the problematic state of Latvian–Russian relations. But, at the same time, against this background it is interesting to observe how the Latvian EU elite manages to put forth scenarios of their country as a gateway between the east and west. Latvia thus, to a certain

Table 6.2 The construction of the EU's geopolitical subjectivity in northern Europe: Latvian views

Component of ordering	Sub-aspect	Summary
Identity projects	Time	Perceptions of slight but important differences between EU time and Latvia's post-Soviet time, but a concomitant effort to link in the common European healing exercise of the past conflicts
	Space	Strong and consistent accent on BSR region-building; resistance to draw new borders to post-Cold War Europe; support for northernness or nordicity both as a route to Europe and as a goal in its own right; preference for an intergovernmental Europe, although the existence of some federalist traits in the contemporary EU is acknowledged
Interest projects	Geo-policy	Cooperative attitude towards the Union's enlargement and Schengen policies; relative activism in the ND policy especially vis-à-vis energy transit questions; neighbourhood policy welcomed but, vis-à-vis the EU's Russian policies, integration should materialize on the basis of EU defined norms; willingness to strengthen the EU's CFSP and ESDP decision-making, provided that the role of NATO is not compromised
	Geo-strategy	Support for the Union to strengthen its subjectivity in northern Europe and Europe as a whole as well as globally; EU and US/NATO seen as compatible, not mutually competing

extent, manages to make up for its deficiencies in Russian relations by promising an integrative input to the enlarging EU that supposedly will help the Union in realizing its broader geo-strategic goals (Table 6.2).

On the basis of this analysis, it seems unlikely that Latvia would become some sort of an 'awkward' partner for the Nordics and EU institutions in the project of strengthening the Union's subjectivity in the northern European region. And Latvia also looks slightly less likely than Estonia to become a 'reluctant' partner for them. However, it should be kept in mind that the practical record of Latvia's inter-ethnic policies, and its Russian relations on the whole, display somewhat different, more introverted and conflictual patterns than are found in EU member countries like Finland and Sweden. One can thus locate important differences between the Latvian and Nordic agendas vis-à-vis the Union's 'north European-ness', but similarly one can observe differences between Latvia and Estonia.

7 New semi-insiders III

Lithuania

This chapter discusses the case of Lithuania's accession into the Union in May 2004. The result of Lithuania's referendum on EU membership was by far the most comfortable one among the three Baltic states and remarkable even within the whole CEE. In May 2003, 91 per cent of those who voted accepted membership. Such a high level of public support is all the more significant in light of the fact that, in contradistinction to Estonia and Latvia, practically the whole of the country's adult population was entitled to vote. Lithuania lacks a large group of mainly Russophone non-citizens, or citizens of Russia, in the way that Estonia and Latvia have. Lithuania's Russophone contingent constitutes just around 10 per cent and Poles about 6 per cent of the country's population of 3.5 million. The different demographic composition of Lithuania implies that, in connection to the country's EU accession, the Union encounters somewhat different issues from the security concerns associated with Estonia's and Latvia's initially slow start in integrating their Russophone minorities.

But, at the same time, it is of course true that in Lithuania's case the Union encounters a newcomer into EU integration in the very same manner as in the cases of Estonia and Latvia. However, whereas Estonia and Latvia have as political entities only a short-lived history of almost desperately seeking connections with Europe and the West in general during the interwar era in 1918–40, Lithuania has a long-standing, though fairly distant, history as a European great power. By the late fourteenth century, a Lithuanian–Polish agreement aligned together the then vast Lithuanian-ruled territories, which extended far into Russian and Belarusian-speaking lands to the east, and the Catholic lands inhabited by Poles. The birth of the Lithuanian–Polish union marked the beginning of a slow process of polonization of what can in Eric Hobsbawm's (1992) terms be called the proto-Lithuanian nation. The purpose of the Lithuanian–Polish union was to resist the invasions of the Tatars from the (south-)east and the Teutonic knights from the north and west. The famous treaty of Lublin in 1569 formalized the process of Lithuania's transformation from an empire-like formation into a junior partner of Poland. More than two centuries later Russian, Prussian and Austrian forces partitioned Poland–Lithuania into three divisions. Lithuania gradually ended up being ruled by the rising Tsarist Russian empire during the late eighteenth and early nineteenth centuries (Lane 2002: xx–xxiv). Thereafter Lithuania's fate was relatively similar to Estonia's and Latvia's: two decades of independence as a small Lithuanian nation-state between the world wars culminated in failed efforts at tightrope-dancing between the great power games of the Soviet Union and Germany in the late 1930s and early 1940s. Ultimately this led to succumbing into a Soviet republic for half a century. Lithuania regained its independence in August 1991 in a totally different geopolitical context from the one of the interwar years.

During the early 1990s, however, Lithuania's great power history failed to smooth over the emergence of difficult negotiations with Russia on the withdrawal of the remaining Soviet/Russian troops from the country as were witnessed in the foreign relations of the restored republics of Estonia and Latvia. The Lithuanians likewise restored their independence, but never adopted the type of restorationist state-building model which handicapped Estonia and Latvia in their own negotiations. The Lithuanians were rather confronted by the issue of Russia's transit to and from its Kaliningrad region, which as a result of Lithuania's regaining of independence became landlocked from mainland Russia by Lithuanian and Belarusian territories. The Kaliningrad question opened up a whole array of problems for Lithuania's Russian relations, ranging from the hypothetical question of to whom the area historically belonged to Lithuania's internal divisions in foreign policy issues along left–right cleavages, which for their own part complicated the negotiations.

The leftist government of Adolfas Šleževičius (March 1993–February 1996) and President Algirdas Brazauskas (February 1993–February 1998) adopted pragmatic tactics in the troop withdrawal question in order to press for a most-favoured-nation status for Lithuania's Russian trade, to avoid double tariffs in selling Lithuanian goods to the lucrative markets in Russia. Vytautas Landsbergis – hero of the Lithuanian independence movement of 1987–91, Lithuanian president prior to Brazauskas's term during August 1991–February 1993, and the right-wing opposition leader during the leftist government – argued that Brazauskas was making far too many compromises and was secretly returning Lithuania to a Russian sphere of influence. But, importantly, the leftists and rightists agreed on the ultimate goal of reinforcing Lithuanian independence and distancing the country from Russia. Hence, their disagreement was largely over the tactics to be used in the negotiations. In the end, the Brazauskas government dropped the rightist-supported demand for compensation for damages allegedly caused by the Soviet forces during their half-century's stationing in Lithuania, and agreed on terms for Russia's transit to and from Kaliningrad against a more hard-line policy of the rightists.[1] The compromise prompted the Soviet/Russian troops to leave by the end of August 1993, a year earlier than from Estonia and Latvia (Lane 2002: 203–5). Kaliningrad nevertheless remained a major issue in Lithuanian–Russian relations. Consequently, it was only logical that it was taken up during Lithuania's EU accession negotiations (see below).

Yet, on balance, it must be said that in Russian relations, among the Balts, the Lithuanians were somewhat privileged throughout the 1990s by not having adopted the restorationist state-building model. In that way they avoided the same sort of disputes on the citizenship rights of the Russophone minority population as Estonia and Latvia had with Russia and the majority of their Russophone population, and which later became items in their EU accession negotiations. Thanks to the relatively small share of Russophone and Polish minorities in Lithuania, the Lithuanians felt they could afford a non-restorationist citizenship policy not discriminating between the titular nation and those who arrived during the Soviet era. And in Lithuania's post-Soviet politics, the historically built apprehensions were not exclusively directed at Russians, but partly at Poles, until the Lithuanian–Polish rapprochement at the interstate level helped to smoothen relations towards the mid-1990s. In 1993, Lithuania and Poland agreed on Polish training for Lithuanian soldiers, coordinated airspace control, and purchase of Polish armaments by the Lithuanian defence forces. The treaty on friendship and cooperation was signed in 1994. In 1997 a 'strategic partnership' between Lithuania and Poland was declared with the creation of joint institutions.[2] The military cooperation side was further strengthened by the launching of the Polish–Lithuanian peacekeeping battalion LITPOLBAT project. On the whole, the Lithuanian pattern of enmities accounted for a lesser degree of societal polarization along ethnic lines than found in Estonia or Latvia. This helped to build good neighbourly relations, but failed to translate into a comparative advantage in the sense of speeding up the development of EU relations.

Lithuania's free trade agreement with the EU was signed in July 1994, with a six-year transition period agreed for the Lithuanian side, after which tariffs could still be maintained for some groups of retail goods. The longer transition period than granted to Estonia (none) or Latvia (four years) indicates the relative slowness of Lithuania's economic transformation. The European Commission cited the lack of a functioning market economy as the chief reason for not inviting Lithuania into membership until late 1999, the fate shared by Latvia. The EU also posed demands for the closure of the Soviet-built Ignalina nuclear power plant (European Commission 1997b; see below). The Lithuanians complained of having been treated unfairly by the Union's alleged application of outdated statistics not taking into account Lithuania's rapid progress towards the late 1990s. The Lithuanians also voiced concerns that the Union was simply thinking of ensuring Russia's access to Kaliningrad at Lithuania's expense, and that it wanted to prevent Lithuania from selling cheap electricity from its Ignalina plant to European markets (Lane 2002: 215).

The next section will take a more detailed look at what type of political economy issues were involved in the Union's enlargement into Lithuania. Today, combined with the good neighbourly relations that Lithuania has determinedly and relatively consistently pursued since the mid-1990s, they make Lithuania fairly well placed in the context of the making of the Union's wider northern Europe. Thereafter the security issues tied to the Kaliningrad question are explored in more depth with an eye on the Lithuanian–EU side of the story (for the EU–Russian side, see Chapter 8). The dispute on the closure of the Ignalina plant will also be taken up. The chapter will then proceed into an analysis of the views of Lithuanian EU elites towards the Union's project of developing its northern European subjectivity.

Issues of political economy in Lithuania's EU accession

Lithuania never opted for the same sort of economic 'shock therapy' as Estonia did almost immediately after the regaining of independence. Lithuania's relatively large heavy industry sector, willingness to maintain the markets in Russia and the rest of the CIS, and decision to grant citizenship to all residents contributed to this. Many of the Russophone and Polish industrial workers who were enfranchised in 1991 worked for USSR-wide enterprises with vested interests in the continuity of state subsidies. Hence they were prone to support only gradual rather than shock reforms of the Estonian style. Among further factors contributing to the Lithuanian gradualism can be included left–right divisions on the pace of economic reforms and Lithuania's rural-based, romantic Catholicism as opposed to the Protestantism of the majority of Estonians and Latvians. This cultural heritage helped to maintain ideas of collective solidarity and to resist liberal economic ideas (Lane 2002: 165–6). In 1998, Christopher Marsh argued that Lithuania was still balancing between the post-Soviet orbit and European economic orientation (Marsh 1998: 162).

In 2001, the imports of the EU-15 from Lithuania made up just 2.53 billion euros. This is a smaller figure than considerably tinier Estonia was able to put up (Statistics Lithuania 2004a; Chapter 5 above). In 2002, the Lithuanian GDP per capita stood at just 38 per cent of the EU-15 level, thus constituting a burden for the Union's assistance programmes (see European Commission 2004d). The EU administered a total of 482.3 million euros of aid to Lithuania during 2000–2. This figure consisted of 126 million euros for PHARE, plus a top-up of 18.5 million for reinforcement of administrative capacity during 2002; 90 million for SAPARD, plus an indicative allocation of 31.8 million for 2002; 155 million for ISPA, plus indicative allocation of 61 million euros for 2002 (European Commission 2004d). These funds were expected to account annually for about 4 per cent of the Lithuanian budget (Valionis 2003a). Lithuania's trade with the EU picked up only slowly, because of the eastern sales of products like Lithuanian foodstuffs and electricity exports from the Ignalina plant to Kaliningrad and Belarus. The balance between the eastern and western European directions finally shifted in favour of the latter only after the mid-1990s. The Russian economic collapse of 1998 functioned as a major economic shock and a political watershed in this respect. Since then, trade with EU members, in particular with Germany, provided the pull for offsetting Lithuania's reliance on eastern markets (Table 7.1).

Arguably, Lithuania's potential position as a bridge of transport routes is its best economic asset in European integration. Lithuania has good infrastructure and good transport potential, and stands at the intersection of major east–west and north–south transport corridors. Two out of the nine EU-designed Trans-European transport corridors, the development of which into the CEE was announced in 1995 by the EU, pass through Lithuanian territory. The Via Baltica runs from Tallinn through Riga and Kaunas to Warsaw, with a spur to St Petersburg, and the projected Via Hanseatica from Kiel to St Petersburg through Hamburg, Gdansk, Kaliningrad, Lithuania and Riga.[3] The ice-free Lithuanian port of Klaipėda was an important port for shipping heavy products such as raw materials and grain

Table 7.1 Lithuania's foreign trade with the EU-15 and CIS, 1993–2003 (% of value)

	1993	1994	1995	1996	1997	1998	1999	2000	2001	2002	2003
Imports/ EU	18.7	26.4	37.1	42.4	46.5	50.2	49.7	46.5	44.0	44.5	44.5
Exports/ EU	16.9	25.8	36.4	32.9	32.5	38.0	50.1	47.9	47.8	48.4	42.0
Imports/ CIS	67.5	50.3	42.0	32.9	29.3	24.7	23.6	30.7	29.4	26.0	25.3
Exports/ CIS	57.1	46.7	42.3	45.4	46.4	35.7	18.2	16.3	19.7	19.2	17.0

Sources: 2001–3 figures for exports: Statistics Lithuania (2004a); for imports, Statistics Lithuania (2004b); rest of figures: J. Köll (2003: 373–4).

already during the Soviet era. Now it offers one of the cheapest routes from the Baltic to Belarus, Ukraine and southwest Russia. Its modernization projects made it during the 1990s the fifth largest single port on the Baltic Sea, although in 1999 Lithuania's share of the total Baltic Sea cargo constituted only 9 per cent, owing to the country's reliance on one main port. But Klaipėda's competitiveness in relation to Estonian and Latvian ports centres on its lesser reliance on Russian markets, with about 80 per cent of the port's transit going to and from Belarus and Ukraine. Hence, out of Russia's westbound transit trade, in 1999 Lithuania accounted for only 6 per cent. This transit income made up an estimated 4–6 per cent of Lithuania's GDP (Lane 2002: 190–2; Laurila 2003: 41–9).

Lithuania's gateway function is supported by its oil infrastructure. That signifies not only the country's own largely unexploited, though very modest, oil reserves, but also the merged energy complex consisting of the Mažeikiai oil refinery – the only one in the Baltic states – the Būtingė oil terminal, which enables the supply of crude oil, thus reducing further the dependence on Russian supplies, and the Biržai oil pipeline. One-third of this complex was sold to the US company Williams in 1998 in return for investments, ahead of interest from the Russian company LUKoil, and as a security measure, to deter Russian capital perceived to be too closely associated with the Russian government. In April 1999, LUKoil did indeed halt oil supplies into Mažeikiai for a short period. But in 2001, the Lithuanian prime minister Brazauskas (July 2001–) expressed his unhappiness at Mažeikiai losses during the year and signalled willingness to receive additional investment from the Russian company Yukos, which was perceived to be considerably more independent than LUKoil. During the lengthy negotiations for the control of Mažeikiai, the Lithuanian president, Valdas Adamkus (February 1998–February 2003; July 2004–), who spent the Cold War as an immigrant first in Germany and then in the US, complained that the Russian company's involvement was negotiated behind closed doors (Adamkus 2002b). The deal maintained the position of Williams as the main operator of the refinery, supposedly guaranteed long-term crude oil supplies into Mažeikiai, and gave both Williams and Yukos a 28.85 per cent stake. The Lithuanian government retained a 40.66 per cent share (Rosbalt 2001, 2002). Since then, Williams has given up its stake and, with the dissolution of Yukos during 2004–5, takeover of the Yukos stake by Russian government-bound companies looked likely, and the future of the complex was left wide open again. Yet, even so, the whole story contrasts favourably with the problems and missed opportunities faced by Latvia's Ventspils (Chapter 6).

Security issues in Lithuania's EU accession

Lithuania, alongside Poland and Germany, is one of the countries that in principle could claim a right to Kaliningrad on historical grounds. References to a 'Lithuania minor' or to the Lithuanian past of Karaliaucius were occasionally seen made during the early 1990s, for example by representatives of the Lithuanian emigrant community.[4] At the turn of the millennium, around half of the Lithuanian population continued to support territorial claims (Vesa and Möller 2003: 50). However, territorial claims never became an approved policy of the Lithuanian government, which was well aware of the fact that the Lithuanian capital Vilnius was a Polish territory during the interwar period, and that Russia could have claimed the area of Klaipėda, which was appended to the territory of the Lithuanian SSR during the Soviet era.[5] In this way, Lithuanian foreign policy makers acknowledged early on Lithuania's status as a beneficiary of the 1975 Helsinki consensus on the inviolability of borders in Europe. They also understood how any territorial claims would have thwarted Lithuania's EU and NATO membership bids, as was attested in the instances of Estonia and Latvia relatively quickly dropping their own claims after realizing their counter-productivity at the broader strategic level (Joenniemi *et al.* 2000: 5; Joenniemi and Prawitz 1998: 236).

The Lithuanian–Russian agreement on Kaliningrad in 1991 meant a system where the borders of Kaliningrad were recognized, rights of ethnic minorities were respected on both sides, and cooperation in the economic, trade and cultural sectors was encouraged. Both the Lithuanians and Kaliningraders were allowed visa-free cross-border visits for up to thirty days, with the Lithuanian party accepting the old Soviet era internal passports. As for Russia's military transit through Lithuanian railways to the Soviet-built base in Kaliningrad, during the Soviet/ Russian troop withdrawal negotiations, the leftist government demanded twenty-one days' notice before any proposed journey, limits on the number of unarmed servicemen to be transported on any one occasion and the presence of Lithuanian guards in the transit trains. Russia never bowed to these demands. Assurances from the EU were needed that the maintenance of a less demanding system would not thwart Lithuania's EU membership bid. At that time, Kaliningrad did indeed represent a threat in the eyes of the Lithuanians. The rightists in particular treated the military transit issue as a threat to Lithuania's national security, and called for reductions in the numbers of troops stationed in Kaliningrad. The document 'Basics of National Security in Lithuania' adopted by the Seimas in 1996 called for Kaliningrad's demilitarization. And suggestions were even heard for a new internationally agreed status for Kaliningrad. However, the Kaliningrad issue gradually transformed from a source of various threat perceptions into an opportunity to play a constructive role in the Baltic Sea region (Lane 2002: 201–7; Miniotaitė 2001: 14; Stanyte-Toločkienė 2001: 243).

Lithuania has in this spirit gone on to participate in four euroregion projects linking it with Kaliningrad, as well as with Belarusian, Latvian, Danish, Polish and Swedish municipalities and regions. The Council for Long-term Cooperation between Regions of the Republic of Lithuania and the Kaliningrad Region of the Russian Federation was established in June 2000, with commissions on policy sectors like agriculture; culture, sports and health care; economic cooperation, trade and energy; cross-border cooperation and euroregions; environmental protection; transport; border checkpoints; and emergency prevention and liquidation. There is also a Lithuanian–Kaliningrad Region Parliamentary Forum established in 2002, and a Lithuanian–Kaliningradian association for non-governmental organizations (NGOs). In the more explicit realm of 'hard security', Lithuania and Russia have agreed on the exchange of information on Russia's military forces in Kaliningrad on the basis of the Conventional Forces in Europe (CFE) treaty, to which Lithuania is not even an original signatory party.

However, despite the EU's many regionalizing policies discussed in Chapter 3, it was clear that from the EU perspective, as expressed during the accession negotiations, the simplified visa regime and military transit on the Lithuanian–Kaliningradian border compromised or even endangered the enlarged Union's universalizing project of building Schengen borders around itself. Therefore, as said, the Union required Lithuania to abolish the simplified border crossing regime and implement Schengen borders, which led into the intense EU–Russian dispute in 2002. And, as will be discussed below, as a testimony to the Union's power, Lithuania had little choice but to respect the EU's requirements, and thereafter became a mere spectator in the EU–Russian negotiations. Yet, Lithuania's reaching of a border agreement with Russia in 1997, in stark contrast to Estonia and Latvia who at that time were still locked in border disputes with Russia, was taken as a very positive signal by the EU side. The border treaty was ratified by the Russian Duma in 2003 as part of the EU–Russian agreement on Russia's transit to and from Kaliningrad.

The remaining security issue peculiar to Lithuania's case is the EU's unconditional request for the decommissioning of the Ignalina nuclear power plant. Ignalina has a similar type of reactor to the one that exploded with catastrophic consequences in Chernobyl in the Ukrainian Soviet Republic in 1986. The EU bodies deemed it insufficient to address the Ignalina issue by means of the gradualist approach applied to many other post-communist and post-Soviet soft security transformation problems, which indicated a belief that the perceived problems could be corrected through time and by means of EU assistance, economic development, and eventual convergence with the standards prevailing among the older member states.

In Soviet Lithuania, the environmental lobby Žemyna and the popular front Sajūdis started in 1987–8 to publicly oppose the planned building of a third reactor at the Ignalina plant. This helped to gather popular momentum to the nascent independence movement. In 1988, the Lithuanian Communist Party halted the plans for a third reactor, and the largely symbolic decision by the local party was not contested by the central authorities in Moscow, who ultimately decided on such policy questions. In March 1990, after Lithuania declared its independence to be restored, Moscow put Lithuania into an energy blockade, which in a paradoxical manner made Ignalina an important symbol of national sovereignty, as it helped to guarantee electricity supply to the threatened Lithuanians. Thereafter the plant assumed a central position in Lithuania's economic recovery by providing cashflow from energy exports. Subsequently, in the face of demands for closure by the EU, Ignalina's position as a symbol of Lithuanian sovereignty became strengthened even more. Its old status as a symbol of Soviet power was thus altered completely (Vähä-Sipilä 2004a: 78–85).

In other words, Ignalina quickly lost its original environmental significance. Its closure became a difficult issue even for the Lithuanian environmentalists to defend (!), let alone Lithuanian governments. The costs of closure are phenomenal for a small state like Lithuania. The Seimas estimates the costs for the closure of the first reactor alone to be about 10 billion euros. The European Commission, meanwhile, reserved only 70 million euros a year during 2004–7, although it also committed itself to further assistance thereafter, until the closure of the first and second reactors in 2005 and 2009 respectively.[6] However, in practice the issue of settling both direct and indirect final costs remains unresolved (Vähä-Sipilä 2004a: 86–95).

In comparison to Estonia and Latvia, it can be said that, looking from the EU side, the Kaliningrad transit and Ignalina nuclear power plant issues dwarf Estonia's and Latvia's security problems of national integration of their large Russophone minorities. This is not to belittle the perceived threats of poor national cohesion and the connections of the Russophones to Russia and its 'near abroad' policy within the framework of the enlarged Union. Instead, at issue is an acknowledgement of the scale of funding and amount of negotiation required for addressing the security issues peculiar to Lithuania's case. Truly big security related issues thus opened up for the EU in the case of Lithuania's EU accession, which on a purely formal plane of EU decision-making connotes only seven votes in the EU's Council (2 per cent) and thirteen seats in the European Parliament (1.6 per cent during 2004–7). To find out how the Lithuanians balance off their obvious disadvantages and small size, it is a useful exercise to take a detailed look at the views of Lithuanian foreign policy makers and EU experts regarding the Union's project of strengthening its subjectivity in northern Europe. The systematic examination relies on an extensive body of empirical material[7] and the model of geopolitical subjectivity introduced in Chapter 3.[8]

Lithuanian views of the EU's identity projects in northern Europe

Time

The familiar 'return to Europe' discourses assume slightly different forms in Lithuania when compared to Estonia and Latvia. In the background can be seen the fact that the Lithuanian identity project has extensive roots as a European great power, but also a history of struggling to maintain the sovereignty of the Lithuanian nation. On the one hand, there is the view of the contemporary EU providing a new linkage to the European modernization process of which Lithuania was long part within the context of the Polish–Lithuanian union (Lane 2002: xxiii–xxiv; Pavlovaite 2003: 200, 212–4). On the other hand, there is the relatively popular yet politically rather powerless view of the EU threatening the well established Lithuanian cultural traditions, which are also coloured by the indigenous paganism that was able to sustain itself even when Western Christianity was making inroads in the Polish–Lithuanian union, as well as thereafter. These tensions notwithstanding, it is correct to say that EU integration is widely accepted as some sort of a second part of Lithuania's modernization project (cf. Vähä-Sipilä 2004b). The Lithuanian foreign minister, Algirdas Saudargas, wanted to make this historical continuity clear in his speech at the Danish Institute of International Affairs in February 1997:

> For centuries, Lithuania has sought to become an equal partner in European affairs (the coronation of King Mindaugas in July 1253, the failed coronation of Grand Duke Vytautas in 1430 were actually steps in that direction), fulfilling its duty to the Continent by stopping incursions from the East and assuming a balancing position at times of peace.
>
> (quoted in Jæger 1997: 25)

The continuity and 'return to Europe' arguments are accompanied by a very sober acknowledgement of the differences between Lithuania's post-Soviet time and EU time. Compared to Estonia and Latvia, this acknowledgement is a slightly more multifaceted one and is made more explicit time and again in the statements of Lithuanian policy makers. First, like Latvia, Lithuania had to catch up with the five CEE countries who had already been invited into EU accession negotiations in 1997. However, after Lithuania's invitation into the negotiations together with the other remaining CEE candidates in late 1999, the Lithuanian foreign minister, Antanas Valionis, was relieved to state that 'now we have an opportunity to catch the first train of enlargement. Not only do we have this opportunity, but also must use it not to be left in waiting for the arrival of another TGV. We know well at what speed the train is moving and we can plan our steps' (Valionis 2001).

Second, representatives of the Lithuanian EU elite have developed a habit of reiterating the remaining differences in development levels between the EU-15 and CEE entrants (e.g. Adamkus 2002c,d; Paksas 2003a, 2004). As in Latvia, some attention is drawn to Lithuania's own efforts to join contemporary EU time. If this would not take place by performing outright economic growth miracles, then at least the Lithuanian leaders are determined to come to terms with Lithuania's part in the Holocaust and in that way participate in the common exercise of overcoming Europe's historical conflicts and hostilities (e.g. Adamkus 2002e; Brazauskas 2004). Yet, during the course of the accession process, the Lithuanians found themselves implementing reforms characteristic of late modern European societies, such as data protection and combating sexual harassment. Such reforms were not in tune with the public's ideas of what should be prioritized in the country's transformation process (Lithuanian EU policy maker, November 2002; Lithuanian EU observer, November 2002).

Third, there are worries that, during the rushed accession negotiation process, the EU-15 and the CEE countries did not manage to familiarize themselves with each other properly. They failed to find a unifying vision bridging the divide between old and new members (Adamkus 2001a, 2002f). As new semi-insiders, new members like Lithuania had a difficulty of judging which aspects of the Union the old members wanted to correct in the future of Europe debate, and why. The Lithuanians were, however, learning fast to conceive of the historically evolved communitarian method as the glue that had made the EU what it currently is. The application of this method dissociates the EU from the Soviet Union (Grybauskaitė 2001; Martikonis 2001).

Space

In stark contrast to Estonia and Latvia, Lithuania's history as a European great power bears strong continental characteristics. The Lithuanian-ruled and Lithuanian-speaking territories of the Lithuanian–Polish union had only a limited access to the Baltic Sea. The traditional direction of expansion was the southeast where the current Belarusian lands lie and where the European neighbourhood policy focuses upon. This means that Lithuania's current position as a small Baltic littoral and EU member state represents a historical reorientation, and that its relationship with Belarus is complicated because of their shared past (Pavlovaite 2003: 203; Vareikis 2002: 277). The relatively thin historical attachment to the Baltic Sea and a strong legacy of the Lithuanian–Polish union mean that a Central European orientation was open to Lithuania in a completely different manner from Estonia and Latvia. In 1996, the Lithuanian foreign minister, Algirdas Saudargas, dismissed ideas of Baltic unity in the context of their EU and NATO accession bids, and referred to Lithuania as a Central European, or at best, a 'Central Baltic European country' (Miniotaitė 2003).

The messy-looking identity political label of Lithuania as a 'Central Baltic European country' is in fact entirely logical in the Lithuanian context. Lithuanian foreign policy makers wish to make Lithuania an 'interpreter' between the East and West (Paleckis 2002). Lithuania's wish to become a geopolitical hub, linking the various edges of northern Europe with Europe's continental parts, is well expressed by the Lithuanian presidents Rolandas Paksas (February 2003–April 2004) and Valdas Adamkus:[9]

> Good neighbour relations and regional co-operation are the major priorities of Lithuania's foreign policy . . . We shall devote special attention to the Baltic Sea region. At the same time, we are ready to continue fostering the strategic partnership with Poland, to support the European integration aspirations of Ukraine and democratic transformations in Belarus as well as to step up the relations with the countries of South Caucasus. We can clearly identify two political vectors in the Baltic Sea region. First, adequate protection of the interests of our countries in the European Union and development

of our infrastructure require enhancement of co-operation with the Nordic and Baltic countries. Second, it is crucial at the same time to fully eliminate the remaining dividing lines in the region. Therefore, we need to strengthen our relations with Russia's northwestern region.

(Paksas 2003b)

Lithuania can be a truly promising north-east centre of logistics in the EU. Two main axes can be singled out here. First, in the north–south direction connecting the eastern part of the Baltic Sea. Second, in the west–east direction, which could become a large-capacity multi-modal logistic centre . . .

(Adamkus 2002g)

There is, however, a need to maintain perspective here. As has been said, the divisions between rightist and leftist political forces have coloured Lithuanian politics since the regaining of independence. They agree on the basic importance of the EU and NATO directions and on the need to maintain distance from the Russian sphere of influence. But vis-à-vis Russia the leftist tactics have been pragmatic and flexible, reminiscent of Finnish–Russian relations at their best, whereas the rightist tactics have been closer to the Russophobic and doctrinaire end of the identity political continuum (cf. Lane 2002: 202). The fears of Russia of the rightists in particular also give rise to the not entirely isolated remarks about living close to a 'volcano' which is just about to explode at Lithuania's peril. But Lithuania's direct neighbour, the Russian region of Kaliningrad, is not portrayed as part of this volcano. It is rather a site where Lithuania offers the EU a good track record of cooperation with Russia, as well as considerable expertise (Pavlovaite 2003: 201–2, 204–5).

Lithuania's orientation towards the northern and Nordic directions lacks the rather explicit tone that was detected in the Estonian and Latvian cases. One rather finds repeated assertions on the need to connect the northern and central, or northern and southern spheres of Europe (e.g. Adamkus 2002a,g,h). However, on the basis of already existing links, it is clear to the Lithuanians that within the enlarged Union the Nordic countries, for example, will provide a more natural direction than southern countries like France, Italy and Spain (Lithuanian policy maker, November 2002; Lithuanian civil society activist, November 2002).

Several Lithuanian documents portray EU space in much more communitarian, perhaps even covertly federal terms, when compared to Estonian and Latvian views. Although some observers claim to have found an almost exclusively intergovernmentalist preference in Lithuania's views of EU space (Pavlovaite 2003: 209), it is striking how many pivotal Lithuanian documents remind one of Finland's federalist views of strong EU institutions as guaranteeing best the interests of small and minor powers within the Union. The Lithuanian document, 'Guiding Principles of the Government of Lithuania on the Future of the European Union', asserts that:

The EU's evolution indicates that for such states as Lithuania, strong European institutions – Council, Commission, European Parliament, European

Court of Justice, etc. – ensure better participation in the Union than inter-governmental co-operation. We believe that the 'community method' ensures coherence of the EU actions and balances diverse interests of the Member States. The application of this method can be reviewed and extended to more areas of action. On the other hand, the community method should not be op-posed to the intergovernmental method, they are not mutually exclusive.

(Government of Lithuania 2002)

The remark on intergovernmentalism at the end of the quote shows how Lithuanian foreign policy makers operate under popular pressures for maintaining Lithuania's sovereignty (cf. Vähä-Sipilä 2004b). This is not unlike the situations of their Estonian, Latvian or Nordic counterparts. But in Lithuania's case the situ-ation does not translate into extensive calls for intergovernmentalism, although the Lithuanian EU elite wishes to see a Union anchored on the principle of equal-ity between member states and balance of interests between large old member states and newcomers (Adamkus 2001b; Brazauskas 2004; Paksas 2003a; Val-ionis 2001, 2002a).

Lithuanian views of the EU's interest projects in northern Europe

Geo-policy

The take-it-or-leave-it character of EU integration which was detected in the Es-tonian and Latvian cases does not come up in a similar manner in the views of Lithuanians. During the 1990s, Lithuania appeared to be a little closer to NATO membership than Estonia and Latvia. Reasons for these perceptions included Lithuania's more sizeable and better equipped armed forces and its above-men-tioned military cooperation projects with Poland, NATO member since 1999. At the same time, after the settling of the troop withdrawal and Kaliningrad transit issues with Russia by the mid-1990s, serious problems in Lithuania's Russian re-lations were largely absent. In these conditions, at the level of official statements, the EU membership question never seemed to assume a life-and-death character. Nonetheless, it clearly was conceived as an important security measure. And at no stage was there any suggestion of a Norwegian-style alternative to EU integration. The competing, albeit at best hypothetical, option of integrating with the CIS was excluded in the 1996 'Basics of National Security' document, which prohibited joining any political, military, economic or other alliances established on the basis of the former Soviet Union (Miniotaitė 2001: 14).

Originally a laggard in the race for EU membership, Lithuania used substantial energy to convince European policy makers and publics of the benefits of enlarge-ment, especially early in the new millennium, when concerns about the costs and institutional feasibility of the whole project arose within the EU-15. According to the Lithuanians, EU enlargement was not only about fulfilling technical criteria or thinking of short-term economic losses on the part of the existing members. In fact, some of them might be better off in an enlarged Union (Adamkus 2001a,c; Martikonis 2001). Enlargement was about doing historical justice and opening up the EU for new members sharing the same values and pursuing similar goals. A long-term perspective would help to see the 'win–win' character of the process. Enlargement was about preparing to meet the challenges lying ahead and about adding new capacities and strengths into the Union (interviews; Adamkus 2000, 2001b, 2002f,h; Brazauskas 2004; Martikonis 2002a; Valionis 2002a).

According to the interviewed Lithuanian EU experts, the new capacities brought in by Lithuania include for instance the familiar issue of a cheaper but well educated workforce, but also experience of how to work with Russia. However, one of the experts remarked that this may be a myth better reflecting deep-seated Soviet era habits, rather than business requirements of the day; and, as another one put it, most of the debate in Lithuania centres not around what Lithuania can offer to the EU, but vice versa (interviews). Yet the point about having gained experience of relatively smoothly working relations with Russia and Kaliningrad during the last decade or so is important. The Lithuanian president Valdas Adamkus is keen to avoid any suggestions that EU integration would represent Lithuanian 'barricade building'. In his opinion, such behaviour is 'negative and inflexible' and would only serve to distance Lithuania from the principles of 'Euro-Atlantic mainstream' and 'community of western nations'; for him, Lithuania should not remain hostage of history and geography (Miniotaitė 2003). Here it must also be recalled how, during the EU–Russian dispute on Kaliningrad, the Lithuanian prime minister Algirdas Brazauskas indicated Lithuania's willingness to preserve the visa-free regime for the Kaliningraders, provided that the EU and Russia can agree on the issue among each other (Aalto 2002b: 28). His suggestion was almost completely ignored. The Union pressed for Lithuania's 'sovereign right' to join the EU and implement the Schengen border regime, which the Union had itself set as an accession criterion (!). Of course, the Lithuanians perceived themselves as future beneficiaries of the free movement set to come with membership in the Schengen treaty, but it was clear that their alternative proposals hinted at by Brazauskas failed to ring a bell on the Union side. And in the opinion of a Lithuanian EU expert, in the EU–Russian negotiations the Kaliningrad transit issue was resolved in Russia's favour:

> It indeed was a political decision, it is difficult to disagree on that. Now, as to any kind of decision, it probably has its winners and losers, or relative winners and losers, and I clearly see it as a victory for Russia. I am personally surprised that the press and media in the west comment it as the great push through of the EU position, but if you compare negotiating positions . . . previous negotiating positions of Russia and EU, it's obvious that the Russians got almost everything that they wanted . . . if we talk about principles, it is a big concession from the EU side and it remains to be seen, from the technical solutions, whether it was not reached that way at Lithuania's expense.
>
> (Lithuanian policy maker, November 2002)

The same expert commented that the Lithuanian position had to constantly respond and adapt to the evolvement of EU–Russian negotiations. But throughout the Lithuanian position was based on three principles: that Lithuania is interested in good neighbourly relations with Russia; it is not interested in the isolation of Kaliningrad; and any solution would have to be based on the EU *acquis* and should not compromise Lithuania's joining of the Schengen treaty. Moreover, official Lithuanian comments insisted repeatedly that the financial burden resulting from the implementation of the negotiated rules should be shared and not fall on Lithuania's shoulders alone. After the EU–Russia agreement in November 2002, Lithuanian and Russian diplomats rather quickly reached their own technical agreement. By June 2003, they finalized the terms of the new rules, including facilitated transit documents (FTDs) issued to the Kaliningraders instead of regular Schengen visas (see Chapter 8). Lithuania opened a new consulate in Kaliningrad's city of Sovetsk as part of the technical agreement and expanded the capacity of the existing premises in the city of Kaliningrad. And in 2004, as a result of the positive experiences of the conclusion of the dispute, Lithuania offered to host an EU training centre for officers of the member states' national border guards (Paksas 2004).

It is also in the very issue of Kaliningrad that Lithuania is most interested when it comes to responding and contributing to the Union's regionalizing ND policy. However, in the interviews some Lithuanian policy makers confessed that, in their opinion, far too few items of the joint Lithuanian–Russian proposal for regional cooperation, the so-called Nida list presented in February 2000, were incorporated into the first action plan of the ND. But if the EU party was not always responsive enough in the planning of its northern European policies, neither was ND and other regional cooperation always easy with the Russian officials in Kaliningrad, as remarked by another Lithuanian policy maker:

> We in Lithuania had some experience trying to work with people in Kaliningrad, officials in Kaliningrad, but they have limited authority and limited capability to absorb the money coming from the EU, because it goes through Moscow, as I understand it; so, a more direct approach would probably be quite good.
>
> (Lithuanian policy maker, November 2002)

The Lithuanian contribution to the ND policy has been much more substantial and original than the Estonian approach, which for a long period remained relatively passive. In its contribution to the drafting of the second action plan for the ND, Lithuania accentuated the promotion of regional cooperation with the enlarging Union's neighbours in tandem with facilitating the enlargement process. Lithuania also wanted to accentuate the strengthening of civil society and democratic institutions in the ND states, probably with a reference to neighbouring Belarus, as well as Russia and Kaliningrad. Other pivotal amendments proposed by Lithuania included Kaliningrad's connection to the Trans-European

Transport Network; building of spur lines from the planned North European Gas Pipeline to Sweden and new member states; improvement of the existing land supply spur line for supplying gas to Kaliningrad through Lithuania; attention to environmental questions in oil transportation on the Baltic Sea as a response to Finnish concerns; reduction of pollution of transboundary waters and river basins in the Lithuanian–Kaliningradian border areas; attention to environmental safety in oil exploration in the Lithuanian and Kaliningradian coast on the Baltic Sea; construction of wastewater treatment facilities in Neman and Sovetsk in Kaliningrad, enhanced cooperation in the Lithuanian–Kaliningradian euroregion projects; improvement of tourism infrastructure; and, in line with the Latvian proposal, establishment of a Northern Dimension unit within the European Commission for monitoring and consultation activities (Government of Lithuania 2003a). However, alongside the emerging picture of Lithuanian activism, it must be mentioned that in his speech to the Lithuanian diplomatic corps President Paksas somehow managed to confuse NATO as being one of the initiators of the ND policy (!) (Paksas 2003c).

The EU's neighbourhood policy is another sector where Lithuania has displayed a fairly enthusiastic approach. This concerns for instance the need for engaging neighbouring Belarus. Lithuanian policy makers see Belarus as an important transit country for cargo and energy resources, some of which also go through Lithuanian territory. But even more important for them is Ukraine, a country which in their eyes has a clear European vocation and thus should not be shut outside future borders of the Union. Lithuania has proposed joint institutions with Ukraine at all levels of government, in the same manner as it has with Poland. Moreover, Lithuania has participated in economic training in Ukraine in a trilateral project with the other Baltic states and Canada, and is also willing to offer bilateral assistance (Adamkus 2002c; Valionis 2002b, 2003b). Lithuania wants to transmit to these countries Lithuania's own experiences of EU-induced reforms, provided that they are willing to forge ties and converge with the Union (Martikonis 2002b). This aim also helped President Adamkus to act as one the mediators in Ukraine's Orange Revolution at the turn of 2004–5. Here, Lithuania claims to take responsibility not only before the EU, but also before Ukraine itself (Adamkus 2002i). The economic part of the Lithuanian interest in the neighbourhood policy is well put by the foreign minister, Antanas Valionis, whereas another comment by a Lithuanian EU observer helps us to see the dialectics of pragmatic economic interests, on the one hand, and emphasis on EU values, on the other, which guides the Lithuanian approach:

> Incredible economic potential that exists on the eastern rim of the European Union warrants that absolute priority be given to the Union's policies towards the future neighbours in Eastern Europe: Russia, Ukraine, Belarus, Moldova. The concept of a wider Europe has to grow into a comprehensive policy backed by firm political will and adequate resources.

> (Valionis 2002a)

We'll probably try to make European Union's policy towards Russia, towards so-called Eastern neighbours, much more pragmatic, and at the same time to hold on to certain principles. Compromises cannot be made by violating sovereign rights, by violating certain values, and violating international law, and creating some things which change the usual understanding of how international relations should be conducted. The problem is that we are a very young state and it's important for us to say for everybody around that we are a state and, of course, we should keep in mind our limits. It's very important for us, it's actually part of our identity – being strict on these issues.

(Lithuanian EU observer, November 2002).

In the more general questions pertaining to the Union's ability to act as a northern European subject, the Lithuanians are consistently in favour of extending QMV procedures within the Union's decision-making. In a speech at the Centre for European Integration Studies in Bonn, the deputy minister for foreign affairs, Rytis Martikonis, even refers to Lithuania's historical experiences within the Polish–Lithuanian union, of how the application of a veto principle eventually led to the end of Lithuanian sovereignty (Martikonis 2001). In the Convention, the Lithuanians also supported the strengthening of EU foreign policy by creating a post of EU minister of foreign affairs (Government of Lithuania 2003b). But, regardless of these federalist positions that go beyond the Estonian and Latvian insistence on national sovereignty in foreign policy questions, the Lithuanian position is just as much worried about duplication of EU and NATO functions within the sphere of the ESDP, although the idea of a European military force as such was approved early on (Adamkus 2001a; Paksas 2004).

Geo-strategy

Out of the three Baltic states, Lithuanian foreign policy makers display the strongest support for the Union's existing and near future policies intended at developing its subjectivity in the northern European region. The assertion in the Lithuanian government's (2002) document 'Guiding Principles' that '[T]he stronger the EU will be, the better the national interests of Lithuania will be served' is very telling about the official Lithuanian views of strong correlation between national and EU-wide interests. It also reminds one of the fairly unconditional support for a stronger Union characteristic of the Finnish government under the leadership of the federalist prime minister, Paavo Lipponen, the initiator of the ND. And remarkably, in contradistinction to the Estonian case, although from the speeches and declarations of Lithuanian foreign policy makers one can find all the same calls for a strong Union speaking with one voice and real influence in world affairs, the Lithuanian words are backed up by support for the very policies designed to realize this overall goal. However, a dissenting voice must be granted to a Lithuanian EU observer, who consigns the official views to the realm of mere rhetoric:

Of course, I think that the Baltic States, and especially Lithuania out of them, will be the most pro-American countries [within the enlarged Union]. And, concerning defence issues, the so-called European Security and Defence Policy, I'm sure that our priority will always be NATO in these issues . . . We are not saying now this aloud within the sphere of diplomacy . . . It's about trying to be diplomatic and to say that we also support all these things . . . I think it's important not to break up this transatlantic link. I think it's also in American interest not to allow for Europe to be so united, to become some sort of superpower which might be competing with the United States, and therefore this will be our position too, and sometimes we will express this opinion. It's a different question how influential our opinion will be, but I'm sure that the same attitude will be found in Poland, and probably in other Eastern candidate countries like Hungary. These countries suffered much more from the actions of Russians than others.

(Lithuanian EU observer, November 2002)

In Lithuanian foreign and EU policy, the most pronounced pro-US speaker has been President Adamkus, who made his civil career in the US Environment Protection Agency. In listing challenges to the Baltic Sea region after EU and NATO enlargements, in a speech at a conference sponsored by the US Embassy in Stockholm, he lists as priority areas first the improvement of infrastructure, then expanding cooperation with Russia and third reinforcing US involvement in Europe. He also speaks of a 'unique psychological attachment to America that exists in the Baltic and Scandinavian countries, as well as in Poland' (Adamkus 2002a). For Adamkus, European integration seems to be about the parallel enlargements of the EU and NATO. In this sort of thinking, issues like European divisions in the context of the US-led war on Iraq in 2003 were genuinely regrettable (Paksas 2003a). The Lithuanian foreign minister, for his part, acknowledges the American–European differences over political and economic visions and interests, but does not want to conceive of them as insoluble (Valionis 2003c).

These Lithuanian comments on the inherent compatibility of EU and NATO in ordering northern European, European and global space on the whole are not perfectly in tune with all developments within the Union, and the US–EU splits that have emerged after the 'war on terrorism' and on Iraq, among other instances. In the end, despite the Lithuanian support shown to the enlarging EU's geo-strategic posture, one must conclude with certain reservations that the Lithuanians are, just like Estonians, Latvians and many others, still to an extent coming to grips with the EU's strategic posture. The comment by a Lithuanian policy maker about the Lithuanian public's view of the Union and of how its very essence and rationale presumably is not as clear as America's, tells us also something about this:

I would say that now many people associate the EU with the European Commission, because we are negotiating with it right now . . . So I would say that one perception is that the people don't really understand that there is a Council of the European Union, there's a Parliament, and so the EU is for them someone like the enlargement Commissioner who's talking to them . . . Since the Commission is quite a bureaucratic institution, where there are some rules and quite strict requirements, in this way there is an understanding that EU – in a popular way – that the EU is not very good, because they always require something from us, they always want something from us, and sometimes it's standards.

(Lithuanian policy maker, November 2002)

Summary

Lithuania lacks similar foreign policy predicaments to those Estonia and Latvia had especially during the 1990s with their Russophone minorities and particularly with Russia's attention to the status of these minorities. Nonetheless, I have tried to show in this chapter that, in Lithuania's case, the EU has gone to some lengths in order to incorporate this new member and, in doing so, to respond to the Lithuanian calls for inclusion into the widening EU subject. Lithuania is not an

Table 7.2 The construction of the EU's geopolitical subjectivity in northern Europe: Lithuanian views

Component of ordering	Sub-aspect	Summary
Identity projects	Time	Explicit acknowledgement of the difference between Lithuania's post-Soviet time and EU time; frustrating catching-up process in the context of EU accession; worries of development differences and lack of a common vision between the EU-15 and CEE; some efforts to participate in the common European healing exercise, although many contemporary issues of EU politics seen as too late-modern for Lithuania
	Space	Both northern/Nordic and central European routes kept open; vision of Lithuania functioning as the EU's geopolitical hub connecting north and south, and east and west; somewhat divided views on Russia's European engagement along left–right continuum; communitarian preference for the organization of EU space; accent on equality
Interest projects	Geo-policy	Enlargement seen as a 'win–win' process despite doubts; more flexibility and a good-neighbourliness attitude towards the application of Schengen borders regime around Kaliningrad than initially shown by the EU Commission; the Lithuanian–Russian cooperation on Kaliningrad as contribution to the ND; very positive view of the neighbourhood policy; positive attitude towards extending QMV and strengthening of CFSP, and even ESDP, provided that it does not lead to duplication with NATO
	Geo-strategy	Support for the Union to strengthen its subjectivity in Europe and world affairs in general; EU and US/NATO seen as compatible; explicit preference for a continuing US role in northern Europe

important economy to the EU common market, and the issues of arranging Russia's transit to and from Kaliningrad after Lithuania's EU membership, as well as the wrangling over the expensive decommissioning of the Ignalina nuclear power plant, required extensive diplomatic efforts and compromises on the Union's part. But Lithuania's strategic location as a gateway between north–south and east–west transit routes, its oil infrastructure and its relatively good connections to Russia, Kaliningrad, Belarus and Ukraine are in the minds of EU policy makers. Importantly, these issues are also clearly evident in the views that Lithuania's EU accession brings into the process of building the Union's geopolitical subjectivity in northern Europe (Table 7.2).

It seems likely that Lithuania will become a good partner for the Nordics and Germany in their ongoing efforts to promote EU–Russian relations in the European north and on the more general plane. Lithuanian foreign policy makers consistently support initiatives towards extending the Union's experiences from northern European regional cooperation to the enlarging EU's wider neighbourhood. The only signs of possible 'reluctance' to strengthen EU's subjectivity in northern Europe can be seen in the attachment to the US as the ultimate guarantor of Lithuanian and Baltic security at the expense of the EU, with which the Lithuanians are still to an extent coming to terms. Here must be kept in mind Egle Rindzeviciute's (2003: 75) remark on the European identity debate – as it is known to us from debates within the EC since the 1980s – having been imported only recently into Lithuania's intellectual circles. Although the analysis in this chapter sides with her observation about the 'European' still having strong national resonations in Lithuania, in this book that is by no means taken as an exception. Next I will proceed to elaborate the limits of the EU subject in the case of encountering Russia and its northwestern regions.

8 From close outsiders to semi-outsiders?

Russia and its northwestern regions

This chapter elucidates Russia's position with regard to the construction of a concentric EU order in northern Europe that was discussed in Chapter 3. The Russian case will be portrayed in notably different terms from the accession of Estonia, Latvia and Lithuania as new semi-insiders into the Union. Similar semi-insider position is not available for Russia by means of EU accession in the short- or medium-term perspective. Rather, at issue is how Russia and its northwestern regions are situated and situate themselves along the third circle of the concentric EU order, i.e. within the confines of the close outsider and semi-outsider positions. In other words, the question is whether Russia on the whole will remain a close outsider, unable to have a real share of EU integration whilst concomitantly being affected by the Union's expansion, or slightly more integrationist positions will be in sight also for other regions of Russia than those in the country's northwest, which has a direct geographical interface with the Union and access to the Union's regionalizing policies and other cross-border cooperation with funding from the EU area. The more integrationist long-term prospects depend on progress within the EU–Russian strategic partnership and on the future development of regionalizing EU policies.

The relatively marginal positions available for Russia can be seen as a reflection of the uncertainty on the EU's part about how relations should be arranged in the absence of an accession perspective. Although the Union's relations with Russia have approximately as short a history as its relations with the Baltic states, this history is in the first place about indecisiveness with regard to the pace and direction of their development. As a result of the Nordic and Baltic enlargements, EU foreign policy makers became only gradually aware of the thorny question of what the balance should be between the EU order and Russia's ordering ambitions. In particular, how far should the EU order extend into the northern European spaces where Russia has traditionally exercised considerable power? As it is well known, since Peter the Great initiated the building of St Petersburg on Russia's Baltic Sea coast in the early eighteenth century Russia has been struggling to first open and then keep a northern European window onto 'Europe'. In the present context we might want to ask whether St Petersburg and its surroundings, or maybe the more recently acquired region of Kaliningrad, will remain mere 'windows' or rather become some sort of gateways of EU–Russian integration.

As a background for the uncertainties and resulting undetermined character of EU–Russian relations must be seen several structural and historically developed factors. The most obvious one is the fact that in Russia the Union encounters a successor state to a former superpower and in the present context a potential great power competitor armed with nuclear weapons. This is in contrast to the mostly minor and small powers that the Union encounters in the CEE, with the exception of would-be great power Poland, which, however, is in the process of becoming voluntarily integrated further into the EU order just as are the Balts. And geographically, Russia extends to the Far East and the Caspian and Black Seas. Only some of these territories pertain to currently outlined or projected ordering ambitions of EU foreign policy makers and member states. Moreover, Russia's population of 145 million people, covering various ethnicities and national languages, clearly surpasses the demographic weight of any current EU member states. Although Russia's population is currently shrinking rapidly and remains well below the Union's total of around 450 million people, not too many in the present-day Union would consider it palatable to give up to one-quarter of the voting power within the Union's institutions for Russia's representatives as existing vote weighing agreements would stipulate.

The obvious structural discrepancies between the EU and Russia are made only worse by the lack of perceptions of such a moral–historical bond as witnessed in the case of the EU's relations with the Baltic states and Poland. To cut short the long history of European–Russian relations, we can point to the telling example of how the nineteenth-century European system, in which Russia took part as one of Europe's great powers, was characterized by shifting alliances and balance-of-power relations. Such anarchic arrangements were not conducive to the emergence of perceptions of a historically based 'moral' imperative to engage Russia in the inner circles of contemporary European integration. The aftermath of the First World War witnessed the birth of communist Russia, which mostly provoked hostility among its immediate neighbours like Finland, the Baltic states and Poland, as well as among the geographically more distant European powers who at that time predominantly clung to liberal or conservative right-wing values, or in some cases to social democracy. The weight of Soviet sympathizers, like Fabian socialists in the UK and communist groups and parties outside Russia, was never enough to ease Europe's isolation of Soviet Russia, which was of course partly self-imposed by the autarchic economic policies of the Soviet state. Neither did the West–Soviet alliance in the Second World War manage to turn the tide more permanently. The Soviet Union did, however, try to establish economic relations with the EC's economic pillar, the European Economic Community (EEC), during the final stages of the Cold War, but the EEC refused to base relations on working with the Soviet-led economic bloc, the Council for Mutual Economic Assistance (CMEA). Only Mikhail Gorbachev's rise to power in the Soviet Union in 1985, his 'new thinking' and proposal for a 'Common European House' finally helped to change the setting (Herrberg 1998: 88–91).

Gorbachev's idea of a Common European House represented the culmination of a fundamental change in East–West relations in Europe, and today continues to tell us something about Russia's position in relation to the EU. Initially, for Gorbachev, a Common European House would pertain to reducing superpower tensions in Europe. Then, gradually, he turned towards accepting the idea of a Common European House as a means for accommodating the erosion of the Soviet-led Eastern European bloc and thus the Soviet Union's altered position vis-à-vis the EC, which was slowly awakening as a European centre of gravity with the conclusion of its Maastricht treaty. In the final stages of Gorbachev's promotion of the idea, it would facilitate the Soviet Union's europeanization (Malcolm 1991: 50–73). In order to get a grasp of this important legacy of contemporary Russian–European relations, it is worth quoting Gorbachev at length. In 1990, he characterized the Common European House as:

> An interstate and inter-ethnic community, constructed on the basis of universally shared values . . . an integral political, legal, economic and cultural space, and alliance of states with common structures maintaining military and ecological security and ensuring a high level of multifarious interaction.
>
> (Gorbachev, October 1990; quoted in Malcolm 1991: 46)

A decade and a half since Gorbachev's introduction of his vision in these terms – speaking of 'integral political, legal, economic and cultural space' as well as 'common structures' – it is clear that the evolution of EU–Russian relations has so far failed to deliver all the desired goods. Negotiations for the EU–Russia PCA were started in 1992 and the treaty text was agreed on in 1994. The entering into force of the PCA was, however, delayed until December 1997, as a result of condemnation by the EU and its member states of Russia's first war in Chechnya during 1994–6. The pivotal documents of the EU–Russian strategic partnership – the EU's CSR introduced in 1999, and Russia's reply to it, the Medium-Term Strategy towards the EU (2000–10) – were often said to display widely differing views of each other. As discussed in Chapter 4, the CSR speaks of universalizing EU goals and common values which, if realized in Russia, would approach the fulfilment of the Union's Copenhagen criteria. Russia's document, by contrast, fails to mention any common values like democracy and rule of law. But it does mention the term 'socially oriented market economy', which can be found in the EU's Constitutional Treaty in the form of 'competitive social market economy' (Inter-Governmental Conference of the European Union 2004). Yet, on the whole, Russia's document speaks more of issues reminiscent of traditional great power behaviour such as its self-declared sphere of influence within the CIS, and of Russia's efforts to reduce the US-centredness of post-Cold War international politics (e.g. Haukkala 2001b: 6–8; see below).

Given an uneasy history like this, the EU–Russia agreement at the St Petersburg summit in 2003 to develop their strategic partnership by the creation of four 'common spaces' shows some promise of positioning Russia in a more mutually satisfactory manner into the context of expanding EU. The next section will take a look at progress within the Common European Economic Space (CEES) project as well as the common spaces on internal security, external security, and culture and education, with a view to assessing how the EU engages Russia and its north-western regions whilst simultaneously promoting its own order project.

From economic to common security spaces

During the new millennium, in the absence of an accession perspective, EU–Russian integration efforts have taken place mainly on the economic plane. This follows the Union's frustration with its inability to influence Russia's Chechnya policy by suspending the entering into force of the PCA and in that way trying to force its 'common values' on Russia. Such a focus on common values has since then lessened somewhat. It consequently has remained questionable whether the EU's declared common values have ever stood anywhere close to Gorbachev's mention of the same term in his characterization of the fundamentals of the Common European House concept, let alone contemporary Russian understandings of what the common values might imply. EU–Russian integration efforts have in this manner become quietly but steadily diverted from the problematic value-based questions into sectors where progress is more likely to be rapid, and where the starting point is more attuned towards common interests than identities. In this light, it is only natural that interest-based political economy issues within the CEES project advance more rapidly than integration within other sectors of the common spaces endeavour.

Common European Economic Space (CEES)

The official launching of the CEES dates back to the EU–Russia summit of October 2001 that took place well before the common spaces concept was announced. But in fact, the roots of the CEES go even further back, to the provisions for an eventual free trade area mentioned in the PCA. In the ensuing discussions of possible models for the practical arranging of the CEES – e.g. by relying on the EEA, EFTA or EU–Switzerland experiences – Russian policy makers repeatedly raise the conviction that 'the most important task today is to prevent the emergence of new dividing lines in Europe that in the past came at a very high price to all parts of our continent' (Gusarev 2002: 179). The goal of the CEES is declared to be more than a mere free trade area, encompassing 'the four freedoms' of the single market – goods, services, capital and labour. In practice, these goals would translate into Russia's partial inclusion in the EU's single market without any right to participate in EU decision-making. This would represent an association relationship with the EU, which Russia's EU strategy considers an unacceptable prospect (see Russian Federation 1999). The several attempts at economic reintegration within the CIS area – including the Russian–Belarusian Union State project, and the project launched in September 2003 between Russia, Belarus, Kazakhstan and

Ukraine – would also pose serious obstacles for European–Russian integration if they were implemented. However, so far they have either collapsed due to mutual economic problems or remained more or less dead letters (Vahl 2003).

The CEES is based on a relatively high EU–Russian economic interdependence. As it became evident in the Baltic case studies in the previous three chapters, these countries compete to function, with variable success, as transport corridors or gateways for exporting Russia's energy resources into the Union as part of their positioning vis-à-vis the EU. The EU is partially dependent on Russia's energy resources, and the dependence is only set to grow with the Union exhausting the bulk of its oil reserves in the next two decades or so (Peters 2003: 34–5). The ongoing EU enlargements into the CEE countries, many of which are dependent on Russian energy supplies, strengthen the Union's dependence. By 2020, the Union's overall dependence on energy imports is estimated to rise from 50 per cent to 70 per cent. Here, the Russian energy resources provide a good alternative to the politically unstable and US-dominated Middle East. In fact, over thirty years Russia has never cut its supplies to the EU (cf. ibid.: 40). The energy interdependence hence forms the driving force of the CEES (Table 8.1). This was accepted already in October 2000 when the EU–Russian 'energy dialogue' was launched. Projects are planned for additional gas and oil pipelines linking the EU and Russia even more comprehensively than they already are. Interconnection of the Nordic, Baltic, other EU and Russian electricity networks is also a priority area, as is the materialization of the already agreed on European transport corridors and telecommunications networks to practically facilitate the energy and other trade.

The largest buyers of Russia's oil and gas in the EU area include Germany, Poland and Italy, with the Czech Republic, France and Hungary also featuring among big customers. Around 80 per cent of the Russian gas delivered to European markets by Gazprom goes through Ukraine. As for oil, again through Ukraine, the Druzhba pipeline delivers approximately half of the volume of Russia's exports directly into their main markets in continental Europe (Myers Jaffe and Manning 2001: 134–7).

The EU–Russian interface in northern Europe adds some region-specific issues to the energy dialogue. These include EU-assisted pilot projects on energy efficiency promotion in Archangelsk and Kaliningrad, and the sizeable but largely unexploited energy resources of the Timan-Pechora region within the Archangelsk *oblast'* and the bed of the Barents Sea. In addition, during winter 2002–3, Finland drew the Union's attention to Russia's development of new oil exportation ports in Batareina, Primorsk, Vysotsk and Ust-Luga near St Petersburg, by raising concerns about maritime safety as a result of Russia's increased oil shipments on the

Table 8.1 EU–Russian energy trade interdependence, 2003 (% of value)

EU		Russia	
Oil imports from Russia	16	Oil exports to the EU	56
Gas imports from Russia	20	Gas exports to the EU	62

Sources: European Commission Delegation in Russia (2003); European Commission (2004e).

environmentally fragile Baltic Sea. As seen in the previous chapters, the Finnish concerns were quickly seconded by the Balts in their contributions to the second ND action plan. This sequence added a new northern environmental dimension to the energy dialogue which may not be entirely welcome among the Russian bureaucrats and oil lobbyists even within Russia's northwest. Otherwise, all other aspects of the energy dialogue are present within Russia's northern interface with the EU. These factors combined seem to imply that a 'testing ground' function for energy dialogue activities is on the cards for Russia's northwestern regions. This is reflected in the way in which the energy provisions in the ND documents replicate previous EU documents for developing trans-European energy networks (Romanova 2004).

The EU has not outright opposed Russia's port-building projects on its Baltic Sea coast. These projects are motivated by aims of winning back some of the 1.5–2 billion US dollars paid each year for transport services in the Baltic states and Finland. A simultaneous aim is of course to divide and rule the Baltic Sea ports in competing for the remaining transit services, and give a snub to Latvia's Ventspils. But, significantly, the European Bank for Reconstruction and Development (EBRD) declined finance to the most grandiose among the port projects, the Primorsk oil terminal. The projected costs for the non-ice-free port of Primorsk are 4–5 billion euros during the ten years of its building in two stages, the first of which was finalized in 2001. Investing 10–20 per cent of this amount would have sufficed to increase the capacity of Latvia's normally ice-free Ventspils to meet any foreseeable increases in Russia's oil exports. On these grounds the EBRD, and many other international financial corporations, refused funding for Primorsk. The EBRD instead lent funds for the modernization of existing transit capacity (Laurila 2003: 46).

The overall figures for EU–Russian trade represent a less advantageous platform for Russian foreign policy makers to influence the terms and form of EU–Russian integration than the energy dialogue does. Apart from the energy resources, the Union also imports, albeit in relatively low quantities, some other non-renewable and renewable resources from Russia: wood, pulp and paper manufactures; various metals and metal manufactures; and chemicals. Russia, by contrast, is strongly dependent on imports from the EU, ranging from machin-

Table 8.2 EU–Russian trade (EU-15 unless otherwise indicated), 1993–2002 (% of value)

	1993	1997	1999	2000	2001	2002	2002 (EU-15 + ten accession states)
EU/share of Russia's foreign trade	40.0	33.8	34.9	35.0	36.0	36.6	62% of exports 61% of imports
Russia/share of EU's foreign trade	3.2	3.7	2.7	3.4	3.4	3.5	4% of exports 7% of imports

Sources: Borko (2003); EC Commission Delegation in Russia (2004b).

ery and chemicals to foodstuffs, and even beverages and tobacco (Pinder 2002: 17–19). The 2004 EU enlargement into the CEE increased Russia's dependence on EU markets dramatically, as its important trade partners became EU members (Table 8.2). To this can be added that, by 2001, cumulatively about 70 per cent of badly needed foreign investment had come from the EU area (European Commission Delegation in Russia 2004a).

Dependence on the EU direction also characterizes most of Russia's northwestern regions. Among them a special case is Kaliningrad, which is 90 per cent dependent on imported foodstuffs from neighbouring Lithuania and elsewhere, while 80 per cent of the region's energy comes from Lithuania's Ignalina nuclear power plant as a legacy of the Soviet era. In an attempt to maintain its grip on Kaliningrad in the context of the region's strong external dependence, Russia's federal centre has preferred to regulate its status directly under presidential and governmental control. The centre first granted Kaliningrad the status of a tax-free Free Economic Zone (FEZ) in 1991, which was transformed into a less 'Hong Kongish' Special Economic Zone (SEZ) in 1996. The SEZ arrangement maintained some of the tax and customs privileges, but took away a lot of the powers of the Kaliningrad regional administration to conduct foreign relations on its own (Sergounin 2001: 162–7). Both the FEZ and SEZ policies have been subject to considerable wrangling between the federal centre and the *oblast'*, but neither of them has managed to attract any significant amounts of investment into the region. Instead, by 2000, foreign investments totalled about one-fifth of the Russian average. Income levels of the population were lower than elsewhere in northwest Russia, yet living costs were not any lower (Khlopetskii and Fedorov 2000: 687–8).[1]

Apart from the EU dependence of Kaliningrad and the rest of northwest Russia stands only the geographically remote Murmansk region, whose imports and exports with the EU-15 as share of the region's total foreign trade are notably below Russia's overall level. The Murmansk region is also alongside St Petersburg the only region with significant trade with the CIS – imports from the CIS being, respectively, 17 per cent and 9 per cent in 2000. Generally, the trade of Russia's northwestern regions with the CIS hovers around the 5 per cent mark (Köll 2003: 453–78).

The strong dependence of Russia and the bulk of its northwest on EU markets is cast in an even more asymmetric light by a comparison of the EU's and Russia's shares of world GDP – around 22 per cent and a mere 1.5 per cent, respectively. In 2002, the purchasing power-corrected GDP per capita in Russia was 30 per cent of the EU-15 level, i.e. well below the Baltic states' non-purchasing power-corrected levels of 35–42 per cent. Russia's economy was lagging far behind the EU's despite the impressive growth totalling 40 per cent since the country's economic collapse and the rouble's devaluation crisis in 1998 (Komulainen *et al.* 2004: 5; see Chapters 5–7). The standard of living difference is particularly striking on the Finnish–Russian border, where comparisons to the US–Mexico border are not out of the question. And the Lithuanian–Kaliningradian border is certainly not far behind in this respect.

On the whole, it can be said that the CEES represents the most important aspect of the EU–Russian strategic partnership. And, at this plane of economic integration, the close outsider perspective remains the dominant position available for Russia in the short to medium term. However, through the energy dialogue in particular it seems that interests-based synergy benefits might in the long run open up some practical integration platforms, which through time may feed into the identity political side, thus allowing more integrationist considerations. When it comes to Russia's northwestern EU border, it does not seem that the sites of Russia's port-building projects – the Leningrad district and St Petersburg area – will be fully able to capitalize on their semi-outsider position as the Union's direct neighbours. Although these regions gain investment, and are becoming gateways for Russian oil into EU markets, they remain firmly within Moscow's grip, much more so than they were during the 1990s. This is a consequence of President Putin's effective stopping of the power struggles that characterized relations between the centre and the regions during Boris Yeltsin's rule. Putin's 'vertical reforms' and division of Russia into seven Federal Districts led by his own representative, including actions like the abolition of individual treaties between the centre and regions, stripping regional governors of their automatic seats in the Federation Council – the upper chamber of the Russian Parliament – and the 2004 law on the president's right to appoint regional governors, have changed the balance in favour of the federal centre.

Common space of freedom, security and justice (common space of internal security)

The main issue within this space is the long-term prospect of an EU–Russia visa-free regime. As will be discussed below, the issue originally arose in the midst of the EU–Russia dispute on Kaliningrad in 2002. The concrete steps so far include an agreement between Russia and Europol, the drafting of an Action Plan on organized crime, signing a readmission treaty with a three-year transition period for third country nationals and stateless people, and the agreement in October 2005 to facilitate and speed up visa granting procedures. Here a source of sheer frustration for the European Commission is the way in which France, Germany and Italy agreed in 2003 with Russia on the easing of visa procedures for businessmen, politicians, athletes and academics. The Union was sidelined. The 2005 EU–Russia agreement reduces visa fees to 35 euros and waives them for some groups of passengers like students, close relatives and the disabled, with diplomats exempted from visa procedures altogether.

The list of issues to settle includes most likely Russia's signature to the long since agreed border treaty with Estonia. And achieving the long-term goal of complete visa freedom will also probably mean the EU taking some responsibility for helping Russia in the massive task of closing its porous borders with the CIS countries that are routes for smuggling people and goods from Asia to the European continent. This is a task Russia has only started. This all implies that, in the absence of simplified access to the Schengen area for the majority of

Russians, the close outsider position is what best characterizes their situation on this plane. The Union side, in particular the Commission, wants to protect its own order and the insiders and semi-insiders within it from the post-Soviet threats presumably emanating from Russia. Therefore, the simplified visa regimes on the Lithuanian–Kaliningradian and Estonian–Russian borders came to an end. This also shrank the prospects for Russia's northwest to practically capitalize on its semi-outsider position.

Common space of cooperation in the field of external security

This common space represents some convergence of interests but relatively little practical integration so far. Russia is the only non-EU country to have gained access to the Union's Political and Security Committee, the main decision-making body of the ESDP. This access takes place through monthly consultations. The EU–Russia summit in Moscow 2002 announced the aim of a common crisis management approach and the start of bilateral military contacts. Russia also agreed to participate in the EU police mission in Bosnia. Moreover, both parties underline their commitment to the central role of the United Nations in global questions. They also have similar positions on specific questions such as Iraq, Middle East settlement, Cyprus, Afghanistan and the spread of weapons of mass destruction ('Joint Statement, EU–Russia Summit' 2003; 'Russia–European Union PPC' 2004).

However, at the same time at least four different factors can be listed that have hindered closer integration on the external security plane. First, both the EU and Russia tend to look towards the US in developing their security policies rather than towards each other. Second, given its bureaucratic and slow decision-making process, the EU tends to ignore Russia and other third parties when taking decisions on the ESDP, whereas Russia seems to prefer a wait-and-see attitude after making an overly activist start to the security relationship. Third, the EU has doubts about Russia's values and strategic culture as manifested in the handling of the war in Chechnya. Fourth, at least for the moment, the parties pay insufficient attention to each other's power and status in connection to potential cooperation within crisis management loci such as the CIS (Forsberg 2004: 256–64).

These factors mean that the common space on external security displays Russia as mostly having a close outsider perspective in relation to EU order. There is no differentiation into more integrationist perspectives within Russia's northwestern regions. Russia's regions simply have no independent role to play here. The historically developed, underlying threat perceptions of Russia's military capability that are still somewhat covertly held by some of Russia's neighbours in northern Europe also contribute to the lack of regional differentiation. Finland and the Baltic states are former parts of the Russian empire and the Baltic states belonged to the Soviet Union for fifty years, whereas Poland has been partitioned by Russia and other powers. Finland's covert threat perceptions of Russia are evident in the country's refusal to rule out in the 2004 national security and defence policy report a large-scale traditional invasion in the medium term in the way Sweden has done by scaling down its armed forces. Similarly, the Baltic states' and Poland's NATO membership must be primarily understood as a very traditional security measure against the fears of Russian revisionism, and EU memberships as corresponding soft measures. In sum, on neither side of northern Europe's EU–Russia border is there any willingness to privilege border regions in questions of external security.

Common space of research and education, including cultural issues

The EU and Russia have an agreement on science and technology cooperation. Some Russian universities have agreed upon entering the Bologna process of creating comparable university degree structures across the European education area, and a European Studies Institute is to be established in Moscow. On the northern European plane, the CBSS included Kaliningrad State University in its Eurofaculty programme of supporting the development of university level teaching of EU integration. In addition, several universities in Russia's northwestern regions have committed themselves to participating in the Cross-Border University project initiated by the Finnish Ministry of Education, which is set to begin after a pilot stage in 2007. Through these processes Russia's northwest will underline its semi-outsider position, if not gain access to a semi-insider one, as a party in the development of joint curricula. However, with all fairness, this educational cooperation will not, for years to come, define the EU–Russia relationship in general or their northern European encounter in particular. The socialization effects of future political and business elites engaged in student exchanges and graduating from joint higher education programmes can be very dramatic, but they are not bound to be quick.

On the whole, it is clear that the common spaces concept in the first place pertains to the EU–Russian strategic partnership. Relatively few issues within it are specific to Russia's northern European interface with the Union. This is of course not to deny that Russia's northwestern regions could function as pilot regions in EU–Russian integration – a function which they already largely fulfil – but to simply state that the common spaces concept, coupled with Russia's centralization tendencies, fails to make the most of their integration prospects.

In the long term, the implementation of the common spaces concept naturally may produce outcomes presently only looming far in the horizon. To put the record straight for these prospects, we need to take a detailed look at how the Russians themselves view them. The officially held views among the federal level foreign policy makers will be privileged in the ensuing analysis because of their more empowered position especially after the vertical reforms introduced during Putin's rule. What in these conditions remains of the semi-outsider perspectives of Russia's northwest is thereafter briefly discussed by referring to views held by regional level actors in Kaliningrad. There, if anywhere, should one be able to find views more attuned to European integration than in the corridors of Moscow. The Kaliningrad region is completely surrounded by EU territories, strongly dependent on them, and widely regarded as the Russian region most capable of playing a part in EU–Russian integration as a pilot region, a prospect already mentioned in Russia's EU strategy (cf. Hedenskog 2002).[2] The systematic empirical analysis of Russian views is based on a representative body of material and will be conducted on the basis of the model of geopolitical subjectivity developed in Chapter 3.[3] The main question to be asked in the analysis is: how do Russia and its northwestern regions respond to the expansion of EU order into their neighbourhood and possibly even further?

Russian views of the EU's identity projects in northern Europe

Time

The early 1990s witnessed a short-lived period in which the Russian ruling elite viewed the Soviet era as an unfortunate distortion in Russia's centuries-old mission to approach the West (Aalto 2003c: 259; Baranovsky 2002: 12–13). This relatively undifferentiated westernizing view, which has quite a lot in common with the early 1990s views in the Baltic states and Poland, was most closely associated with President Boris Yeltsin's foreign minister, Andrey Kozyrev. Since then, Russia's identity political soul-searching from the mid- to late 1990s is well documented and includes such temporally coloured ideas as a 'near abroad' policy directed at maintaining the ties between Russians in 'Russia proper' and those scattered throughout the FSU as a result of the Soviet era migration and the policies of resettling peoples; 'eurasianism' both in its traditional–mythical and more contemporary forms; and ideas of a return to the *derzhava* (great power) of the Soviet Union (e.g. G. Smith 1999).

Here it is of note that, with Putin's presidency, this soul-searching has resulted in a view of the EU as the most important source of modernization for Russia. This would aid the grander purpose of rebuilding Russia's traditional great power status (Bordachev 2003: 31; Likhachev 2000). At the same time, Russian observers disagree among themselves to what extent the Russians have developed a correct idea of the contemporary processes transforming the relationship of 'Europe' and the EU. A large number of observers portray the Russian elite as lacking a correct idea of the extent to which 'Europe' is becoming synonymous with the EU (e.g. Bordachev 2003: 51; Leshukov 2000: 38; Trenin 2000: 24, 35). But Russia's EU strategy takes note of the 'widening supranational powers of the EU bodies under the Amsterdam treaty' (Russian Federation 1999). And according to Russia's permanent representative in the European Communities, Russians have increasingly started to think of the EU as a magnet for far-reaching integration efforts within the continent (Likhachev 2000: 116). The 1999–2003 Duma chairman Gennady Seleznev even takes note of the federalist tendencies in the Union, warning of how 'the European Union is a very clever organization that adopted all useful things from the Soviet Union' (quoted in Baranovsky 2002: 25).

It is also hard to avoid noticing how often Russian foreign policy makers refer to some sort of a 'historical opportunity' in EU–Russian relations. The Russian foreign minister, Igor Ivanov, echoes well the dominant EU view in saying that 'the history of Europe is a succession of evolving and disintegrating military–political alliances, the struggles between which led to confrontation and oftentimes also to wars on our continent'. At the same time, he is careful to stress that Russia and EU should now 'think in strategic terms, showing concern about the future' (Ivanov 2000: 107). And while commenting on Russia's new European orientation he says that 'perhaps never before in the history of Europe have there been so many opportunities for building a truly united democratic Europe without dividing lines' (Ivanov 2001a: 5). President Putin also refers to the unique opportunity offered by the new historical context when speaking to students of the Kaliningrad State University:

> You surely remember very well the history of Königsberg and the history of Kaliningrad. Let me assure you that no one, except a few most foolish people, is preparing to return to 1937, thinking of giving up the region and so on. Such ideas are not needed in Europe and therefore they have no future. This understanding is shared both in our country and in Europe. Indeed, the future is something completely different – unification.
>
> (Putin 2003a)

The accent on what promising future prospects of 'unification' the evolution of EU–Russian relations is opening up does not, however, imply a similarly blind outward-orientedness as was in evidence in the euphoric times of the early 1990s. In his state of the nation address in May 2003, President Putin continues with his pragmatic foreign policy that springs up from open acknowledgement of Russia's transformation problems, and declares that '... real integration with Europe ... of course is a complicated and long-term process. But this is our historical choice. It has been made' (Putin 2003b: 13–14). And, for help in alleviating Russia's continuing transformation problems, expectations towards the EU are very high. For example, that the EU started proceedings for recognizing Russia's market economy status in May 2002 indicated 'principled' and 'moral–political' significance that the Russian president also expects to materialize in concrete and measurable returns (Putin 2002a). The act of accepting Russia's market economy status signified an acknowledgement that Cold War era structures – referring to Russia's forced isolation from economic integration in Europe despite its efforts to the contrary – are finally breaking. But, interestingly enough, from Russia, similar statements to those from the Baltic states – somewhat covertly admitting the baggage of 'post-Soviet time' – have been in short supply. Instead, Russia has in various connections declared itself as free from Cold War era chains and demanded the same from the contemporary EU.

Space

During the early 1990s, officially Russia was portrayed as an undifferentiated part of the 'West', which Russia attempted to approach as an equal partner. Somewhat similar views were heard at the same time from the Baltic states. But where the

Balts manifested a small state syndrome of having violently been cut off from 'Europe' and the 'West' for fifty years, in the Russian case at issue was a great power complex of having been excluded from the joint ordering of European and global affairs. And, as already implied above in the analysis under the aspect of time, such very relative similarities between the Balts and Russia proved short-lived. Russian foreign policy makers and the intelligentsia soon started to develop more differentiated views of the 'West' and 'Europe', and of Russia's position on that plane.

Of the various ideas, those can be mentioned which continue to have relevance in the Putin era. The Soviet nostalgia primarily applies to the older generations, which are gradually passing away. Towards the late 1990s, the 'near abroad' policy also gradually started losing its relevance in the Baltic, and thus European, direction, although since the build-up to the EU's 2004 enlargement the same concerns were often repeated again. Most likely this was in order to press the EU on other questions (cf. Aalto 2003a). But, while the rights of Baltic Russian-speakers can be considered a bargaining chip for Russian foreign policy makers in the contemporary context, *eurasianism* continues to carry intrinsic relevance for understanding Russia's views of European space. Eurasianism originates in nineteenth century slavophilism. Its supporters include those who have for long been out of political power at the highest level, like the Communists; those who occasionally, in particular during the late 1990s, seemed to manage to influence the political process, like representatives of the new Russian right (e.g. Aleksandr Dugin, Vladimir Zhirinovsky); those more or less 'democratic statists' appointed during President Yeltsin's rule (G. Smith 1999), whose power, though, has been shrinking during the Putin regime; and finally, those recruited to power in Putin's Russia have occasionally displayed some eurasianist colours too. This broad support base means that eurasianism is a very flexible, even ambiguous idea that can take several forms. Its basic nature was well captured by Dugin himself when commenting on the policies of the former Russian foreign and prime minister, Yevgenii Primakov:

> Today, Eurasianism is coming softly . . . Primakov's policy is Eurasian-ist policy. This is left-wing economic policies at home, helping Arab states abroad, orientation toward the East, helping traditional friends like Serbia, strengthening the integration of the former Soviet Union. This is Eurasian-ism, the policy of the heartland.
>
> (quoted in Clover 1999: 13)

That some traces of Primakov's policy have continued to surface in Putin's Russia speaks for the fact that eurasianist views are deeply embedded in the coun-try. Russia's 2000 Foreign Policy Concept refers to broadly understood eurasian-ism in the following manner: 'a distinctive feature of Russian foreign policy is its balanced nature. This is predicated on its geopolitical position as a major Eurasian power, which requires an optimum mix of efforts in every direction' (Russian Federation 2000). Eurasianism also helps us to obtain an idea of how the CIS has maintained its place as a high priority in Russian foreign policy. But at the same time it is interesting to see how 'Europe' and the 'EU' have consistently climbed in terms of perceived importance, now almost equalling the importance attached to the CIS.

In the 1993 Foreign Policy Concept the CIS was mentioned as the first priority direction. 'Europe' was assigned only the fifth place after arms control issues and relations with the US, and was allocated relatively little space (Baranovsky 2002: 17). In the 2000 Foreign Policy Concept, relations with 'European nations' are mentioned in the second place. Under the 'European' heading we find mentions of the OSCE, Council of Europe and EU, indicating 'key relevance' for these three. President Putin's speech in January 2001 on priorities for Russian diplomacy maintains the number two place for 'Europe', speaking of it as 'traditionally a very important region for us', although concomitantly asserting that 'it would be wrong to gauge which is a higher priority to us: Europe or Asia' (Putin 2001a: 4).

Putin's speech in July 2002 on 'key tasks for Russian diplomacy', for its part, reflects Russia's joining of the then particularly hot US-led 'war on terrorism', and mentions first global scope fora such as the UN Security Council and relations with the US, then 'European partners', and Russia's main task of 'direct participation in building a unified economic area' in the European direction. The CIS is mentioned only after 'Europe', but once again the presentation ends with references to Russia's geographic position, which makes it present 'in Europe and Asia, north and south' (Putin 2002b: 3). The 2003 state of the nation address mentions first the UN Security Council, then the CIS, and 'broad rapprochement and real integration with Europe', including strategic partnership with the EU (Putin 2003b: 12–14). In his 2005 speech to the Federal Assembly, Putin identifies Russia 'above all else ... as a major European power', which, however, has a 'civilizing mission in the Eurasian continent' (Putin 2005: 2, 10). The persisting prevalence of eurasianism in the Russian view of European space results in an idea of balance between the European/EU and CIS directions.

Within this framework, notions like 'ties' and 'dialogue' – not 'association' or 'accession' – imply how EU relations are portrayed as the western cornerstone of Russia's multivector, broadly eurasianist policies. Russia's representative in the EU admits that the developments within the Union's space have a global and regional extent, commenting, 'our interests cannot but be influenced by the processes that unfold within the EU and symbolize its potential (introduction of the euro, expansion of membership, common security and defence policy, and others)' (Likhachev 2003: 60; see also Alekseev 2001: 41). Yet, although Russia recognizes the manner in which EU space increasingly comes to border Russia's own, clear limits to the EU–Russian strategic partnership are set. This is done in order to try to preserve its character as a partnership, rather than to let it transform into an asymmetrical expansion of EU space as witnessed in the EU accession process. Hence, Russia has mostly accepted the Baltic states' inclusion into EU space but, as regards the rest of the FSU, Russia's EU strategy expresses opposition to 'any possible attempts to hamper the economic integration in the CIS, in particular, through maintaining "special relations" with individual countries of the Commonwealth to the detriment of Russia's interests'. Indeed, 'the development of partnership with the EU should contribute to consolidating Russia's role as a leading power in shaping up a new system of interstate political and economic relations in the CIS area' (Russian Federation 1999). This idea of two mutually recognized and respected 'dialogic poles' of regional and global politics in the shape of the Union and Russia is clearly influenced by ideas of multipolarity, which Russia declared it is seeking as a strategic goal in its 2000 Foreign Policy Concept in order to counter the unipolar aspirations of the US for dominating world affairs (Russian Federation 2000).

On the whole, compared to the Balts, who already have developed a relatively coherent idea of the sometimes surfacing federalist pressures within the EU, Russian policy makers display their lesser degree of integration with the EU centre. Regardless of the already noted comments by Gennady Seleznev on the EU's reaching of a more federal form, the mainstream Russian views of the Union remain strongly intergovernmentalist. Only very rarely do they include any assumptions of the Union developing in a more federal direction. This comes up inescapably in how Russian policy makers continue to attach relevance for bilateral ties especially with large EU member states. As a Russian federal level policy maker comments:

> If the European Commission assumes significant additional competencies, it is true that such a situation has some sort of an impact on the balance of the foreign policy orientation of the Russian Federation. But I think that, for the upcoming few years, if not for a whole decade, the national factor in foreign policy undoubtedly remains, and contacts along the lines Moscow–Berlin, Moscow–Paris, Moscow–Rome, Warsaw, etc., will remain. They are necessary elements in the construction of foreign policy.
>
> (Russian federal level policy maker, November 2002)

This may not at first sound entirely dissimilar to, for instance, Estonian views of how to conceive of the Union spatially. However, Igor Ivanov's statement that 'We regard all-round co-operation with the EU as *one* of the top priorities of our European policy' (Ivanov 2000: 106; emphasis added) reveals a difference of emphasis. For a new EU member like Estonia – a small country with limited diplomatic resources – the EU is increasingly becoming *the* focus of day-to-day European policy, regardless of the continuing flirtation with NATO, and practically because of the alliance's relative inactivity in northern Europe. For Russia, similar 'europeanization' of foreign policy is not at issue. Although both Estonia (Chapter 5) and Russia have been found to have an intergovernmentalist bias in their views of the EU, for Russia this bias has a distinct 'great game' tone. At the face of the thus constructed grand game between the EU and Russian 'centres', one can find some, but not always entirely consistently expressed, support for the EU to promote a northern European project and for Russia's northwestern regions to make use of their geographic position.

The Council on Foreign and Defence Policy (*Sovet po vneshnei i oboronnoi politike*, SVOP) used to be influential in the shaping of federal policy until the beginning of the new millennium (Pynnöniemi 2003: 22). In its special report

'Russian interests in Northern Europe', published in 2001, SVOP mentions Russia's northwestern regions as enjoying the most peaceful border that Russia has anywhere. The report adopts predominantly an intergovernmental approach, and asserts that 'today it is appropriate to pay the utmost attention to the further development of contacts and relations at the regional level, the most important Russian regions being those bordering on Finland and Norway' (Council of Foreign and Defence Policy 2001). With regard to the Baltic states, already in its 1997 report on Russia and the Baltic states SVOP proposed a more dialogic and geo-economically oriented approach towards them, viewing them as some sort of stepping-stone to European economic integration and markets in the context of EU enlargement into the Baltics. It was also vaguely hinted already that the disputed status of the Russophone minorities in Estonia and Latvia was slowly turning into an EU–Baltic issue rather than continuing to be a bilateral Russo–Baltic affair (Ozhobischev and Iurgens 2001: 70–3).

And, as mentioned above, Russia's EU strategy puts forth the often-quoted idea of Kaliningrad as a possible pilot region in EU–Russian integration. Similarly, there are the occasional references to the rather well-functioning Finnish–Russian border and the mostly unproblematic Finnish–Russian relations, as suitable and/or successful meeting grounds for the EU and Russia. However, the integration potential assigned to the northern European platform is put into the broader strategic context by the Russian foreign minister, Igor Ivanov, in his column in the newsletter of the CBSS, where he asserts that a solution to the problems of the Baltic Sea region is unthinkable outside the wider European processes (Ivanov 2001b).

In summary, from time to time Russian foreign policy makers and analysts single out northern European locations such as Kaliningrad, the Baltic states or the Finnish–Russian border. However, meeting grounds of this kind are not taken to exhaust EU–Russian relations but rather complement the wider picture. Overall, Russian views of EU space in northern Europe have evolved considerably since the 1990s and, as these variously successful examples suggest, the space allotted for the EU in this region is not fixed, but rather open-ended and almost constantly changing. But it can be observed, though, how the limits set for EU involvement have gradually moved from the Baltic states towards Russia's own borders and the CIS, thus recognizing the EU's space as increasingly wide in northern Europe. Yet, importantly, the CIS is still regarded as a space of Russian responsibility, and the gradually awakening acceptance of expanding EU space in the wider northern European region is made conditional upon the unfolding of the overall EU–Russian strategic partnership.

Russian views of the EU's interest projects in northern Europe

Geo-policy

The Union's enlargement policy naturally has its biggest impact within the acceding states. However, it can be argued on good grounds that it is also the single most important EU policy that Russia confronts in northern Europe, with eight of the BSR states having become EU members by May 2004. Russia's EU strategy notes that enlargement has an 'ambivalent' impact on EU–Russian cooperation and on Russian interests, with both positive and negative aspects (Russian Federation 1999). Such ambivalence comes up well in President Putin's remarks during the EU–Russia summit in May 2003, on the need to find a 'solution which would allow us to turn the upcoming expansion of the European Union into a factor which will bring our nations and peoples closer together' (Putin 2003c). If such a 'solution' was still needed in spring 2003, at a time when the EU had given its blessing for the CEE enlargement, obviously from Russia's point of view its hopes and concerns vis-à-vis enlargement had remained inadequately addressed by the Union and its member states.

The positive aspects of enlargement as seen through the Russian eyes are to an extent constructed by a negation. Russian foreign policy makers signalled Russia's approval of EU enlargement partly because it was positively contrasted to NATO enlargement, which Russia vehemently opposed for a long time (cf. Baranovsky 2002: 172). In addition, as a Russian federal level policy maker commented in an interview, the EU accession of the Baltic states and Poland may help the northern direction to gain more attention within the Union. This can provide advantages to Russia. However, simultaneously, new dividing lines are bound to form along Russia's borders as a result of enlargement (e.g. Alekseev 2001: 42).

Such negative aspects became the central focus in 2002, when the Union and Russia were engaged in a heated debate over the impact of Kaliningrad's encirclement by Lithuania's and Poland's EU accession. After first offering Kaliningrad as a 'pilot region' for developing EU–Russian relations in a cooperative manner, Russian foreign policy makers actually made the region a 'test case' measuring the extent to which the Union was willing to meet Russia's interests. In this case, Russian interests were declared to be about the continued free movement of the Kaliningraders to and from Russia proper. More covertly, one may read efforts to safeguard Russia's territorial integrity and seek equal access to the EU's policy radar (Aalto 2002a). Such a changed, more demanding test case approach reflected Russia's growing frustration at the failure of Brussels to listen to Russia's proposals such as a 'Baltic Schengen' arrangement and the maintenance of a visa-free regime for the Kaliningraders' transit through Lithuania (Sergounin 2001: 189). The Union proved consistently unwilling to compromise on its Schengen policy, speaking only of increased, but still in the Russian eyes inadequate, technical assistance for alleviating the Kaliningraders' problems (e.g. European Commission 2001).

The privileging of the visa issue can of course be justified by the fact that the Kaliningraders make about eight million transborder trips a year (Fairley 2001: 10). But, at the same time, it naturally took place at the expense of other burning issues. In Kaliningrad's case alone, they include the socio-economic disparities between the *oblast'* and its EU-assisted neighbours, which underlie the many social problems perceived by the Union and its member states as emanating from the region. The prospects of economic development in the region after EU enlargement were also overshadowed. Russian analysts suggested that, as a consequence of reduction in the shuttle trade, which gave livelihood to an estimated 10,000 people, and the introduction of tighter monitoring on flows of goods, people and money, open unemployment in Kaliningrad could soar from the present 1.0–1.5 per cent to 15–20 per cent. This could then have an impact on local consumer demand, retail trade, small businesses and ultimately Kaliningrad's tax revenue. Moreover, lower tariffs resulting from EU enlargement could also work to Kaliningrad's disadvantage. An inflow of higher quality, affordably priced goods from Lithuania and Poland could put pressure on Kaliningrad's agriculture and industry (e.g. Smorodinskaya 2001: 64). To respond to the new situation, modernization of Kaliningrad's economic infrastructure would cost an estimated 650 million euros and addressing the environmental problems approximately 3 billion euros (Sergounin 2001: 159; Smorodinskaya 2001: 67). According to estimates by the Institute of Economics, Russian Academy of Sciences, lifting Kaliningrad's economy to the EU level would take about 36 billion US dollars until 2010 (Kortunov 2003: 114).

After seeing several negotiation rounds ending up inconclusively, President Putin nominated the incumbent chairman of the Duma's International Committee, Dmitry Rogozin, as his special envoy to conduct shuttle diplomacy on the Kaliningrad question. Putin himself asserted in the tense EU–Russia summit in May 2002:

> All of our proposals on guaranteeing the transit of people and goods between the Kaliningrad *oblast'* and the rest of Russia unfortunately do not find understanding in Brussels. In fact I need to put this even more clearly: what is being required from us in essence means only one thing – that the right of Russians for free contacts with their fellow countrymen living in one or other part of the country be made dependent on decisions by another country . . . Dear colleagues, I count on your understanding. Today, when the Cold War has already been buried, returning to approaches of this kind is absolutely incomprehensible . . . To us [resolving this issue] represents the absolute criterion for determining the quality of our cooperation, a 'litmus test' of our cooperation.
>
> (Putin 2002a)

The vital interests that the Kaliningrad question symbolized to Russian foreign policy makers is vindicated by the fact that finally reaching a political compromise on the transit issue in the next summit in November 2002 only worked to raise further questions related to the EU's Schengen borders. Russia proposed to scrap visas between EU and Russia altogether. Later this led to the problematic visa freedom debates and the launching of the EU–Russian common space on internal security. In the November 2002 summit, it was agreed that, for single trips by train to and from Kaliningrad, a facilitated transit document (FTD) in place of a Schengen visa could be obtained by producing a passport when purchasing a ticket. For multiple entry transit by all forms of land traffic, an FTD could be obtained from a Lithuanian consulate, subject to necessary checks. For both types of FTD it was agreed that the old Soviet/Russian internal passports were valid until the end of

2004. After that an internationally accepted passport was required (Joenniemi and Sergounin 2003: 100). A plan for building a high-speed, non-stop train connection linking Kaliningrad with mainland Russia through Lithuanian territory was also agreed (Rosbalt 2003h), although after initial feasibility studies the project failed to gather pace. The centre-to-centre character of how the political agreement was reached was evident in the decision to leave to Lithuanian–Russian bilateral negotiations all technical questions as to how the provisions are practically implemented, although Russia had repeatedly during the build-up expressed its preference for Lithuania to be more closely consulted and involved. Yet, as noted in Chapter 7, all remaining technical issues were solved by summer 2003 (Joenniemi and Sergounin 2003: 100–1).

Hence the EU made minor changes to its Schengen regulations by agreeing on the FTD concept and increased its technical assistance to the *oblast'* by promising 15 million euros more of TACIS funding during the external relations commissioner Chris Patten's visit to Kaliningrad in 2001.[4] Russia, for its part, accepted Lithuanian/EU control over the eligibility of Kaliningraders for multiple entry transit through Lithuania. Judging by the approving comments of the Russian leadership, it seems obvious that the solution witnesses the EU passing Russia's 'test' for considering deeper relations. At the same time, it is perfectly clear that the Russian side also itself faced a 'test' in the Kaliningrad question, which taught it a lot about the goal-orientedness and rigorous nature of the Union's geo-policies, and of the Union's subjectivity more broadly. In a word, Russian foreign policy makers faced a Union which is becoming the major subject of northern Europe, and requested a sufficient degree of recognition of Russian interests in the building of such a subject.

With the 'test' passed, and the FTD arrangement functioning smoothly,[5] in his meeting with students of the Kaliningrad State University in June 2003, President Putin mentions Kaliningrad merely as '*one* of the first [Russian regions] where the inhabitants can enjoy the advantages of Russia's increasing integration with the EU' (Putin 2003a; emphasis added). Although some Russian observers and political actors still call for Kaliningrad's continued pivotal position in EU–Russian relations (e.g. Kortunov 2003), it seems that, in the eyes of the Russian leadership, the region has fulfilled a large part of its task. This has reduced Kaliningrad's potential as a pilot region in EU–Russian relations. Kaliningrad has lost some of its capacity to symbolize Russia's interests, and the diplomatic activity has been channelled into the more large-scale common space projects.

But even at the grand scale of the common space projects, Russia remains critical of the universalizing tendencies in the Union's geo-policies. From the Russian point of view, the universalizing EU order appears somewhat intrusive and too much EU-centred, failing to take into account Russia's interests:

> [There is] 'subjectivism' in EU behavior. Some cases in point are the politicization of economic disputes, long-lasting reluctance to recognize, despite realities, Russia's market status, imposition of criteria that go beyond the generally recognized world standards on Russia's accession to the WTO,

failure to honor in due measure the Russian concerns in connection with the EU expansion, including regard of the Kaliningrad problem, restrictions on trade in nuclear materials, etc.

(V. Likhachev, Russia's Permanent Representative to the European Communities, 2003: 59)

[There are in the EU] mechanisms of governance that presuppose centraliza- tion . . . And that may mean that the uniqueness of some types of individual regions suffers. As for example the Kaliningrad *oblast'* suffers today.

(Russian federal level policy maker, November 2002)

It seems fairly clear that the TACIS funding the EU has offered for Russia since the early 1990s has not been enough to persuade Russian foreign policy makers to embrace the Union's universalizing policies in a similar take-it-or-leave-it manner as has happened in the accession states (see Chapters 5–7). In terms of funds al- located per capita, TACIS offers a fraction of what the accession states receive. In addition, most of these funds have gone for environmental and nuclear safety, not for structural reforms, as in the case of the accession states. Even though Russian views of TACIS have varied from highly positive to outright rejection, it is clear that, on the whole, the programme has failed to provide incentives for implement- ing the reforms expected by the EU for the deepening of relations (Khudoley 2003: 21–2).[6]

Against the background of the Russian criticism of universalizing EU policies, Russia's somewhat different view of the EU's regionalizing ND initiative should be noted. After early hesitation, this more open side of the EU's policies towards northern Europe received a fairly positive reaction from Russia (Joenniemi and Sergounin 2003: 37–8). Under the heading of 'transboundary cooperation', the initiative received a positive mention in Russia's EU strategy. 'Joint efforts' were mentioned as a way to substantiate the initiative (Russian Federation 1999). Foreign Minister Ivanov commented in the first ministerial conference on the ND that:

In the North of the continent, unique experience has been acquired in broad- scale equality-based interaction among states which have such unifying factors as geography, history, mutual desire to strengthen relations and the urge to seek together ways of meeting the challenges of our time. Our re- gion should convince, as an example, all the Europeans of the feasibility of ensuring security, stability and prosperity through meaningful and equal international co-operation. Here we see the main political objective of the Northern Dimension concept.

(Ivanov in 2000, cited in Joenniemi and Sergounin 2003: 38)

In 1999, in its first official reply to the ND initiative, Russia singled out north- west Russia and Kaliningrad as regions needing special attention. Russia also sug- gested including Belarus as a participant, in the light of its traditional economic ties with northern European countries, its geographical position, and its economic and customs union with Russia (Joenniemi *et al.* 2000). Such activism encouraged by the EU's initiative was complemented by the Lithuanian–Russian 'Nida' initiative in 2000 on how to address Kaliningrad's problems by means of the ND (Chapter 7). Nevertheless, in connection with the drafting of the second ND action plan (2004–6), the Russian side complained that far too few of the earlier proposals had actually arrived on the ND agenda, and urged that further steps in ND policy should be taken on the basis of equal participation (Government of the Russian Federation 2003a,b).

These comments suggest that, regardless of the emergence of a positive Russian response to the ND, words of caution are due. First, the heading of 'transboundary cooperation', under which the ND appears in Russia's EU strategy, tells us that the initiative is viewed in the context of regional cooperation, not in the context of the EU–Russian strategic partnership. Such a comparatively low status assigned to the ND is also evident in the difficulties of obtaining financial contributions from Russia to the projects under the ND umbrella, and in Russia's contribution to the drafting of the second action plan, speaking of the ND as an '*additional* tool of comprehensive development of Russia's North-west' (Government of the Russian Federation 2003b; emphasis added). In fact, the ND was not even viewed as weighty enough to entirely cover its intended scope of EU–Russian interaction in northern Europe. This was evident in how Russia's contribution dropped Kaliningrad from the ND agenda and requested that it be dealt with separately in the context of the strategic partnership. The usual absence of any mentions of the ND in the president's and foreign ministers' most important speeches on EU–Russian relations and on Russian foreign policy at large also speaks for the same tendency. Russia has striven to develop the ND into an important regional forum, and hopes of a grand new opening in EU–Russian relations on the whole have been sidelined. High-ranking observers such as Iuri Deriabin, who is a former ambassador to Finland, have probably been at least to some degree let down in their expectations for the initiative's capacity to contribute to the EU–Russian strategic partnership (Deriabin 2000: 49).

Second, especially in the early stages of the ND's development, the Russians expressed criticism of what they perceived to be a sinister aim of merely gaining access to and making use of the natural resources in northwest Russia. They feared the EU side was only interested in developing infrastructure for resource extraction in these mostly remote locations, in some places under permafrost, but without any real willingness to develop the overall industrial potential of Russia's north (e.g. Haukkala 2001c). Therefore, in the early stages of the initiative's development, Russia recommended making environmental issues a central part of the ND (Baranovsky 2002: 82–3). The development of the EU–Russian energy dialogue since its launch in October 2000 meant, however, Russia's acceptance of its role as the Union's single most important external energy supplier. This resulted in energy issues becoming too big to be dealt with in the ND context alone, although there also they have become perhaps the dominant issue (Lausala 2002: 194; Moisio 2003b: 95). But environmental issues within the ND context, which are significantly related to energy extraction, have since then become the target of Russian criticism. In the midst of Russia's transition problems, addressing environmental problems has become perceived as not so pressing an issue as the Nordic countries and the Commission have insisted.

Third, Russian criticism has also targeted the relatively modest amount of earmarked ND funds, most of which have been assigned to the ND Environmental Partnership. The difficulties in using the TACIS funds in combination with the PHARE and Interreg programmes intended for the (enlarged) EU side were also frequently cited as frustrating (Government of the Russian Federation 2003a). Although the synchronization problems are being corrected, frustration with the ND's implementation led Russian policy makers to complain of their lack of voice and subjectivity in developing the ND policy (e.g. Haukkala 2001c; Leshukov 2000: 45).

Russia's response to the EU's new neighbourhood policy is crucial to any efforts at bridging the gap between the Union's universalizing and regionalizing policies. We have seen some broadly eurasianist Russian comments directed at maintaining Russia's sphere of influence in the CIS region even in conditions of the EU and US becoming more active there. Some observers in fact expected Russia to end up viewing the neighbourhood policy in zero-sum terms, as a sphere of interest game with the EU (see Raik and Palosaari 2004: 36). But what has happened is Russia's refusal to be treated as one of the neighbourhood policy target countries, regardless of the likelihood of the country's northwestern regions to benefit from the funds under the new Neighbourhood Instrument. This example illuminates the ambivalent reception of EU policies on the Russian side. The Union's double-edged, both universalizing and regionalizing policies are matched by Russia's equally dual views of and practices vis-à-vis them. Russia's ambivalence and its policy-specific views lend credence to many competing interpretations. Another implication is that Russia's response is shifting and mostly reactive, not predominantly proactive.

Geo-strategy

> Today, economic coalitions are counted by dozens not all of them being equally mature. The most advanced of them is the European Union which has posed itself a task of developing into a fully-fledged political subject and a pole of international relations with a single currency and economic, foreign and defence policies to reflect the consolidated interests and functions of the EU member-states. We are witnessing a unique historical experiment in which a cooperated superpower of a new kind in Europe is born.
>
> (Lev Klepatskii, Deputy Director of the Department of Foreign Political Planning at the Ministry of Foreign Affairs of Russia, 2000: 82)

Lev Klepatskii's references to the EU as currently developing into a 'fully-fledged political subject' and 'superpower of a new kind' represent perhaps the most explicit end of Russian views of the Union's geo-strategy. More common-place statements limit themselves to mentioning the Union as one of the strategic poles in international and European politics (e.g. Meshkov 2002: 20; Putin 2001b, 2002a). Regardless of Russia's ambivalent view of the EU's geo-policies, in the end Russian foreign policy makers think they constitute a self-conscious Union with fairly clearly defined goals that also occasionally give rise to 'centralizing tendencies', or 'subjectivist' or 'egoistic' behaviour (Russian federal level poli-cy maker, November 2002). This makes the EU a 'tough customer' (Likhachev 2003: 59).

In order to contextualize this sort of a view, it can be noted how the new semi-insiders, the Baltic states, are coming to grips with the Union's increased significance. But each of them has somewhat different ideas on how far and by what means they wish to be involved in efforts to strengthen the Union both in-ternationally and in the northern European context, ranging from Estonia's early scepticism towards the ND to Lithuania's hopes of bridging the east and west and north and south of the wider Europe area. The Russians, by contrast, mostly as close outsiders take the Union's international dimensions and its 'wider Europe' and north European projects as facts of life with which one has to cope. Their dominant tendency is to seek for an equal and pragmatic partnership with the Un-ion (see Putin 2003b: 14). Yet it has to be granted that they simultaneously have fears of unintended association or inclusion of Russia's northwestern regions in the Union. Thus, compared to the Balts, the perspective of a close outsider again comes into play in the Russians' disinclination, as a non-participant in the inner dynamics of European integration, to deliberate very explicitly over the Union's geo-strategy, except in regions and issue areas where it meets Russian interests.

Another difference vis-à-vis the Balts is that, whereas they, at least for the time being, wish to reserve the US a place in European and also in northern European politics alongside the Union, for Russia, such a weighing of options comes in the shape of more encompassing multipolarity thinking and the related idea of the beneficial effects of multipolarity for the promotion of Russia's interests. This means that, regardless of the increasing frequency of references to the EU, the Union is unlikely to become the *sole* focus of Russian foreign policy, in the face of problems and opportunities perceived in other directions, such as the US, NATO and China (cf. Baranovsky 2002: 44; Khudoley 2003: 27). It is noteworthy that both the Balts and Russia wish to leave other options open, especially with an eye on hard-core military security issues. And they do so for the same reason: the perception of the Union as still being largely a *civilian power*, despite the occasional acknowledgements of its developing foreign political and security and defence dimensions.

From federal to regional level views in Kaliningrad

In the views of EU's subjectivity held by the Kaliningraders the tension between the close outsider and semi-outsider perspectives comes clearly into play. As il-lustrated by Kaliningrad's transformation from a pilot region into a 'test case', for Russian foreign policy makers Kaliningrad remains subjected to Russia's broader strategic aims. This is because of their identity political emplotment of Kaliningrad as a war conquest and reminder of Russia's heroics in the Second World War against Nazi Germany (Aalto 2002a). By contrast, for the Kaliningraders themselves, the more distant European history of the region has become a topic of interest. Especially its history as German Königsberg has been reinvoked. Old German era buildings have been restored, excavations revealing German and Lithuanian graves have been made, and memorial sites constructed (Oldberg 2000: 275–8). More restorations and memorial sites were prepared for 2005 when the city of Kaliningrad celebrated its 750th anniversary. However, it is notable that no similar investment was promised from the federal centre to that which St Petersburg received in connection with its grandiose 300th anniversary celebrations in 2003. Neither was the name Königsberg allowed to appear in a prominent place in this connection (Rosbalt 2003l).

In the space aspect, it is fair to say that the majority, especially the adult and older generations of the Kaliningraders, seem to echo the official views in viewing the region as part of Russia in political terms. Consequently, they also view the EU as lying 'outside' the *oblast'*. This is perfectly in line with the fact that almost all except the youngest of the Kaliningraders represent Soviet people – i.e. voluntary or involuntary Soviet immigrants, or their children, who arrived in the *oblast'* to replace the expelled Germans in the aftermath of the Second World War. At the same time, on account of an opinion poll conducted in May 2001, a sizable group of people, constituting from one-third to around half of the region's residents, would like to see the status of the *oblast'* changed within the Russian federation, to reflect its special location outside the Union, but not outside in the same way as the bulk of Russia (see Holtom 2002: 54). Although they see the present status of the region as elementarily linked to Russia, EU enlargement into the neighbouring regions gives rise for considerable confusion as well as expectations:

> Today, naturally, the priority in favour of the Russian side is unambiguous . . . all agricultural mechanisms, political mechanisms, judicial – everything is harmonized with Russia apart from those spheres which provide some sort of exceptions. And in addition, there are also the socio-cultural ties. When it comes to the future, it is very difficult to say. I certainly would not set these two priorities against each other. This is because in my view, in the future, integration between EU and Russia will take place – again the question is only about its extent.
>
> (Kaliningradian EU observer, November 2002)

This statement by a Kaliningradian EU observer does not yet in itself imply a clear departure from Russia's official policy, nor from President Putin's above-quoted references to upcoming 'unification' with Europe when speaking with students of Kaliningrad State University in 2003. However, when asked whether Kaliningrad has any better prospects for European integration than other Russian regions within the northwest Federal District, the same expert continues:

> Kaliningrad has more opportunities for integrating with the EU because it is

actually separated from the borders of the rest of Russia. By 'integration', we first and foremost speak of economic space. Everything else is, so to say, for entertainment only. The basis is, I think, the economy. And therefore I think there is no problem. And the plus here is that, taking the share of Kaliningraders who have been abroad, I think, who have business or other ties, personal ties, contacts and so on, is far greater than even among St Petersburgers or those in the Karelian Republic. In that sense I see us as more integrated already now. That is a fact. We have a lot more opportunities for integration than the other Russian regions. And this is strengthened by the fact that we are forced to intersect with foreign governments. This was the case also earlier. In other words, we feel the influence of the EU much more than the others . . .

(Kaliningradian EU observer, November 2002)

Such references to Kaliningrad's better prospects for economy-based integration with the EU and to other long-standing perceptions of the Kaliningraders as more integrated make a good case for the close outsider/semi-outsider distinction. The import of this distinction also becomes evident in the comments by Alexander Songal, head of the external relations unit of the Kaliningrad *oblast'* Duma, who, however, places Kaliningrad on an equal footing with other northwestern regions: 'the westernmost part of Russia has lived the last decade under conditions different from those of the remaining, "continental part" of the country . . . elements of experience have accumulated which have no relevance to that of the people on the "continent"' (Songal 2001: 109). However, both observers would probably agree with the statement of the governor of Kaliningrad, Vladimir Egorov, when asked how he views Kaliningrad's development prospects: 'the fate of history has placed Kaliningrad in the very centre of integrating Europe' (Egorov 2001).

Nevertheless, at best, these views imply a perception of a semi-outsider status, which is certainly not quite 'in', but not entirely 'out' either. Such a perception falls clearly short of the more minority views such as the proposals of Sergei Pasko, of the small Baltic Republican Party, who suggested setting up a Baltic Republic in the region. It would be part of Russia, or an associate member of the federation, but also integrated into the EU as a subject of international law. Moreover, some of the young people seem to support an even more pro-European view. Sergei Kortunov reports that, in an anonymous opinion poll presumably conducted in early 2002, 60 per cent of those under twenty-eight years of age wanted separation from Russia. This opinion may have something to do with the fact that 90 per cent of the young Kaliningraders have visited Poland, Lithuania and Germany several times, without having ever been to Russia proper (Kortunov 2003: 122). In another poll conducted by researchers from the Kaliningrad State University in June 2001, a higher proportion of the younger generations, up to forty years old, are anxious about the exclave status of the region (17–20 per cent) compared to the older generations (5–10 per cent). Yet, only around one-tenth of the respondents in all age groups wanted to see Kaliningrad as an 'independent state' (Klemeshev and Fedorov 2002: 27). In any case, there are some generation-based differences in spatial orientation among the Kaliningraders.

But it is important to point out that the eurasianist traits in the official spatial

conceptions, with their accent on a multivector orientation also assigning a prominent place for directions such as the CIS and China, is most likely not very widely
shared as a priority from the Kaliningradian point of view. For the majority of the
Kaliningraders, the Russian and EU spaces combined are close to exhausting the
spatial dimensions relevant to them. When ties with Russia and its various regions
are, as a rule, seen as clearly insufficient on their own to help to alleviate the
Kaliningraders' problems (Khlopetskii and Fedorov 2000: 219), it is questionable
whether adding any eurasianist priorities would help to improve the situation.

Second, in terms of interest projects, the Kaliningraders share the ambivalence
of the federal centre vis-à-vis the consequences of the most important EU geo-
policy, the enlargement project. Most of the interviewed euro-experts expect *some*
negative consequences for Kaliningrad, but they disagree among themselves as
to how grave and long lasting these are going to be. Contradicting some Russian
estimates heard from Moscow (Smorodinskaya 2001: 64), all but one of them
expect only a short initial shock and then foresee predominantly positive opportunities. However, they all have a clear regionalist bias in their views of EU enlargement. This is well summarized by the head of the international relations unit of
the Kaliningrad regional administration, Viktor Romanovsky: 'The present day
situation in Europe resulting from the process of EU enlargement considerably
affects the viability of the region. For us, the people living there, all these issues
are not "high politics". It is our daily life' (Romanovsky 2001: 21). This statement
is made in an international conference with Russian federal level participation,
and represents direct criticism of the federal centre, towards which Kaliningrad's
regional elite commonly felt severe disappointment at the turn of the millennium.
The federal policy was perceived as unstable, with its continuous wavering on the
FEZ/SEZ question, and failures to meet the financial contributions targets in the
first and second federal programmes for the region (1998–2000; 2002–10). The
federal programmes themselves were often seen as inadequate, even if fully realized, and both implicit and explicit references were made to the inadequate degree
of regional autonomy granted to the region and to its unstable and ill-defined character (e.g. Khlopetskii and Fedorov 2000: 688–9, 699, 706; Romanovsky 2001:
89; Songal 2001: 109–12; interviews).

The regionalist bias is also evident in the manner in which the Kaliningraders
resist reducing the question of the *oblast'* to the visas issue as Russia did in 2002.
The prospect of denied entry not only to Russia but also to the enlarging EU, on
which the Kaliningraders are badly dependent as well, was seen as a problem at
the beginning of the new millennium. However, it was not made a high politics issue, rather a practical question which needed to be solved alongside more serious
problems such as the growing socio-economic gap between Kaliningrad and its EU
neighbours. In September 2002, Valery Ustyugov, Kaliningrad's representative in
Russia's Federation Council commented shortly after his resignation, which was
motivated by his open disagreement with his government's policy, that:

> Moscow continues to try and resolve Kaliningrad's problems with one stroke
> (although this is a long process with many stages), and has reduced them to
> one narrow issue – visa-free transit . . . The most important thing is to reach

an agreement with Europe and not threaten her with a worsening of relations, like Dmitry Rogozin [the president's Kaliningrad envoy] is doing. And we shouldn't try to frighten our neighbours, Poland and Lithuania, because they can't resolve the visa issue, only Brussels can . . . Let's finally come to terms with the fact that we are not trying to resolve the issue of people from Vladivostok or any other Russian town travelling to Kaliningrad. We are trying to ensure the survival of the Kaliningrad region's one million or so people.

(Rosbalt 2003m)

With regard to the Union's geo-strategy, Ustyugov goes on to comment that 'today, the EU is a superpower. It is developing dynamically, and is economically and politically more powerful than Russia' (ibid.). Although the notion of a superpower might not be what is widely shared among the Kaliningraders, they certainly think the Union is having a major and increasing impact upon their everyday lives. This impact differs greatly from the centre-to-centre dialogue between the EU and the Russian federation on the ordering of northern Europe.

Summary

I have argued in this chapter that Russia's position in relation to the construction of a concentric EU order is best understood as a mixture of two somewhat different perspectives that were termed close outsider and semi-outsider positions. Owing to Russia's sheer geographical size and the lack of a perception on the EU side of a historically developed 'moral' imperative to include Russia, there is no accession perspective in sight, and the parties are limiting themselves to forming four common spaces that link them in the spheres of the economy, internal and external security, and socio-cultural and educational ties. The economic sphere, and in particular the energy trade issues within it, carry notable long-term potential for transforming Russia's current close outsider position into a more integrationist semi-outsider position, from which Russia's northwestern regions already benefit to a limited extent, while being concomitantly subject to centralizing tendencies from the federal centre. The views of the Union's subjectivity held by Russian foreign policy makers and regional elites in Russia's Kaliningrad region reproduce these discrepancies (Table 8.3).

In the case of Russia and its northwestern regions, most notably Kaliningrad, the EU has clearly encountered the question of the limits of its ordering project. This observation applies both to the EU's own hesitations in extending its umbrella onto Russian territory and to Russian reservations ultimately pertaining to Russia's own broadly eurasianist great power project, where the EU, however, functions as an important western cornerstone and Russia's most important interlocutor. This situation can well be understood as a mutual learning project that was clearly in evidence in the solving of the Kaliningrad transit issue in 2002. This helped to open up room for finding a more integrationist *modus operandi* in the longer run, and it is these future prospects that are discussed in the final chapter of this book.

Table 8.3 The construction of the EU's geopolitical subjectivity in northern Europe: Russian views

Component of ordering	Sub-aspect	Summary
Identity projects	Time	Expectations of the EU to function as Russia's most important source of modernization, and concomitant demands for it to leave behind the remnants of its Cold War era tendency to disregard Russian interests. Perceptions of a historical moment for bridging earlier East/West divide in Europe. In Kaliningrad, concomitant interest in the region's pre-Soviet European past
	Space	Deriving from eurasianism, rejection of association with the EU. Strategic partnership between equal poles of international and European politics preferred. Various northern European locations offered for developing the partnership, but EU–Russian regional integration in northern Europe subjected to developments at the strategic partnership level. Yet, in Kaliningrad, eurasianist ideas rejected as irrelevant to the local context, where experience of being affected by enlarging EU space is very immediate
Interest projects	Geo-policy	Ambivalent view of the Union's universalizing policies such as enlargement and Schengen borders, and their consequences in particular as regards Kaliningrad. The more regionalizing ND policy positively received, but concomitantly viewed as insufficient on its own, and as suffering from implementation problems. In Kaliningrad, perceptions of Russia focusing narrowly on the Schengen issues at the face of more burning issues
	Geo-strategy	Perception of the EU as a significant pole of international and European politics, which also increasingly influences Russia's strategic thinking, but without exhausting it entirely as regards world politics on the whole. In Kaliningrad's case, the impact of the EU felt in a very practical manner

9   Future prospects of an EU-led wider northern Europe

The final chapter of this book revisits some of the differences that were detected in the preceding case study chapters on the second and third circles of the concentric EU order in northern Europe. In the case study chapters, the Baltic states were portrayed as new semi-insiders who remain located mainly in the second circle of the Union until they are able to participate fully in all sectors of EU policy and thus integrate further into the evolving EU order. Nonetheless, in each of the Baltic states, the semi-insider position was shown to allow the formation of somewhat different views of the construction of EU order and one's own position within it. Among the Baltic states, Estonia was found to be potentially the most reluctant partner for the Nordics (and Germany) in the making of a wider northern Europe. Lithuania was found most consistently receptive to the idea, especially with regard to engaging Russia, and its exclave of Kaliningrad, and the western members of the CIS by means of the EU's neighbourhood policy. Nevertheless, Russia and its northwestern regions were termed close outsiders and semi-outsiders. They remain located in the third circle of the Union's order because of their more limited integration prospects in the short to medium term. The close outsider/semi-outsider distinction was invoked in order to account for how the underlying politico-economic factors and experiences of being 'outside' were to a degree different between Russia as a whole and the country's northwestern regions, in particular in the special case of the Kaliningrad region.

The aim here is to probe more systematically into the Union's concentric geopolitical form and some of the related divisions that have been forming in the post-Soviet north since the launch of the Baltic enlargement process and the deepening of relations with Russia. This will be done by making use of Q methodology (Stephenson 1953; Brown 1980; also Aalto 2003a,b), which will help us to look at subjective views of foreign policy makers and EU observers from the Baltic states and Russia's Kaliningrad region. Some interview quotes pertaining to their subjective views have already been presented in the previous chapters, but here more emphasis will be put on outlining alternative and eurosceptic views as well, besides the discussed official views of Estonia, Latvia and Lithuania. Also, it will be examined whether the Balts share some views with the Kaliningraders, who were found to occupy the most EU-integrationist positions among the Russians.

These comparisons will tell us how it matters at the subjective level where among the Union's concentric circles one is located, and how people in the post-Soviet north view the interface between the second and third circles, where the delimiting function of the EU's otherwise fuzzy borders is at its greatest, with policies like the Schengen borders regime and asymmetric amounts of EU funds provided for different sides of the border. Likewise, the Q methodological comparisons will help us to realize the normative-theoretical objective running through this book: to maintain the construction of the Union's geopolitical subjectivity as an *intersubjective process* and ultimately close to its constituent parts, the human subjects. Realizing this objective will help us to elucidate *what views people in the Union's northern fringes bring into its negotiation tables and foreign policy activities, and what diplomatic challenges they may offer to the Union.*

On the basis of the examination of subjectively perceived and constructed positions and cleavages in the post-Soviet north, towards the end of the chapter some overall conclusions will also be drawn on future prospects of EU-led wider northern Europe. What shape it is likely to assume as a result of intersubjective games between the EU centre and the northerners, which have been the subject of this book, will also tell us something about EU foreign policy in a wider sense.

The construction of EU order through subjective views

To address more detailed questions about the differences between the second and third circles, and simultaneously scale down to the individual level, the notion of the EU as the main geopolitical subject of northern Europe needs to be broken down to its constituent parts again. As suggested throughout the book, the breakdown of the concept of geopolitical subjectivity into identity and interest projects and into their sub-aspects results in four analytically separable foci of statements that can be presented about the EU's subjectivity in northern Europe: statements on (A) time; (B) space; (C) geo-policy; and (D) geo-strategy. This division can be combined with an analytical distinction between speakers situated in different circles pertaining to the Union's subjectivity: (a) insiders (centre and first circle); (b) semi-insiders (second circle); (c) semi-outsiders and/or close outsiders (third circle); (d) other (independent observer, e.g. scholar). The cross-tabulation of the thus formed four by four dimensions results in a sixteen-cell theoretical model of the EU's geopolitical subjectivity in northern Europe (Table 9.1). In this way, the model maps the intersubjective construction of EU's geopolitical subjectivity in northern Europe as a result of statements that people can present about the process.

The model was used to place altogether 340 statements picked from various textual sources including policy documents, speeches, printed interviews, previous literature and some newspaper excerpts, with an accent on issues pertaining to the post-Soviet north. The source material included texts and comments in English, Russian, Estonian or Finnish, which were authored or uttered by representatives of EU institutions, by representatives of various northern EU member countries including for example Finland and Sweden, and by representatives of

Table 9.1 Theoretical model: the construction of the EU's geopolitical subjectivity in northern Europe

Foci of statement/ speaker		a. Insiders (centre and first circle)	b. Semi-insiders (second circle)	c. Semi-outsiders and/or close outsiders (third circle)	d. Other (independent observer, e.g. scholar)
Identity projects	A. Time	Aa	Ab	Ac	Ad
	B. Space	Ba	Bb	Bc	Bd
Interest projects	C. Geo-policy	Ca	Cb	Cc	Cd
	D. Geo-strategy	Da	Db	Dc	Dd

the Baltic states, Russia and Kaliningrad. The time range of the source material was from the Union's Nice agreement in summer 2000, in which the Union's institutional preparedness for enlargement was finally declared and a timetable agreed, to autumn 2002 when accession negotiations were close to conclusion and the Kaliningrad issue had already emerged. For example the statement, 'Enlargement is European Union's historic duty. Enlargement closes one chapter in Europe's history and lays the basis for building the future,' was picked almost as it originally appeared in the speech by the Chairman of the European Commission, Romano Prodi, to the European Parliament in Strasbourg on 12 November 2001. The statement focuses on temporal considerations in European integration (time aspect) and is presented by a speaker within the very centre of the Union. Consequently, it falls into the Aa cell of the model and represents statement number two in the final statement sample (*Q sample*; see Appendix).

By selecting a maximum of three statements in this manner for each cell of the model and eliminating unnecessary overlap between the statements, the initially fairly large body of statements was reduced to a more manageable set of forty-three statements. The criteria in selecting the final statements for the Q sample were that they should display as much variation as possible and be of both theoretical and substantial interest. Purely random sampling of statements would be prone to lead to an unbalanced sample, as some types of statements appear in the debates more often than some others (Brown 1986). That the final statement sample is bound to be judgmental does not, however, pose problems of validity in the traditional sense.

First, in Q methodology, the statements do not, unlike survey items, have any predetermined meaning. They do not purport to measure any particular characteristic or trait (ibid.). They are simply picked in order to provide suitable 'raw material' for the purpose of arranging fieldwork experiments, in which participants from the target population are asked to respond to them. In this case, statements were picked in order to administer them to a group of EU experts in the Baltic states and Kaliningrad – including policy-makers, politicians and observers closely associated with EU integration issues. They were asked to sort (rank-order) the statements into an array arranged in a quasi-normal distribution, along a scale ranging from –5 through 0 to +5 (*Q sort*) (Figure 9.1). In other words, the participants of these Q methodological experiments were provided with an opportunity to express their subjective view and express *their theory* of what form of subjectivity the EU should display in their own regional context. *They* were asked to determine what statements were salient and meaningful, and what interconnections between them could be established. Thus, not the sample of statements but the Q sorts provided by the participants are the primary issue of interest. The Q sorts are subjectively valid, since there can be no outside criterion to evaluate the participants' viewpoints about themselves (Brown 1980: 18, 55).[1] Yet the Q sorts are observable and open for scholarly analysis.

The participant group included altogether thirty-six EU experts from Estonia, Latvia, Lithuania and Kaliningrad. This is actually a relatively high number of participants, because Q works best with small groups. All but three of the thirty-six experiments were organized by myself as one-to-one sessions with each participant during November–December 2002.[2] Depending on the case, the Russian, English and Estonian languages were used as communication media. The compiled Q sorts were then factor analysed.[3] Table 9.2 expresses each participant's gender, country/region of residence and *factor loading* on the three extracted factors, i.e. statistical association with each factor, ranging from 1.0 (strong positive correlation with the factor) to –1.0 (strong negative correlation with the factor). However, in Q methodology, the factor loadings are not of primary interest, but factor interpretation, which is conducted by examining *factor scores*, i.e. the arrays of idealized Q sorts for each factor (Appendix).[4] I will first discuss the common ground among the extracted three factors before proceeding to factor interpretation.

One EU subject or many?

The first observation is that there is a rather low consensus among the consulted thirty-six Baltic and Kaliningradian EU experts on the desired form of the EU's geopolitical subjectivity with regard to ordering the post-Soviet north. Whilst looking for different factorial solutions, it emerged that the unrotated first principal

Most unlike my view (please write number of statement)						Most like my view (please write number of statement)				
-5	-4	-3	-2	-1	0	+1	+2	+3	+4	+5

Figure 9.1 Forced Q-sorting grid.

Table 9.2 The participants and factor loadings (*N* = 36)

Participant	Gender	Country/region	FI	FII	FIII
1	F	Kaliningrad	0.55	0.45	0.07
2	F	Kaliningrad	0.63	0.45	0.30
3	M	Kaliningrad	0.48	0.40	−0.03
4	F	Kaliningrad	0.21	0.22	*0.42*
5	F	Kaliningrad	*0.64*	0.34	0.31
6	M	Kaliningrad	−0.04	0.27	0.38
7	M	Kaliningrad	0.24	*0.57*	0.14
8.	M	Kaliningrad	0.30	*0.69*	0.02
9	M	Kaliningrad	0.14	*0.40*	−0.18
10	M	Kaliningrad	*0.59*	0.36	0.30
11	M	Kaliningrad	0.39	*0.63*	−0.23
12	M	Lithuania	*0.55*	−0.03	0.21
13	M	Lithuania	*0.46*	0.17	0.31
14	F	Lithuania	*0.65*	0.39	0.35
15	M	Lithuania	*0.81*	0.19	0.07
16	M	Lithuania	*0.57*	−0.16	0.32
17	M	Lithuania	*0.80*	−0.09	0.04
18	F	Lithuania	*0.62*	0.08	0.18
19	M	Lithuania	*0.53*	−0.29	0.27
20	M	Latvia	*0.75*	−0.03	−0.05
21	F	Latvia	0.27	−0.12	*0.64*
22	F	Latvia	0.11	−0.16	*0.52*
23	M	Latvia	0.33	−0.11	0.07
24	M	Latvia	*0.77*	0.15	−0.05
25	M	Latvia	0.45	0.36	0.09
26	F	Latvia	*0.67*	0.25	0.22
27	F	Latvia	*0.85*	−0.01	0.04
28	F	Estonia	*0.74*	−0.12	0.05
29	M	Estonia	-0.31	−0.08	0.11
30	F	Estonia	*0.53*	−0.17	0.05
31	M	Estonia	*0.45*	−0.05	−0.25
32	M	Estonia	*0.61*	−0.05	0.12
33	F	Estonia	*0.56*	−0.19	0.16
34	M	Estonia	-0.45	0.05	0.16
35	M	Estonia	0.05	−0.34	*0.50*
36	M	Estonia	0.17	−0.10	0.30

Defining loadings (> 0.39) are shown in italics. Symbols: M = male, F = female.

component – which by definition expresses the highest possible extent of consensus – explains only 36 per cent of the variation among the Q sorts. Moreover, two of the consulted people have a negative factor loading on the first principal component (–0.32 and –0.38), and many others have a fairly low loading (for example as low as 0.13, 0.16 and 0.22). Interpreting the first principal component cannot thus be considered meaningful, as wide-reaching consensus extending to several aspects of the Union's geopolitical subjectivity is not at issue among these experts. However, the existing, relatively thin common ground is elucidated by the consensus statements, i.e. statements which all the participants, on whatever factor, evaluate in a fairly similar manner.[5] These indicate what issues these EU experts can agree on (Table 9.3).

There is a substantial yet rather abstract agreement on the importance of protecting the several very peculiar border areas within the region and maintaining at least some of the historically developed cross-border contacts within them. True, on the policy-making level the record of helping to maintain these cross-border contacts, for example on the Estonian–Russian and Lithuanian–Kaliningradian borders, is rather mixed. This is very evident in the Schengen-induced abolition of the simplified border crossing regimes that since the early 1990s had been in place on these two border areas for those with a need for frequent crossing. For Estonian policy makers, this seemed to be a fairly low-key and mostly welcome item in the EU accession process, whereas the Lithuanians' feelings were more mixed owing to their sidelining in the EU–Russia negotiations. For Russian policy makers at the federal level, it became a major issue to oppose, whereas for the Kaliningraders it represented mostly an unwelcome issue, but one not overriding the problem of the overall socio-economic effects of the asymmetrical spreading of EU order that is making the *oblast'* continually poorer than its neighbours (Chapters 4, 7 and 8).

Table 9.3 Consensus statements

Statement		FI	FII	FIII
13	Border regions are important laboratories for developing a Europe closer to the people, a democratic counterweight to globalization and europeanization.	+3	+2	+2
11	Enlargement should not cause any new division of Europe. Cross-border contacts that often go back hundreds of years should not be made impossible or unbearably difficult, especially in areas where the same language is spoken on both sides of the border and close cultural links exist.	+2	+5	+4
17	The EU can hardly be my most preferred choice for organizing the European political space.	–4	–1	–3
26	More active EU involvement is necessary in order to develop international transport corridors, which will connect two formerly separated regions of northern and central Europe.	+5	+2	+2
16	I tend to perceive the EU as something 'strange' and threatening to my national values.	–5	–4	–5
4	Increasing EU integration may result in the weakening of nation-states, which may provoke war in Europe.	–5	–5	–3

Although the EU's policy-making record in the sphere of cross-border contacts is mixed, there seems to be a consensus among the consulted EU experts that the EU centre should understand that those currently located in the Union's outer circles have something valuable to offer for European integration and that the Europeans should respect and embrace the peculiar cultures there. This account of border region peculiarities is in no way intended as a statement preferring an isolationist stance with regard to European integration. On the contrary: none of the groups supports the claim of the EU 'hardly being my most preferred choice for organizing the European political space'. In this light, there is very little out-right opposition to the Union's contemporary position within the wider European area. With a reference to more specific northern European issues, the EU should assist in linking the region to the wider area of Central and Eastern Europe by means of subsidizing and supporting the development of international transport corridors. Moreover, these EU experts agree that EU integration should not be perceived from a very narrow nation-state or national sovereignty framework. This comes up in their refusal to conceive of integration as such in a negative or threatening light with respect to national identities. Notably, this consensus on the EU's leading role and its non-threatening nature with regard to national identities challenges some of the intergovernmentalist pressures identified in the analysis of the official views of Estonia and Latvia.

On balance, it has to be said that the located fairly abstract consensus on most accounts falls short of reaching the policy-making level because it fails to suggest a detailed and all-encompassing, widely agreed on model of subjectivity to the EU vis-à-vis the post-Soviet north. This is because the located consensus pat-terns leave a lot of room for envisaging mutually incompatible ideas and policies for the Union in this regional context. In this respect, dissimilarities rather than similarities among the perceptions of the Baltic and Kaliningradian EU experts are what calls for a more detailed analysis. These dissimilarities are best exam-ined by interpreting the three extracted factors and by then briefly looking at the strongly eurosceptic views conveyed by the two negative loadings on the first factor (Table 9.2).

FI: The EU as a benevolent subject correcting the wrongs of the Cold War era division

The nineteen participants defining this factor – those with a significant loading on this factor only – include eight Lithuanians, four Latvians, five Estonians and two Kaliningraders. Although these figures cannot be taken as representative of views held by broader population, it is nevertheless clear that the rather wide range of participants on the factor reflects on the relatively strong position that the views it conveys enjoy among policy makers and EU observers in the Baltic states. And, as for the two Kaliningradian participants on this factor, they are persons working with or for international organizations that have good cooperation with various EU bodies. These people receive their livelihood from these organizations and have largely socialized themselves into the rather positive views that these organizations promote of the Union or of international cooperation in general.

In short, this view echoes the internalization of official EU views of the Union as a benevolent subject engaged in correcting the wrongs of the Cold War era division of Europe (Chapter 4). According to this view, the Union is not drawing any new boundaries or imposing its own laws and traditions on its new subject territories, as it mostly relies on voluntary association and consent. As such, the Union cannot be compared to the Soviet Union or any other historical empire – a term which for these people easily evokes negative associations. Such connotations must be resisted as they might harm the realization of their preference for the Union to include the Baltic states quickly and conclusively (Table 9.4).

This view sets out to champion the cause of EU enlargement and makes some references to a 'Europe without dividing lines', a policy aim often heard from Russian foreign policy makers. Nonetheless, this view declines to criticize the EU for failing to think of the possibility of Russia's inclusion within the Union. As reasons for a reserved stance towards Russia are cited practical obstacles for Russia's convergence with the EU and the obvious fact that Russia has not handed in any formal application for membership. This should be Russia's own decision, and a possibility which the Union should not really try to contemplate at all at the moment (40, 14, 18).[6] As for Kaliningrad, this view identifies several soft security threats as emanating from there and posits that the region should stay outside

Table 9.4 FI and the Union as a benevolent subject

	Statement	FI	(FII)	F(III)
2	Enlargement is the European Union's historic duty. Enlargement closes one chapter in Europe's history and lays the basis for building the future.	+5	0	+1
17	The EU can hardly be my most preferred choice for organizing the European political space.	–4	–1	–3
21	Speaking of the dividing lines in Europe, the true barriers are likely to be erected between those who belong to the European Union and those who are left outside it. The barriers resulting from EU enlargement will thus be greater than those resulting from NATO enlargement.	–2	+4	–2
31	It is a problem that European laws are largely 'imposed' from outside with little regard for local habits, tradition, preferences and resources.	–2	–4	+5
7	The future of the EU will be settled neither by economic integration and free movement of working force, nor by a joint financial system and even joint armed forces – this all used to exist in the Soviet Union. The Europeans should be more serious about the experience of another Union that has recently collapsed.	–4	0	+3
5	An empire is an empire. It is not important what name we give it – EU or anything else. I would just like to avoid the scenario of the EU empire being ruled by a few narrow-based interest groups or even a dictator.	–3	–5	0

Schengenland for the time being. Yet, here, this view merely echoes the overwhelming majority of policy makers and observers within the current Union, and alongside with them, counts Russians among the beneficiaries from the enlarged Schengen area even though they are set to remain outside of it. At the same time, all claims that the Union is trying to separate Kaliningrad from Russia should be vehemently resisted (12, 23, 29, 33).

Departing from the premise that Russia and Kaliningrad should remain outside the Union for the foreseeable future, this view lends some modest support for the ND policy as a tool for finding a proper place for Russia in Europe or, rather, a place in the wider northern Europe. However, the ND and other EU policy instruments are criticized for their lack of coordination within the Union itself and also for a lack of consultation with other donors and actors in the region for avoiding duplication of projects. The focus in the ND should be on problems with significant transboundary effects such as nuclear waste, organized crime and environmental problems in the Baltic region (19, 22, 24, 27).

Overall, this view echoes the prevalent tendencies within the Union that the EU is needed to promote stability, predictability, security and prosperity not only around its immediate neighbourhood but also in contemporary international politics in general. The Union is seen as doing a good job in spreading its own identity and interest projects and in trying to acquire a stronger military–political dimension in order to be able to display increased subjectivity whilst tackling particularly thorny cases. Concomitantly, it is stressed, along the lines of official Baltic views, that in assuming a stronger role in Europe and the world at large the Union should resist any temptation to become a US-like superpower. The Union should not try to compete with the US or NATO in the military sphere. It should maintain its double-edged character as a Union and an intergovernmental entity (3, 38, 41, 43; interviews).

FII: The EU as a boundary-constructing subject in need of opening up towards its new neighbours

The four participants defining this factor are all Kaliningraders, i.e. semi-outsiders on the third circle and thus with no perspective of a rapid EU accession. The view expressed by this factor disputes the view of FI of the EU as a benevolent subject engaged in a process of correcting the historical wrongs and bridging the former dividing lines. Rather, the EU is seen as a rather determined subject that is currently engaged in a harmful process of erecting new dividing lines through selective enlargement. Such a posture fails to take into account properly the Russian and Kaliningradian interest of seeking closer ties with the Union. Indeed, the Union does not need a military–political dimension to develop its subjectivity. For example, in the case of Kaliningrad, the effects of the Union's subjectivity – e.g. in the Schengen borders question and in the issue of promoting asymmetrical socio-economic standards across the post-Soviet north – are already now clearly felt, without any presence or involvement of military power (18, 21, 38, 41, 42).

Starting from the premise of building a greater Europe without dividing lines (40), this view puts forth several policy recommendations on how the Union could command more authority and loyalty towards its actions among the Kaliningraders and Russians in general. The Union should not only support Kaliningrad's neighbours, but also open up towards its new neighbours and take a note of their interests in a much more direct manner than it has done so far (Table 9.5).

Regardless of the criticism posed towards the forms of subjectivity that the Union has displayed towards the post-Soviet north so far, this view does not manifest any fears that the cross-border cooperation activities practised by the Union and its member states could harm Kaliningrad in any way. One of the reasons suggested for this is that cross-border cooperation is simply something that takes place naturally on the basis of local needs. The EU is not the most important *initiator* in this policy sector (Kaliningradian policy maker, November 2002). At the same time, the ND is seen as a highly positive initiative. Despite the fact that its implementation has faced problems as a result of the unclear and complicated division of labour among the various participants to the cooperation it promotes, this initiative goes a rather long way towards engaging the Kaliningraders and Russia in a right manner, at least when compared to the asymmetric effects of EU enlargement across the second and third circles. Moreover, trying to solve the nuclear waste, organized crime and environmental problems under the ND framework represents something that can benefit Kaliningrad and the rest of northwest Russia (19, 22, 27). Although the visa and transit issues – which were raised as questions of prestige by Russian foreign policy makers in 2002 – do affect the

Table 9.5 FII on the desirable form of the Union's subjectivity vis-à-vis Kaliningrad

Statement		FII	(FI)	(FIII)
23	More attention should be given to 'soft security' hazards arising from the social and economic crisis in the Kaliningrad region and from the unstable conditions there.	+4	+4	–5
32	Kaliningrad presents a 'unique situation' within the context of EU enlargement. The EU officials should be ready to undertake 'unique' or 'non-standard' approaches to solve the problems.	+5	–1	–1
33	I would like to see Kaliningrad included in the Schengen area at the same time as the region's neighbours.	+2	–3	–4
25	It is the very moment to start discussion on cross-border and regional cooperation with Belarus and problems connected with it. I am not interested in the international isolation or self-isolation of Belarus.	+4	+1	0
36	The objective of the EU's relations with Russia should be to construct a wider European area of peace, stability and prosperity – a 'new European order', a 'pax europea' between equal partners.	+3	+1	–3

Kaliningraders significantly, on balance the soft security and socio-economically based issues are much more fundamental (interviews).

FIII: The EU as a concentric empire in the making with too rapidly forming outer circles

The four participants defining this factor include one participant from Kaliningrad, two from Latvia and one from Estonia. Along with the second factor, the position conveyed by this factor also disputes the first factor's view of the EU as a benevolent subject engaged in healing the Cold War era divisions. At the same time, this factor disputes the second factor's view of the EU as engaged in an unfortunate boundary-construction process towards its neighbours. For this factor, EU integration in general, and the grand schemes for increasing the extent of the Union's territorial control in particular, are proceeding at a too rapid pace.

Yet the message is not one of outright but, rather, of mild euroscepticism. EU integration does not pose any direct threat to national identities in the post-Soviet north and in principle offers several valuable benefits to the peoples of the region (4, 16, 17). But the people both in the current member states and in accession states are not yet well enough prepared for building a stronger European dimension within their countries and for a greater transfer of power to the centre in Brussels. There are too many question marks regarding what a greater degree of europeanization would mean in terms of developing a democratic polity and in

Table 9.6 FIII on the Union's emerging imperial geopolitical form

Statement		FIII	(FI)	(FII)
7	The future of the EU will be settled neither by economic integration and free movement of working force, nor by a joint financial system and even joint armed forces – this all used to exist in the Soviet Union. The Europeans should be more serious about the experience of another Union that has recently collapsed.	+3	−4	0
31	It is a problem that European laws are largely 'imposed' from outside with little regard for local habits, tradition, preferences and resources.	+5	−2	+4
28	The EU and its member states should not artificially force the process of border cooperation. Otherwise, it will be difficult to see the difference between cross-border cooperation and the economic, demographic and cultural or religious expansion of contiguous countries.	+3	−1	−4
14	The idea of any union is that some belong to it and some others do not. However, there are plans to include all the European states in the EU, in the worst case also Russia and Turkey. I do not understand such efforts: why force Asian peoples to become Europeans?	+5	−2	−2

terms of identity politics (6, 8, 20). The EU centre seems to be extending its grip of the countries on the second and third circles too rapidly, and in that process its geopolitical form seems to be approaching an imperial formation reminiscent of the Soviet Union (Table 9.6).

Although the view of the factor does not envisage the Baltic states' EU accession as bringing with it any markedly anti-Russian tones to the Union (30), it displays considerable scepticism towards the manner in which the EU–Russian partnership is evolving and gradually assuming a more strategic character. It doubts the importance of the ND and its idea of offering Russia a new northern European location in place of its former marginalization into the 'East'. On the whole, this view is unsure about the whole ND initiative, despite making the general claim that the EU financing instruments require streamlining and improved coordination, so that the different funds can match each other on different sides of borders as is planned in the new Neighbourhood Instrument. And naturally, in this mode of thinking, Russia's EU membership would constitute an unacceptable idea (18, 19, 24, 36, 39). Similarly, the Baltic participants on this factor are not eager to raise the Kaliningrad question to a more prominent position within the Union's agenda and strongly dispute the claim that the Union is trying to separate the region from Russia. However, the Russian participant on this factor would like to make Kaliningrad a special case in EU–Russian relations especially in connection to the Schengen issue (23, 29, 32, 33).

Nevertheless, regardless of all the reservations that this view has towards the EU's policies and its current geo-strategy towards the outer circles, it suggests a strong regional and global role for the Union. In this sense, the desirable geo-strategy is reminiscent of the positive attitudes towards a more effective and visible subjectivity for the Union that are manifested by supporters of FI and by the efforts of some of the present-day insiders. But, importantly, the view promoted by FIII stands for keeping the use of military–political instruments strictly in the hands of national governments and is not interested in traditional geopolitical games of international politics (3, 35, 41, 42, 43). Hence, whilst the first factor stands for a careful and balanced increase in the Union's traditional geopolitical subjectivity – provided it does not compromise the role of NATO (interviews) – and the second factor views the Union's influence as clearly felt already now without the military dimension, this view argues for what has been termed a 'civilian' and, somewhat differently, a 'normative' power Europe (see Manners 2002; interviews).

Strongly eurosceptic voices

Whereas the representatives of the third factor can be termed mild eurosceptics, the two participants from Estonia who had a negative loading on the first factor can be taken as exemplary cases of a strong version of euroscepticism. This is a political orientation which EU lobbyists in Estonia and Latvia feared might escalate in their countries during the EU accession campaigns in 2003, and therefore they rushed to print leaflets countering the claims of strong eurosceptics each time they got publicity (see Mikkel and Pridham 2004: 731–8; interviews).

In fact, the strong euroscepticism represented by these two Estonians could better be termed outright opposition to the EU. These people identify far-reaching federalist pressures within the EU which have not been disclosed to the public in their entirety. One of them equates the EU directly with classical empires such as the Soviet Union. The EU simply aims at controlling its own subject states by means like the common agricultural policy, which makes member states dependent on subsidies and regulation from the EU centre, in the same way as the Soviet Socialist Republics were made dependent from Moscow's regulation and distribution of all-Union resources. Although the classical imperial aims of controlling extensive territories are there, the means this time are much more subtle. They are linked to the financial muscle of the liberal international economic order, which allegedly is a conspiracy project of the Freemasons: banks, companies, corporations and international economic organizations that in general profit from this order and utilize the EU as their tool of colonial domination. The other participant thinks somewhat differently of the EU originally as a conspiracy project started by big capital: a sub-theatre of their mostly American playing field, which also serves as a launching pad for aims of conquering the whole world. Now, however, the former apprentice EU is trying to distance itself from its American patrons by growing to unnatural proportions (interviews).

With an eye on EU foreign policy and the making of a wider northern Europe, these people, being strong eurosceptics, have relatively little to offer in terms of a positive political programme. They concentrate on voicing their opposition to the whole idea of EU integration and especially the CEE enlargement which they think is a mere material exercise of acquiring strategically important bridgehead territories and more resources for the Union, such as Estonia's oil shale in the northeast of the country. Therefore, most of their comments are of the more reactive rather than proactive type compared to the more EU-supportive people in the Baltic states and, as such, remind one of the close outsider view of Russians. Interestingly enough, both of them see strong evidence of Russia becoming some sort of a dominion or even part of the Union in the medium to long term. Moreover, they see considerable popular pressure building at some point against federalist pressures within the EU. This would reintroduce the European nation-state framework, which for these people provides for a much more natural means of arranging economic accumulation and redistribution, as well as for the individual, a natural community for leading a decent life within a tightly knit cultural unit (interviews).

Strongly eurosceptic voices reminiscent of these views were presented by the Estonian 'No to the EU' movement (e.g. Leito 2002; Leito and Silberg 1998), and similar tones appeared also during Latvia's EU membership campaign. The principal opposition movement in Latvia, headed by Janis Sils, equated the EU with the Soviet Union during the build-up to the EU referendum. Thus, both the Estonian and Latvian 'no' movements relied on identity political and national catchwords. For example, they directed attention to how the word for 'union' is in the national languages the same for the European Union and the Soviet Union: in Latvian *savieniba* and in Estonian *liit*. Yet in neither country did the strong eurosceptics manage to gather any notable political support for their programme (Mikkel and Pridham 2004).

The future of the concentric EU order in northern Europe

The main finding of the Q methodological analysis was the low degree of consensus among the consulted Baltic and Kaliningradian EU experts on the desirable characteristics of the Union's geopolitical subjectivity in the post-Soviet north. But importantly, at the same time, the views conveyed by the first factor, portraying the EU as a benevolent subject correcting past wrongs in the region, were assumed to be fairly widely shared among Baltic EU experts. This gives us grounds to propose that many of them relate relatively positively and with relatively few reservations towards EU enlargement into the post-Soviet north, and towards the Union's growing subjectivity in the wider northern European region (FI). It is quite possible that *some* Kaliningraders can broadly agree with them on this point. Yet, in the Q methodological analysis a very distinct Kaliningradian voice disputing this opinion and instead speaking of new boundary construction practices of the Union was also detected (FII), as were both mild versions of eurosceptism (FIII) and strong ones, both of which operate with negatively perceived notions of the Union as too reminiscent of imperial tendencies.

Somewhat differently, though, an empire-like geopolitical form consisting of concentric circles of EU order was also offered in Chapter 3 as the most apt characterization of the effects of the EU's use of power in the northern European region, including the post-Soviet north, and of the extent to which it can be held responsible for the division of political space there. Paradoxically, it will be now claimed that the EU experts on the first factor in fact support views that are ultimately prone to lend added credence to the concentric model despite their vehement opposition to any notions of EU empire. How is this apparent paradox possible?

To start with, evidently the term 'empire' evokes different associations for those policy makers and observers from its use in this book – as a shortcut to how the EU uses and divides political power in peculiar ways that its subject states and citizens predominantly think is legitimate. But the important point is that the people on the first factor in broad terms accept the differentiated manner in which the EU presently exercises power and divides political spaces. Moreover, they favour a clear division into Union and member state capacities in opposition to a Union reminiscent of the US, or of the centralization of a possible Westphalian-federal formation. When translated into the contemporary political practice of European integration and EU foreign policy-making, this preference will most likely only serve to maintain the present concentric form where the exercise of power and division into Union and member state capacities varies from one country to another, and from one circle to another. In other words, this view will not allow development into a federation where Union regulation would be highly and equally binding on all members, because it will be far too difficult to agree on how the capacities in a Union with more and more diversity should be universally divided. And likewise, it is clear as well that proponents of this view will not want to see the Union stripped down to a mere international organization that would be equally little binding on all of its members.

If the views reflected by the first factor are in practice prone to maintain diversity and the concentric EU order of the Union, what about the alternative views offered by the second and third factors? The views and expectations of the Kaliningraders and Balts on the second and third factors reflect contestation and critique towards widely circulated views of the present-day Union as a benevolent subject. Such a critique will not be accepted easily by the ruling elites in the Baltics, or Nordic states, let alone the EU centre with its federalist pressures.

The perception of the second factor of strong identity and interest projects of the Union that often leave a lot to be desired and in an unfortunate manner create a clearly felt insider/outsider distinction at the Union's borders, expresses a degree of frustration in many senses reminiscent of Russia's official policy. As a message to EU foreign policy makers, this frustration is only prone to translate into continued gradualist efforts at integration mainly focusing on individual policy sectors such as the economy, where progress is most likely. The critical views of semi-outsiders like Kaliningraders, even if slightly more integrationist than those in Russia on the whole, is not very likely in political practice to suffice to kick-start wide-ranging efforts for fast-tracking the region's integration. At worst, they may even make some EU and Russian officials more cautious than now. In the short to medium term, the sectoral patterns of mutual trade and energy supply dependencies between Russia and the Union that were detected in Chapter 8 are thus likely to continue. In the foreseeable future, for the Russians this will mean a continued position at the margins.

Further, the existence of such mildly eurosceptic and popular, if not populist, pressures within old and new member states alike as expressed by factor three is likely to help preserve the existing concentric arrangements as the only viable option. This means variation in the capacities between the Union and member states, as well as variation in the degree of integration. Where such pressures are strong, as they are in many policy sectors for instance in Denmark, or in the sector of defence, potentially in non-aligned Finland or Sweden or some of the Baltic states, opt-outs will continue. Where sheer capacity to integrate further for example in the monetary sector does not measure up to the Union's requirements, as can happen in some of the Baltic or other CEE states, for a few years at least, opt-outs will continue too.

All these observations from the Q methodological analysis, when coupled with the diverse views that were located in the analyses of official views of the EU in Estonia, Latvia, Lithuania, and Russia and Kaliningrad, represent conflicting expectations towards the Union. Remarkably, this is precisely the environment in which empire-like formations have fared so successfully in the past. Yet this time, somewhat paradoxically though, divide-and-rule policies will have considerable popular and practical support from below, i.e. from new members and neighbours, but without any doubt also from old member states. In the light of these findings, northern Europeans are set to strengthen the concentric EU order even though they may not very often see this as a conscious choice of their own.

However, this conclusion about strengthened concentricness warrants some further examination. The Q methodological analysis also hinted at interesting possibilities of transgressing the concentric circles model at the level of subjective views and perceptions. Some of the Kaliningraders were strongly associated with FI and one with FIII. In other words, not all of them were associated with the semi-outsider view of FII. This fact gives us some grounds to take the circles of the concentric Union as not completely clear-cut but rather a matter of subjectively perceived location. Although, as an empirical result in a broadly constructionist study such as this book, this may not be totally unexpected, in the more theoretical sense, on this basis it seems reasonable to argue that the circles are not entirely concentric but considerably overlapping as well. This means that at the level of subjective perceptions there is complexity and diversity within the Union's borders in northern Europe. In suitable political conditions these perceptions may become better empowered and assume significance in political practices, and consequently shift the balance of prevailing regional order. However, so far for example in Kaliningrad, politically very experimental views have not assumed centrality. In fact, despite the frustration expressed towards the policy of Russia's federal centre (see Chapter 8), with Russia's recent re-centralization we have seen a retreat from the regional experiments of the 1990s. Here, socialization has moved towards slowly finding some elements for a common agenda between the centre and the Kaliningrad region, which is not necessarily a bad thing, although the wrangle between them is probably still unfinished. For the region's EU integration prospects such relative stabilization of centre–regions relations may even be useful. Yet, theoretically it is important to know that there *is* movement within and across the circles.

This finding prompts us to ask: could such movement across the circles, if found more widely and in necessary directions, erode the concentric EU order? Although the emergence of a Westphalian-federal Europe was deemed unlikely, could the possible erosion of concentricness make a regionalized European order, or Europe of Olympic rings, which for some seemed to be on the cards in the early 1990s, a more viable option again? From the perspective of this book, in the metaphorical sense, answering these questions constitutes an important test of falsification.

Out of the various region-building writers who were analysing northern Europe's regionalization prospects in the 1990s, Pertti Joenniemi (1993: 209–15) argued already in 1993 that a concentric Europe may in fact coexist with a more regionalized European order – whether the more mosaic-like Europe of regions or the Europe of Olympic rings variant in which relatively autonomous regional entities centre around an imagined region instead of the EU centre. The coexistence of the concentric and regionalized forms is possible because they both depart from the allegedly weakening bond between the state and nation, and because the EU itself supports both Brussels-centred policies (termed universalizing policies in this book), and subsidiarity-based policies that bear some resemblance to the policies here termed regionalizing. In 1995, Joenniemi argued that regionalization was entering the European scene in particular through the EU's new institution of the Committee of Regions and formation of regions like the Baltic and Barents regions. Yet Joenniemi pointed out that there are concomitant limits to region-alization in Europe. Many authors have seconded him on this point, especially directing attention to how actions of states within the region undermine prospects of bottom-up regionalization (Joenniemi 1995: 346–50; Käkönen 1996: 60–3; Hedegaard and Lindström 2003: 13; D. Smith 2003: 51). Most recently, Joen-niemi and Christopher Browning posited the drive towards the centre as the defin-ing feature of northern Europe's post-Cold War development. In a broad sense, this speaks of strengthening concentricness in Europe. But, in their view, focusing only on Brussels-centred processes unfortunately prevents us from seeing the pos-sibility of the formation of other competing places of importance. Margins may position themselves between the centre and their own marginality, thus creating new political spaces as witnessed in the multi-level region-building in northern Europe since the early 1990s (see Browning and Joenniemi 2004b: 229–30).

The argument offered in this book is that we should indeed pay attention to what is taking place in supposed margins like the Baltic states or, even more so, Russia and Kaliningrad, and that these developments are worth looking into as part of the new, enlarged Union and its neighbourhood. The need is made only more urgent by the fact that here the Union encounters a territory previously unknown to it, the post-Soviet north. In this context, a natural reference point is also the often noted manner in which the EU has evolved as a result of what the newcomers have brought into it: in Finland and Sweden's case, more focus on northern European issues in general, the ND policy, and more emphasis on relations with Russia, although, as implied, Germany and its reunification also played a crucial role in the deepening of EU–Russian relations. While this focus hopefully captures some aspects of how 'marginality' may open up useful viewpoints, and what it is intended to connote, what I have concomitantly tried to highlight throughout this book is the way in which the pull of the centre works in intersubjective processes. It is not only about how margins strive for a more central position by means of EU accession, and partnerships and regional cooperation with the Union, but of how the centre has in fact come 'here'. The European Union's institutions have not simply remained a distant centre somewhere in Brussels around which oth-ers are centring themselves. Actually the centre has *entered the north European region with an increasing decisiveness and goal-orientedness that I have termed 'ordering' and the construction of its geopolitical subjectivity*. Put otherwise, an intersubjective process is at play. Whether we like it or not, the EU has become the main talking point and centre of gravity in relation to which margins and any other players position themselves in northern Europe. Apart from the processes examined at length in this book, another good example that was mentioned in passing in Chapter 1 is how the NEI policy of the US is modelled along the lines of the EU's ND. This surely does not represent a typical approach for US foreign policy (Browning 2001). This again speaks for the EU's centrality in northern Europe.

A different type of argument is provided by Helmut Hubel (2004b), who otherwise writes in line with the concentric model, but maintains some role for regionalization. For Hubel, the Baltic Sea region is becoming a European *sub-region* rather than a distinct region of its own, or a type of 'laboratory' for political experiments as in Hubel's words it was in the early 1990s, immediately after the breaking of the Cold War. In this scheme, the main factors affecting the contours of order within the sub-region are partly inside and mostly outside: (western) European integration, transatlantic relations and the continued importance of NATO for many players in the region (especially Denmark, Norway, the Baltic states and Poland), as well as developments within the Nordic states and post-Soviet space. By contrast, my argument here has been to accentuate the role of European integration and the manner in which it has eaten into the significance of these alternative factors. NATO has simply retreated from political action within the region, although it has maintained an important structural role in the background. Nordics have provided their own input into the (northern) European project, and subsequently *Norden* has largely faded out as an independent formation, although as a concept it continues to offer a means of hindering any too quick merger of Nordic and Baltic identities as seen in the reserved reactions to Estonian and Latvian claims of nordicity. The post-Soviet traits, for their part, have retreated considerably, although important traces of them remain, and despite the fact that there has been a shared EU–Russian hesitation to allow the spreading of EU order further into the parts of post-Soviet space controlled by Russia.

In short, Hubel's vision of a European sub-region shaped by externalities seems to imply mostly a traditional geopolitical view of northern Europe, where the region is defined from the outside. He himself calls it an institutionalist view, but what I have suggested here is rather a story in which the players within the region first invited the centre, which eventually started answering the call and grew stronger in the consequent encounter and eventual integration. This may be called institutionalization, although I have tried to make it clear that the notion of the construction of geopolitical subjectivity grasps better the EU's power, responsibility and goal-orientedness in the making of a new EU-centred order in northern Europe than the terminology of comparative politics or any other approach we are used to thinking of. Rather than a mere 'institution', we are now living with a new geopolitical subject.

Finally, with reference to more traditional geopolitical accounts of order-making in Europe like Mouritzen and Wivel's work on the geopolitics of Euro-Atlantic integration (2005c), it should be clear by now that my argument of a new geopolitical subject in northern Europe very deliberately accentuates the leading role of the EU. Mouritzen and Wivel recognize the EU's position as the main integration machine to which states need to adapt, but they simultaneously want to keep the US and NATO connection on board. However, in this book the focus is not on the Euro-Atlantic area but on northern Europe, where it is argued these two players are no longer particularly visible. At the same time, the commonalities are seen in the way in which this book can also accommodate the type of historically familiar adaptation patterns of northern European powers observed by Mouritzen and Wivel as part of their argument, with the northern Europeans trying to fit into their shifting geopolitical neighbourhood. But this is not the end of the story. Russia's role must be recognized too. Viewed from the northern European angle, Russia is also participating in the definition of the EU subject in a much more important capacity than as the supposed plain 'outsider' that it appears in Mouritzen and Wivel's work. This difference of emphasis means returning to my initial argument that the EU has become the most important power in northern Europe, even to the extent that adjacent powers cannot live as plain outsiders without being impacted and drawn along. Therefore my theoretical conclusion is that the EU's character is not best understood by references to conventionally used categories of political imagination: we need the geopolitical subjectivity approach.

Summary

In this chapter, I have attempted to probe deeper into the structure of the EU's concentric order in northern Europe and especially into the differences between the second and third circle within it. The Q methodological analysis of subjective views of policy makers and EU observers in the Baltic states and Kaliningrad that was introduced for this purpose revealed that the mainstream views within the Union centre and various members, like the Baltic states, somewhat para-doxically support the maintenance and strengthening of this order although they might not necessarily themselves always notice it. At the same time, there are also voices both among the Baltic states and in Kaliningrad adopting a critical at-titude towards the prevailing order. But these views and proposals are unlikely to change the course towards strengthened concentricness of the Union in northern Europe. For this reason the alternative model of Westphalian-federal Europe was deemed unlikely. Interestingly enough, there were some indications that some of the Kaliningraders challenge their own semi-outsider position and express views that one would mostly expect only from quite differently positioned agents. Yet, this potential that the Kaliningraders showed for transgressing one's own position within the Union's various circles was not deemed conducive towards a regional-ized northern European order, but rather as evidence of the partially overlapping and cross-cutting nature of the circles of the concentric EU order. In the light of the findings introduced in this book, this concentric order also looks the most likely future course for the Union's northern European engagement.

Appendix

Factor scores (idealized Q sorts)

	Statement	FI	FII	FIII
1	More than fifty years on from the end of the Second World War, we should have learnt to look forward. We have more important things to do than to run around in circles pursuing the same old arguments. There is still so much to do in the process of uniting Europe; we cannot afford to waste time and energy on pointless debates on the numerous past wrongs and sufferings.	0	+1	+1
2	Enlargement is the European Union's historic duty. Enlargement closes one chapter in Europe's history and lays the basis for building the future.	+5	0	+1
3	The world now more than ever needs a strong European Union which is sure of its values, which encourages stability, predictability, security and prosperity around it, and which is active internationally.	+4	+1	+4
4	Increasing EU integration may result in the weakening of nation-states, which may provoke war in Europe.	−5	−5	−3
5	An empire is an empire. It is not important what name we give it – EU or anything else. I would just like to avoid the scenario of the EU empire being ruled by a few narrow-based interest groups or even a dictator.	−3	−5	0
6	The societies on both sides of the continent are too little informed about the prospects of the European Union. The unifying vision, which will lie at the core of our new, wider identity, is yet to be born.	+1	−3	+3
7	The future of the EU will be settled neither by economic integration and free movement of working force, nor by a joint financial system and even joint armed forces – this all used to exist in the Soviet Union. The Europeans should be more serious about the experience of another Union that has recently collapsed.	−4	0	+3
8	A basic problem in contemplating the EU's future international role is that we don't know what direction European politics will take. For example the rise to power of xenophobic politicians would make European politics look less than progressive. We should therefore be circumspect about any centres of power and this includes the democratic EU.	−1	0	+2
9	Europe should not be afraid of the Russians, 'Islamic fundamentalism' or anything similar – rather Europe should be afraid of its own past, which should not be allowed to become its future.	−2	−2	0
10	The socio-economic ideal of the EU has always been the social market model, which demands a vast amount of collaboration among the social partners. This means that the Union cannot behave towards its neighbours as an unrestrained imperialist.	0	−1	+4
11	Enlargement should not cause any new division of Europe. Cross-border contacts that often go back hundreds of years should not be made impossible or unbearably difficult, especially in areas where the same language is spoken on both sides of the border and close cultural links exist.	+2	+5	+4

#	Statement				
12	It is important to note that non-EU nationals, including Russian citizens, will benefit from an enlarged EU area of freedom, security and justice. This includes the possibility of circulating without internal border controls.	+3	+3	0	−1
13	Border regions are important laboratories for developing a Europe closer to the people, a democratic counterweight to globalization and europeanization.	+3	+2	+2	+2
14	The idea of any union is that some belong to it and some others do not. However, there are plans to include all the European states in the EU, in the worst case also Russia and Turkey. I do not understand such efforts: why force Asian peoples to become Europeans?	−2	−2	−2	+5
15	The Union should be open to all countries that want to belong to the Community, satisfy the membership criteria and are able to assume and implement obligations.	0	0	−2	−1
16	I tend to perceive the EU as something 'strange' and threatening to my national values.	−5	−5	−4	−5
17	The EU can hardly be my most preferred choice for organizing the European political space.	−4	−4	−1	−3
18	The EU should be criticized for not considering the prospect of Russia's future membership of the Union.	−3	+3	+3	−4
19	The Northern Dimension could be regarded as one of the most promising directions in the EU's Russian policy. The fact is that Russia cannot and will not enter the European Union in any foreseeable future, but it has a real chance of eventually becoming part of one integrated entity – the European north.	+2	+2	+5	−3
20	After fifty years of European integration there still is no 'European public space' – there is only a juxtaposition of national public spaces, capped by a jumble of intergovernmental and supranational bureaucracies.	−1	−1	−1	+1
21	Speaking of the dividing lines in Europe, the true barriers are likely to be erected between those who belong to the European Union and those who are left outside it. The barriers resulting from EU enlargement will thus be greater than those resulting from NATO enlargement.	−2	−2	+4	−2
22	For the Northern Dimension a clearer structure for cooperation with the regional organizations, euroregions, international financial institutions, private enterprises and other states active in the region (USA, Canada, EEA countries) needs to be established in order to divide responsibilities and ensure that duplication of projects is minimized.	+3	+3	+3	+1
23	More attention should be given to 'soft security' hazards arising from the social and economic crisis in the Kaliningrad region and from the unstable conditions there.	+4	+4	+4	−5
24	The EU financing instruments require streamlining and improved coordination, so that the different funds can match each other on different sides of borders in the EU countries, in the future member states and in Russia.	+4	+4	+1	+3

Appendix *continued*

	Statement	FI	FII	FIII
25	It is the very moment to start discussion on cross-border and regional cooperation with Belarus and problems connected with it. I am not interested in the international isolation or self-isolation of Belarus.	+1	+4	0
26	More active EU involvement is necessary in order to develop international transport corridors, which will connect two formerly separated regions of northern and central Europe.	+5	+2	+2
27	The best way to achieve results in the Northern Dimension programme is to focus on priorities that will have an impact throughout Europe. These include working with Russia to tackle nuclear waste, addressing causes of environmental pollution throughout the Baltic region and striving to combat organized crime.	+3	+3	0
28	The EU and its member states should not artificially force the process of border cooperation. Otherwise, it will be difficult to see the difference between cross-border cooperation and the economic, demographic and cultural or religious expansion of contiguous countries.	−1	−4	+3
29	The EU is trying to separate Kaliningrad from Russia.	−5	0	−5
30	It is unfortunate that the new EU members will be anti-Russian from the outset. This will have a negative impact on EU–Russian relations.	−3	+1	−2
31	It is a problem that European laws are largely 'imposed' from outside with little regard for local habits, tradition, preferences and resources.	−2	−4	+5
32	Kaliningrad presents a 'unique situation' within the context of EU enlargement. The EU officials should be ready to undertake 'unique' or 'non-standard' approaches to solve the problems.	−1	+5	−1
33	I would like to see Kaliningrad included in the Schengen area at the same time as the region's neighbours.	−3	+2	−4
34	I firmly believe that the Union, having put its own economic house in good order, should export stability to the southern Mediterranean area and to the enlarged Union's 'new neighbours' – Russia, Ukraine and the Caucasus countries.	+1	−1	−4

35	I do not share the vision of the EU as a future superpower, but rather as a new kind of strong international actor that can mitigate and cover problems caused by power politics and superpower behaviour around the world.	+1	+1	+2
36	The objective of the EU's relations with Russia should be to construct a wider European area of peace, stability and prosperity – a 'new European order', a 'pax europea' between equal partners.	+1	+3	–3
37	Incredible economic potential that exists on the eastern rim of the European Union warrants that absolute priority be given to the Union's policies towards the future neighbours in Eastern Europe: Russia, Ukraine, Belarus, Moldova. The concept of a wider Europe has to grow into a comprehensive policy backed by firm political will and adequate resources.	0	–3	0
38	The goals of the EU are very unclear. It seems that the Union simply serves the interests of a small circle of well-paid officials.	–4	–5	–1
39	The Northern Dimension initiative is a manifestation of an eternal geopolitical rivalry between Russia and the West. In contrast with the past, the West prefers economic rather than military instruments for putting pressure on Russia, in order to secure its status as the West's 'younger partner' and a source of cheap natural resources and labour force.	–1	–3	–2
40	I am indeed a supporter of a Greater Europe without dividing lines.	+2	+2	–1
41	The European Union's acquisition of a military–political dimension in addition to its economic dimension is welcome.	+2	–3	–2
42	A 'civilian' Europe without any military capability can only be a second-rate actor on the diplomatic and strategic chessboard of world affairs.	0	–2	+1
43	I would like to see the EU remain a flexible actor in international relations able to determine the scale of its actions on a case-by-case basis. The EU should act both as a union and through its member-states. It should resist the temptation to become a US-like superpower.	+5	–1	+5

Notes

1 Introduction

1   A third possible alternative, *confederation*, represents an arrangement in which there is variation along the territorial dimension, but not along the functional dimension. This model allows for units of different sizes as in the present-day European Union, but does not allow for the present functional diversity within the Union. This form is historically a relatively rare and unstable occurrence. The fourth option, *consortio*, is an even rarer instance in political organization. In this form, territorial units are fixed and in a hierarchical relationship, and their cooperation along functional tasks is non-fixed and variable. Schmitter's *condominio*, for its part, stands for variation along both the territorial and functional dimensions. Although Schmitter thought of this being an unlikely variant, he ends up thinking of its realization through the Maastricht treaty; and the scheme introduced in this book bears some similarities to Schmitter's idea (see Schmitter 1996: 135–6).
2   The NEI was replaced by the Enhanced Partnership in Northern Europe (e-PINE), which meant downscaling of already modest resources.
3   The Westphalian views of the EU discussed here represent illustrative examples of the literature. For a broadly similar discussion on state-centric EU foreign policy studies, see K. Smith (2003: 3–5); for Westphalian approaches to EU foreign policy, see also Browning (2005a).
4   Until the Union's Amsterdam treaty in 1997, the Schengen borders regime used to be exclusively a III pillar issue. However, in this treaty it was partly transferred to the I pillar.

2 The EU encounters *Norden*

1   Austria also joined the EU in the 1995 enlargement. However, as Austria is not a north European country – despite the similarity of its Cold War era security policies to the Nordic neutrals Finland and Sweden – it is excluded from the analysis in this book.
2   To this could be added Denmark's North American inclinations that result from its position as a state with North Sea coastline on its western shores, its possession of the Faroe Islands and Greenland in the northern Atlantic and, most notably, its membership in NATO. Under its right-wing government that came into power in 2001, Denmark has also been a vocal participant in the US-led 'war on terrorism' that was started after 11 September 2001.
3   One part of the history of EU enlargement is the dilution of the competing free trade area EFTA, which originally included Austria, Denmark, Norway, Portugal, Sweden, Switzerland and the UK. The current EFTA includes only the non-EU members Iceland, Norway, Liechtenstein and Switzerland.

4 During 1992–8, Germany alone contributed about 245 million German marks to PHARE and other EU programmes that were directed to the Baltic states. To this must be added substantial bilateral aid programmes by Germany and the Nordic countries to both the Baltic states and Russia, in the form of financial support for infrastructure and environmental projects, as well as technical aid. In addition, the Baltic states received military equipment donations. During 1991–7, the US provided to the Baltic states 136 million US dollars through the Support for East European Democracy Program. With a capitalization of 50 million US dollars thse Baltic–American Enterprise Fund promoted growth of small and medium sized businesses (see Pabriks and Purs 2002: 133, 138).

3 The EU encounters the post-Soviet north I: A new theoretical approach

1 The EU regulates the position of stateless people with the directive on the Regulated Status of Third Country Nationals Within the EU, adopted in 2003, which granted minimal rights to establish residency in the EU as well as some social guarantees and other basic rights. But stateless people are not allowed visa-free travel in the Union; they are also restricted from seeking employment in any EU country except their own state of residence (Mite 2003).
2 Although not perhaps strictly speaking an 'empire' analyst, Hans Mouritzen presented a bold scenario where the EU is the undisputed centre of European geopolitics and Russia the 'periphery of the periphery' of the Union (1996a: 284–93). However, in his analysis scenarios are defined as 'that which will *not* happen' (p. 282), and the actual developments usually include elements of several scenarios.

4 The EU encounters the post-Soviet north II: EU views

1 The annual budget of ISPA for 2000–6 was set to 1,040 billion euros, whereas SAPARD's was 520 million euros (European Commission 2003a).
2 I first read through previous research and the primary material and simultaneously coded each piece along the lines suggested in the theoretical model (Chapter 3), highlighting the manner in which time, space, geo-policy and geo-strategy aspects come up, if at all. Second, I examined in more detail all material that was found to be related to each aspect, in order to find out the dominant construction along each aspect. Thanks to the amount of available and relevant previous research, most of the reporting of the analysis is based on secondary sources.
3 In Estonia, Konstantin Päts's authoritarian regime followed the democratic experience. It was justified by the claim that in this way Päts countered an attempted *coup d'etat* by the League of Veterans of the 1918–20 War of Independence. In Latvia, Karlis Ulmanis seized authoritarian power as a result of his and his nationalist government allies' frustration with the working of parliamentary democracy in the country. The Latvian governments which had been mostly dominated by him and his closest circles found it difficult to force legislation through the parliament. In Lithuania, young army officers in Kaunas organized a coup on the pretext of countering a communist plot, with the guiding hand of the nationalist Antonas Smetona, who was subsequently elected president, with the silent support of the Christian Democrats (see Smith *et al.* 2002).
4 Later on Fischer seems to have dropped his interest in the 'centre of gravity' and instead speaks of a wider 'continental Europe'. This vision also includes Turkey in order to create a weighty enough EU capable of responding to the pressures of global competition (*Helsingin Sanomat* 2 March 2004).
5 A prime example is the manner in which the Italian prime minister, Silvio Berlusconi, saluted Russia's policies in Chechnya during Italy's EU presidency (autumn 2003). Berlusconi's statements damaged the Union's relatively consistent policy of

expressing concern for the alleged human rights violations by the Russian troops in Chechnya.

5 New semi-insiders I: Estonia

1 It seems that the Russophone people of Estonia held more pessimistic images than ethnic Estonians of the impact of Estonia's EU membership on their own everyday lives (Kivirähk 2003: 15), and on the country's overall economic development (Vetik 2001: 97). However, until July 2001 Russophones showed more support for EU membership than ethnic Estonians. The survey findings were then even for the two groups until July 2003, after which ethnic Estonians' support for membership increased while Russophones' support levels went into a decline. According to an exit poll, 56 per cent of the Russophones eligible for voting and 73 per cent of ethnic Estonians voters said 'yes'. One of the reasons mentioned for the eligible Russophones' different voting pattern is a protest vote to the Estonian government for their treatment, coupled with an adverse reaction against a campaign poster of the Estonian Chamber of Commerce presenting EU membership as a security measure against the historical threat from Russia (Mikkel and Pridham 2004: 741–2).

2 The total volume of the EU's imports from the thirteen candidate countries in 2002 was 143 billion euros and for exports 164 billion euros (European Commission 2004b).

3 Ratification of the Estonian–Russian border treaty seemed close in May 2005 when the Russian side wanted to settle the issue as part of the grand festivities for the sixty years since the end of the Second World War. However, the Estonian Parliament added an introduction to its bill on the border treaty with some references hinting at the Tartu Peace Treaty. The adding of the introduction was deemed by the Russian party a reason to stop the ratification process on its own part.

4 Some observers argue that since then Russia has maintained the trade restrictions by refusing export licences to many Estonian dairy products companies with potential markets in Russia.

5 Earlier versions of the analysis in the rest of the chapter are published in Aalto (2004a) and (2004b). The consulted primary material represents a comprehensive set of official Estonian positions on EU integration presented during a period stretching from the Nice summit of 2000, where the enlargement issue was finally blessed by the Union, to the summer of 2003, when the Convention on the Future of Europe finished its work. The most important source in the material is the Estonian government's document 'Positions of the Estonian Government on the Future of Europe' (Government of Estonia 2003). The primary material also includes a set of nineteen speeches made in 2002–3 by Estonia's representatives at the Convention. In addition, all relevant speeches dealing with the EU and its future shape, made between summer 2000 and summer 2003, were included – speeches by Estonian presidents (Lennart Meri until October 2001, since then Arnold Rüütel), foreign ministers (Toomas Ilves until January 2002, Kristiina Ojuland until February 2005), and the prime minister (Juhan Parts, April 2003–April 2005). A few Estonian documents from autumn 2003 on EU's ND and the neighbourhood policy were also included. On the whole, the material includes both English and Estonian language sources, and a total of sixty documents. Nine expert interviews were also conducted with Estonian policy makers, politicians and observers who are closely involved with EU integration issues. All interviews were conducted in Estonian by the author. One of the interviews was conducted in May 2002, seven in December 2002 and one in February 2003. This material is supported by a selection of key speeches made by members of the Estonian EU elite on the subject of European integration from the late 1990s.

6 I first read through the primary material and simultaneously coded each individual document along the lines suggested in the theoretical model (Chapter 3), highlighting the manner in which time, space, geo-policy and geo-strategy aspects come up, if at

all, in each individual document. Second, I examined in more detail all material that was found to be related to each aspect, in order to find out the dominant construction along each aspect. In this more detailed analysis, the statements in the document 'Positions . . .' (see previous note) were considered the most pivotal ones. Third, I contrasted the findings from the primary material along each aspect with previous research outlining developments since the 1990s. The overall findings that were obtained by following this three-stage procedure are reported in the next section.

7 Of course, it could also be claimed that Estonia's very smallness dictates the take-it-or-leave-it attitude towards EU integration. However, the material surveyed for this paper indicates that EU integration *is* fairly often defended through references to a choice of either staying in the past or embracing the future. However, eurosceptic arguments conspicuously often raise the issue of Estonia's smallness in order to defend the position for staying outside (Estonia being a small, dynamic and flexible state that can well adjust to global flows of capital, etc. without EU integration; for more, see Chapter 9).

6 New semi-insiders II: Latvia

1 The Russian-speakers within Latvia's poor eastern region of Latgale voted mostly against joining. In the city of Daugavpils, where ethnic Latvians constitute only 14 per cent, 67 per cent voted 'no'. However, in some western districts such as Kurzeme, where Russophones constitute more than 40 per cent, the vote was overwhelmingly 'yes' for membership (Mikkel and Pridham 2004: 743–4). Immediately after the country's 'yes' vote, the Russian-speakers organized a protest rally against the Latvian state and its plans to reduce Russian-language tuition in education. However, this was not explicitly an anti-EU rally, but rather organized against the inter-ethnic policies of the Latvian state, which according to these people had failed to look after their well-being and instead focused on easing the ethnic Latvians' Russian fears by means of EU membership.

2 The material includes altogether fifty-five documents, which form a comprehensive set of official Latvian positions on EU integration presented during a period stretching from the Nice summit of 2000, where the enlargement issue was finally blessed by the Union, to the aftermath of the summer of 2003, when the Convention on the Future of Europe finished its work. This includes the most important guideline documents; a set of fifteen speeches and comments made by Latvia's representatives in the European Convention; relevant speeches on the EU and its future shape by the Latvian president Vaira Vīķe-Freiberga (1999–), the foreign ministers Sandra Kalniete (November 2002–February 2004) and Indulis Bērziņš (July 1999–November 2002), and other representatives of the Latvian Ministry of Foreign Affairs; and the Latvian prime ministers Andris Bērziņš (May 2000–November 2002) and Einars Repše (November 2002–February 2004), In addition, eight interviews were held in December 2002 with Latvian EU experts ranging from policy makers to observers and scholars. All this material is contrasted to previous research.

3 The analysis was made in a similar manner to the Estonian case analysis (see note 6, Chapter 5). The same methodological remarks as introduced in the previous chapter on the material and its applicability in determining the accession country views apply also here.

7 New semi-insiders III: Lithuania

1 In 1992, a referendum was organized in which the majority of the Lithuanian public voted for the linking of the troop withdrawal and compensation issues. In 2000, the Lithuanian Parliament or *Seimas* approved a Law on Indemnity for Occupation by

the Soviet Socialist Republics, which obliges each Lithuanian government to demand compensation (Vesa and Möller 2003: 49).

2 They include the following bodies with meetings twice a year: the Consulting Committee of the Presidents of Lithuania and Poland; the United Assembly of the Members of the Parliaments of Lithuania and Poland; the Council of Cooperation between the Governments of Lithuania and Poland.

3 However, note that the Lithuanian president, Valdas Adamkus, has time and again repeated in his speeches how it still takes seven to eight hours to travel by train the 300 km distance from Vilnius to Riga, and ten hours from Warsaw to Vilnius, whereas before the Second World War it only took three hours to cover the same distance (!) (Adamkus 2002a).

4 In the thirteenth century the Teutonic knights conquered the northern part of East Prussia, of which the present Kaliningradian territory is historically part. Lithuanian settlers were later on allowed into the area when the number of German settlers diminished. During the sixteenth century the area acknowledged the supremacy of the king of Poland (Wörster 1995: 156–8).

5 This area is the former northern strip of East Prussia, called Memel until annexation by Lithuania in 1923 after League of Nations administration since 1919. It was occupied by Nazi Germany during the Second World War. In 1945 the area was made part of the Lithuanian SSR.

6 Earlier the EU had already committed 165 million euros. Fifty million euros was also pledged by other donor states (Ministry of Foreign Affairs of Lithuania 2004).

7 The material includes altogether fifty documents, which form a comprehensive set of official Lithuanian positions on EU integration presented during a period stretching from the Nice summit of 2000, where the enlargement issue was finally blessed by the Union, to the aftermath of the summer of 2003, when the Convention on the Future of Europe finished its work. This includes the main governmental documents; four speeches by Lithuania's representatives in the European Convention; relevant speeches on the EU and its future shape by the Lithuanian presidents Valdas Adamkus (1998–February 2003; July 2004–) and Rolandas Paksas (February 2003–April 2004; see note 9), the foreign minister, Antanas Valionis, and other representatives of the Lithuanian Ministry of Foreign Affairs, and the Lithuanian prime minister Algirdas Brazauskas (July 2001–). In addition, nine interviews were conducted in November 2002 with Lithuanian EU experts ranging from policy makers to observers and scholars. All this material is contrasted to previous research.

8 The analysis was made in a similar manner to the Estonian and Latvian case analyses (see note 6, Chapter 5). The same methodological remarks as introduced in Chapter 5 on the material and its applicability in determining the accession country views apply also here.

9 Paksas was removed from office amid allegations of his having as prime minister granted citizenship on shaky grounds to a Russian businessman who eventually supported his presidential campaign financially. Paksas was replaced by caretaker president Artūras Paulauskas from April to July 2004 and then succeeded by Adamkus after early presidential elections.

8 From close outsiders to semi-outsiders? Russia and its northwestern regions

1 In 2001, a new Federal Programme until 2010 was devised for Kaliningrad, envisaging funding to the value of 3.1 billion US dollars, of which 8 per cent would come from the federal budget directly and the rest from the regional budget, Kaliningradian enterprises, loans and other sources such as state-owned companies (Joenniemi and Sergounin 2003: 101–2). After initial difficulties in obtaining the full amount of planned state contributions, the situation seems to have improved. According to Russia's minister for economic development, German Gref, the 2004 total budget for the

region was 1.2 billion US dollars, over twice the figure in the previous year (Rosbalt 2003g).

2 Several authors comment that an obvious competitor, St Petersburg and the surrounding Leningrad district, is so strongly related to the imperial heritage of Russia that prospects for its independent profile-lifting vis-à-vis the EU are not particularly promising (e.g. Hedenskog 2002; Morozov 2002).

3 The material includes altogether forty primary documents that cover well Russia's European policy from the turn of the millennium to the end of 2003. This includes the key documents, President Putin's key speeches on Russia's European and EU relations, speeches and articles by Russian foreign policy makers such as the foreign minister, Igor Ivanov, and other high-ranking officials. In addition, one interview was made in November 2002 with a Russian foreign policy maker and eight EU experts in Kaliningrad, including politicians, officials and observers. News items, conference proceedings and previous literature were also used.

4 In July 2002 the European Commission announced that, depending on Russia's plans for Kaliningrad's future, the Union was ready to allocate another 25 million euros for developing small and medium-sized businesses in Kaliningrad. It was initially hinted that the amount could be paid into a special fund, an arrangement preferred by the Kaliningrad regional administration and some independent experts (e.g. Dewar 2001; Rosbalt 2003i). However, in 2003 it was announced that the fund would be channelled through TACIS, meaning that about 80 per cent of it would go to Western/European consultants, not into investment (Rosbalt 2003i, j; European Commission 2002b).

5 This was declared by the governor of the *oblast'*, Vladimir Egorov, in September 2003. In addition to the FTD-based train service, Kaliningraders can take a ferry to St Petersburg without having to show a passport or sort out a visa. The ferry leaves every other day from the town of Baltiisk. The Russian airline company Aeroflot and the Kaliningrad regional administration have also signed a two-year agreement on a flight connection. The cost of a return flight is less than 30 US dollars and there are four flights a day (Rosbalt 2003k).

6 During 1991–9, the TACIS programme distributed just under 1.3 billion euros in total, and for 2004–6 the allocated amount is 392 million euros (European Commission 2000, 2003f). Even from these figures, which are unlikely to have major impact in a vast country like Russia, about 80 per cent goes for hiring European consultants to prepare various technical recommendations for Russia, and only 20 per cent for investments. However, in this context it is also noteworthy that in the new millennium an increasing share of the funds has gone to reforms carried out by the Russian government, rather than to the promotion of activities that presumably could promote Russia's applicability for deeper EU integration, like civil society education and training actions (Bordachev 2003: 48).

9 Future prospects of an EU-led wider northern Europe

1 In a carefully conducted Q methodological study, neither the detailed composition of the Q sample nor the participant group is likely to affect the final research results. For example, Thomas and Baas (1992/3) compiled, each one individually, separate samples of the same statement universe and proceeded with separate participant groups. Yet their separately arranged Q studies yielded practically the same results.

2 One experiment was conducted as a face-to-face session in February 2003. In two further cases the Q sort material was obtained by distributing instructions by mail.

3 Centroid factor extraction and judgmental rotation were used as is common in Q methodology.

4 As with any of the thirty-six Q sorts here, factor scores range from –5 through 0 to +5. They indicate how an 'idealized' representative of the factor, with a factor loading of 1.0, would score the statements. Factor interpretation involves comparing the scores

that the factor gives to statements dealing with a given area of theoretical or empirical interest, and on that basis determining how the statements are grouped on each factor (e.g. 'factor A rejects statements x, y and z and supports statements a, b, and c', etc.).

5   Only those statements are displayed in Table 9.3 as consensus statements that receive either a notably positive or a notably negative score. Scores around 0 are assumed to manifest either indifference or too much complexity or ambiguity within the statement to the participant. Because such diverse reasons may lead a participant to place a particular statement under or around the 0 mark, in most cases it is not meaningful to speculate what the consensus statements formed in this manner – receiving seemingly 'neutral' scores' – actually signify.

6   The numbers in parentheses refer to statements in the factor scores table and the factor scores they receive on this factor (Appendix).

Bibliography

Books, chapters and articles

Aalto, P. (1997) 'Post-Soviet ethnic conflicts and the level of everyday life', *Finnish Review of East European Studies*, 4: 8–27.

—— (2002a) 'A European geopolitical subject in the making? EU, Russia and the Kaliningrad question', *Geopolitics*, 7: 143–74.

—— (2002b) 'The European empire and Russia: solving the "Kaliningrad puzzle"?', *Íslenska leiðin – tímarit stjórnmálafræðinema*, 2: 28–30.

—— (2003a) 'Revisiting the security/identity puzzle in Russo-Estonian relations', *Journal of Peace Research*, 40: 573–91.

—— (2003b) *Constructing Post-Soviet Geopolitics in Estonia*, London: Frank Cass.

—— (2003c) 'Post-Soviet geopolitics in the north of Europe', in M. Lehti and D. Smith (eds) *Post-Cold War Identity Politics: northern and Baltic experiences*, London: Frank Cass.

—— (2004a) 'Estonian views of the EU as a north European power', in E. Rindzeviciute (ed.) *Contemporary Change in Estonia*, Huddinge: Baltic & East European Graduate School.

—— (2004b) 'European Union's "Wider Northern Europe" and Estonia', in A. Kasekamp (ed.) *The Estonian Foreign Policy Yearbook 2004*, Tallinn: The Estonian Foreign Policy Institute.

Aalto, P. and Berg, E. (2002) 'Spatial practices and time in Estonia: from post-Soviet geopolitics to European governance', *Space and Polity*, 6: 253–70.

Aalto, P., Dalby, S. and Harle, V. (2003) 'The critical geopolitics of northern Europe: identity politics unlimited', *Geopolitics*, 8: 1–19.

Adler, E. (1997) 'Seizing the middle ground: constructivism in world politics', *European Journal of International Relations*, 3: 319–63.

Archer, C. (2002) 'The EU foreign policy in the context of the Baltic Sea region', in H. Hubel (ed.), with A. Bannwart and S. Gänzle, *EU Enlargement and Beyond: the Baltic States and Russia*, Berlin: Berlin Verlag.

Arter, D. (2000) 'Small state influence within the EU: the case of Finland's Northern Dimension initiative', *Journal of Common Market Studies*, 38: 677–97.

Bach, J. and Peters, S. (2002) 'The new spirit of German geopolitics', *Geopolitics*, 7: 1–18.

Baranovsky, V. (2002) *Russia's Attitudes towards the EU: political aspects*, Helsinki and Berlin: UPI-FIIA and Institut für Europäische Politik.

Batt, J. (rapporteur) (1999) 'Final report of the Reflection Group on the long-term implications of EU enlargement: the nature of the new border', Florence: European University Institute.

Berg, E. (2002) 'Schengeni leppega liitumise mõju Eestile', *Praxis Poliitikanalüüs*, 2/2002.

Bordachev, T.V. (2003) 'Strategy and strategies', in A. Moshes (ed.) *Rethinking the Respective Strategies of Russia and the European Union*, Helsinki and Moscow: UPI-FIIA and Carnegie Moscow Center.

Borko, I. (2003) *Ot evropeiskoi idei – k edinoi Evrope*, Moscow: Delovaia literatura.

Bort, E. (2000) 'Under the shadow of Schengen: the borders of Central and Eastern Europe', mimeo, University of Edinburgh.

Broks, J. (2001) 'National and regional integration', in A. Tabuns (ed.) *National, State and Regime Identity in Latvia*, Riga: Baltic Study Centre.

Brown, S.R. (1980) *Political Subjectivity: applications of Q methodology in political science*, New Haven: Yale University Press.

—— (1986) 'Q technique and method: principles and procedures', in W.D. Berry and M.S. Lewis-Beck (eds) *New Tools for Social Scientists: advances and applications in research methods*, Beverly Hills: Sage.

Browning, C.S. (2001) 'A multi-dimensional approach to regional co-operation: the United States and the Northern European Initiative', *European Security*, 10: 84–108.

—— (2002) 'Coming home or moving home? "Westernizing" narratives in Finnish foreign policy and the reinterpretation of past identities', *Cooperation and Conflict*, 37: 47–72.

—— (2005a) 'Westphalian, imperial, neomedieval: the geopolitics of Europe and the role of the north', in C.S. Browning (ed.) *Remaking Europe in the Margins: northern Europe after the enlargements*, Aldershot: Ashgate.

—— (2005b) 'Introduction: remaking Europe at the margins', in C.S. Browning (ed.) *Remaking Europe in the Margins: northern Europe after the enlargements*, Aldershot: Ashgate.

Browning, C.S. and Joenniemi, P. (2003) 'The European Union's two dimensions: the eastern and the northern', *Security Dialogue*, 34: 463–79.

—— (2004a) 'Regionality beyond security? The Baltic Sea region after enlargement', *Cooperation and Conflict*, 39: 233–53.

—— (2004b) 'Introduction: The challenges of EU and NATO enlargement', *Cooperation and Conflict*, 39: 227–31.

Caporaso, J.A. (1996) 'The European Union and forms of state: Westphalian, regulatory or postmodern?', *Journal of Common Market Studies*, 34: 29–52.

Cecchini, P., Jones, E. and Lorentzen, J. (2001) 'Europe and the concept of enlargement', *Survival*, 43: 155–65.

Christiansen, T., Petito, F. and Tonra, B. (2000) 'Fuzzy politics around fuzzy borders: the European Union's "near abroad"', *Cooperation and Conflict*, 35: 389–415.

Clover, C. (1999) 'Dreams of the Eurasian heartland: the reemergence of geopolitics', *Foreign Affairs*, 78: 9–13.

DeBardeleben, J. (2005) 'Multilevel governance and centralization in Russia: implications for EU–Russian relations', paper presented at the ICCEES conference, Berlin, 25–30 July.

Dewar, S. (2001) 'Kaliningrad needs a special development fund', in R. Grönick, M. Kulmala and L. Päiviö (eds) *Kaliningrad –Isolation or Co-operation?*, Helsinki: Finnish Committee for European Security.

Deriabin, I. (2000) *'Severnoe Izmerenie' politiki Evropeiskogo soiuza i interesy Rossii*, Moscow: Ekslibris-Press.

Diez, T. and Whitman, R. (2002) 'Analysing European integration: reflecting on the English school – scenarios for an encounter', *Journal of Common Market Studies*, 40: 43–67.

Duchêne, F. (1973) 'The European Community and the uncertainties of interdependence', in M. Kohnstamm and W. Hager (eds) *A Nation Writ Large? Foreign policy problems in the European Community*, Basingstoke: Macmillan.

van Elsuwege, P. (2002) 'The Baltic states on the road to EU accession: opportunities and challenges', *European Foreign Affairs Review*, 7: 171–92.

Fairley, L.D. (2001) 'Kaliningrad borders in regional context', in L. Fairley and A. Sergounin, *Are Borders Barriers? EU enlargement and the Russian region of Kaliningrad*, Helsinki and Berlin: UPI-FIIA and Institut für Europäische Politik.

Fairley, L.D. and Sergounin, A. (2001) *Are Borders Barriers? EU enlargement and the Russian region of Kaliningrad*, Helsinki and Berlin: UPI-FIIA and Institut für Europäische Politik.

Filtenborg, M.S., Gänzle, S. and Johansson, E. (2002) 'An alternative approach to EU foreign policy: "network governance" and the case of the Northern Dimension', *Cooperation and Conflict*, 37: 387–407.

Forsberg, T. (2004) 'The EU–Russia security partnership: why the opportunity was missed', *European Foreign Affairs Review*, 9: 247–67.

Friis, L. and Murphy, A. (1999) 'The European Union and Central and Eastern Europe: governance and boundaries', *Journal of Common Market Studies*, 37: 211–32.

Fuchs, D. and Klingemann, H.-D. (2002) 'Eastward enlargement of the European Union and the identity of Europe', *West European Politics*, 25: 19–54.

Gänzle, S. (2002) 'The EU's presence and actorness in the Baltic Sea area: multilevel governance beyond its external borders', in H. Hubel (ed.), with A. Bannwart and S. Gänzle, *EU Enlargement and Beyond: the Baltic States and Russia*, Berlin: Berlin Verlag.

Gänzle, S. and Hubel, H. (2002) 'The Council of the Baltic Sea States and the EU: dealing with soft security risks in a European subregion', in H. Hubel (ed.), with A. Bannwart and S. Gänzle, *EU Enlargement and Beyond: the Baltic States and Russia*, Berlin: Berlin Verlag.

George, S. (1998) *An Awkward Partner: Britain in the European Community*, Oxford: Oxford University Press.

Ginsberg, R.H. (1998) 'Conceptualizing the European Union as an international actor: narrowing the theoretical capability–expectations gap', *Journal of Common Market Studies*, 37: 429–54.

Glarbo, K. (1999) 'Wide-awake diplomacy: reconstructing the common foreign and security policy of the European Union', *Journal of European Public Policy*, 6: 634–51.

Goloubeva, M. and Ieleja, D. (2004) 'Conceptualising the fear of losing national identity as a result of European integration: the case of Latvia', in J. Stampehl, D. Brekenfeld, A. Bannwart and U. Plath (eds) *Perceptions of Loss, Decline, and Doom in the Baltic Sea Area*, Berlin: Berliner Wissenschaftsverlag.

Grabbe, H. (2000) 'The sharp edges of Europe: extending Schengen eastwards', *International Affairs*, 76: 519–36.

Hallik, K. (2002) 'Nationalising policies and integration challenges', in M. Lauristin and M. Heidmets (eds) *The Challenge of the Russian Minority: emerging multicultural democracy in Estonia*, Tartu: Tartu University Press.

Hallstrom, L.K. (2003) 'Support for European federalism? An elite view', *European Integration*, 25: 51–72.

van Ham, P. (1999) 'The Baltic States and Europe: identity and institutions', in O.F. Knudsen (ed.) *Stability and Security in the Baltic Sea Region: Russian, Nordic and European aspects*, London: Frank Cass.

Hansen, L. (2002) 'Sustaining sovereignty: the Danish approach to Europe', in L. Hansen and O. Wæver (eds) *European Integration and National Identity*, London: Routledge.

Haukkala, H. (2001a) 'The making of the European Union's Common Strategy on Russia', in H. Haukkala and S. Medvedev (eds) *The EU Common Strategy on Russia: learning the grammar of the CFSP*, Helsinki and Berlin: UPI-FIIA and Institut für Europäische Politik.

—— (2001b) 'Two reluctant regionalizers? The European Union and Russia in Europe's new north', *UPI Working Papers*, 32/2001.

—— (2001c) 'Pohjoinen ulottuvuus "kaunis pakkaus"?' *Aamulehti*, 7 November 2001.

—— (2003a) 'A problematic "strategic partnership"', in D. Lynch (ed.) *EU–Russian Security Dimensions*, Paris: European Union Institute for Security Studies.

—— (2003b) 'A hole in the wall? Dimensionalism and the EU's "new Neighbourhood Policy"', *UPI Working Papers*, 41/2003.

Hedegaard, L. and Lindström, B. (2003) 'The NEBI area ten years later', in L. Hedegaard and B. Lindström (eds) *The NEBI Yearbook: north European and Baltic Sea integration*, Berlin: Springer.

Hedenskog, J. (2002) 'Windows onto Europe or Russian dead ends? The federal centre and the foreign relations of Russia's western regions', in L. Hedegaard and B. Lindström (eds) *The NEBI Yearbook 2001/2002: north European and Baltic Sea integration*, Berlin: Springer.

Heffernan, M. (1998) *The Meaning of Europe: geography and geopolitics*, London: Arnold.

Herrberg, A. (1998) 'The European Union and Russia: toward a new *Ostpolitik*?', in C. Rhodes (ed.) *The European Union in the World Community*, Boulder: Lynne Rienner.

Hill, C. (1993) 'The capability–expectations gap, or conceptualizing Europe's international role', *Journal of Common Market Studies*, 31: 305–28.

Hill, C. and Wallace, W. (1996) 'Introduction: actors and actions', in C. Hill (ed.) *The Actors in Europe's Foreign Policy: key documents*, London: Routledge.

Hobsbawm, Eric (1992) *Nations and Nationalism since 1780: programme, myth, reality*, Cambridge: Cambridge University Press.

Hoffman, S. (2000) 'Towards a Common European Foreign and Security Policy', *Journal of Common Market Studies*, 38: 189–98.

Holtom, P. (2002) 'Kaliningrad in 2001: from periphery to pilot region', in P. Holtom and F. Tassinari (eds) *Russian Participation in Baltic Sea Region-Building: a case study on Kaliningrad*, Gdansk and Berlin: Wydawnictwo Uniwersytetu Gdańskiego and Nordeuropa-Institut der Humboldt-Universität zu Berlin.

Hubel, H. (1999) 'The European Union, the Baltic States and post-Soviet Russia: theoretical problems and possibilities for developing partnership relations in the north-eastern Baltic Sea region', in O.F. Knudsen (ed.) *Stability and Security in the Baltic Sea Region: Russian, Nordic and European aspects*, London: Frank Cass.

—— (2002) 'The European Union in the Baltic Sea area – a general perspective', in H. Hubel (ed.), with A. Bannwart and S. Gänzle, *EU Enlargement and Beyond: the Baltic States and Russia*, Berlin: Berlin Verlag.

—— (2004a) 'The EU's three-level game in dealing with neighbours', *European Foreign Affairs Review*, 9: 347–62.

—— (2004b) 'The Baltic Sea region after dual enlargement', *Cooperation and Conflict*, 39: 283–98.

Ingebritsen, C. (1998) *The Nordic States and European Unity*, Ithaca, NY: Cornell University Press.

Istituto Affari Internazionali (ed.) (2003) *Convention Watch*, Rome: Istituto Affari Internazionali.

Jachtenfuchs, M. (2001) 'The governance approach to European integration', *Journal of Common Market Studies*, 39: 245–64.

Jæger, Ø. (1997) 'Securitising Russia: discursive practices of the Baltic States', *COPRI Working Papers*, 10/1997.

Jauhiainen, J. (2002) 'Territoriality and topocracy of cross-border networks', *Journal of Baltic Studies*, 33: 156–76.

Joenniemi, P. (1993) 'The Baltic countries as deviant cases: small states in search of foreign policies', in P. Joenniemi and P. Vares (eds) *New Actors on the International Arena: the foreign policies of the Baltic countries*, Tampere: TAPRI.

—— (1995) 'Regionality: a sovereign principle of international relations?', in H. Patomäki (ed.) *Peaceful Changes in World Politics*, Tampere: TAPRI.

—— (2002) 'Finland in the new Europe: a Herderian or a Hegelian Project?', in L. Hansen and O. Wæver (eds) *European Integration and National Identity*, London: Routledge.

Joenniemi, P. and Lehti, M. (2003) 'The encounter between the Nordic and the northern: torn apart but meeting again?', in M. Lehti and D.J. Smith (eds) *Post-Cold War Identity Politics: northern and Baltic experiences*, London: Frank Cass.

Joenniemi, P. and Prawitz, J. (1998) 'Kaliningrad: a double periphery?', in P. Joenniemi and J. Prawitz (eds) *Kaliningrad: the European amber region*, Aldershot: Ashgate.

Joenniemi, P. and Sergounin, A. (2003) *Russia and the European Union's Northern Dimension: encounter or a clash of civilisations?*, Nizhny Novgorod: Nizhny Novgorod Linguistic University Press.

Joenniemi, P., Dewar, S. and Fairlie, L.D. (2000) 'The Kaliningrad Puzzle: a Russian region within the European Union', *COPRI Working Papers*, 6/2000.

Joerges, C., Mény, Y. and Weiler, J.H.H. (eds) (2000) *What Kind of a Constitution for What Kind of Polity? Responses to Joschka Fischer*, Florence and Cambridge, MA: Robert Schuman Centre for Advanced Studies, EUI and Harvard Law School.

Johansson, E. (2002) 'EU foreign policy and subregionalization in North-Eastern Europe', in H. Hubel (ed.), with A. Bannwart and S. Gänzle, *EU Enlargement and Beyond: the Baltic States and Russia*, Berlin: Berlin Verlag.

Käkönen, J. (1996) 'Regionalisation and power in the Baltic Sea region', in S. Perko (ed.) *Nordic–Baltic Region in Transition: new actors, new issues, new perspectives,* Tampere: TAPRI.

Karvonen, L. and Sundelius, B. (1996) 'The Nordic neutrals: facing the European Union', in L. Miles (ed.) *The European Union and the Nordic Countries*, London: Routledge.

Kasekamp, A. (2005) 'The north-east', in H. Mouritzen and A. Wivel (eds) *The Geopolitics of Euro-Atlantic Integration*, London: Routledge.

Kelstrup, M. (2000) 'Danish integration dilemmas and options', *COPRI Working Papers*, 18/2000.

Khlopetskii, A. and Fedorov, G. (2000) *Kaliningradskaia oblast': region sotrudnichestva*, Kaliningrad: Iantarnyi skaz.

Khudoley, K. (2003) 'Russia and the European Union: new opportunities, new challenges', in A. Moshes (ed.) *Rethinking the Respective Strategies of Russia and the European Union*, Helsinki and Moscow: UPI-FIIA and Carnegie Moscow Center.

Kivirähk, J. (2003) 'Avalik arvamus Eesti liitumisest Euroopa Liiduga: ülevaade avaliku arvamuse küsitluse tulemustest', Tallinn: Uuringukeskus Faktum.

Klemeshev, A.P. and Fedorov, G. (2002) 'Perspektivy formirovaniia i rasvitiia kaliningradskogo sotsiuma', in A.P. Klemeshev (ed.) *Kaliningradskii sotsium v evropeiskom kontekste*, Kaliningrad: Izd-vo KGU.

Knudsen, O.F. (1999) 'Security on the great power fringe: dilemmas old and new', in O.F. Knudsen (ed.) *Stability and Security in the Baltic Sea Region: Russian, Nordic and European aspects*, London: Frank Cass.

Komulainen, T., Korhonen, V., Lainela, S. Rautava, J. and Sutela, P. (2004) 'Venäjän talous Putinin aikana', *BOFIT Online*, 4/2004. Online. Available at http://www.bof.fi/bofit/fin/7online/04abs/04pdf/bon0404.pdf (accessed 25 January 2005).

Kortunov, S. (2003) 'Kaliningrad and Russia – Europe partnership', *International Affairs* (Moscow), 49: 111–31.

Kristinsson, G.H. (1996) 'Iceland and the European Union: non-decision on membership', in L. Miles (ed.) *The European Union and the Nordic Countries*, London: Routledge.

Kuus, M. (2002a) 'European integration in identity narratives in Estonia: a quest for security', *Journal of Peace Research* 39: 91–108.

—— (2002b) 'Toward cooperative security? International integration and the construction of security in Estonia', *Millennium: Journal of International Studies*, 31: 297–317.

Lagerspetz, M. (1999) 'Post-socialism as a return: notes on a discursive strategy', *East European Politics and Societies*, 13: 377–90.

Lane, T. (2002) 'Lithuania: stepping westward', in D.J. Smith, A. Pabriks, A. Purs and T. Lane (2002) *The Baltic States: Estonia, Latvia and Lithuania*, part III, London: Routledge.

Laurila, J. (2003) 'Transit transport between Russia and the European Union in light of geopolitics and economics', *Emerging Markets Finance and Trade*, 39: 27–57.

Lauristin, M. and Vihalemm, P. with Rosengren, K.E. and Weibull, L. (eds) (1997) *Return to the Western World: cultural and political perspectives on the Estonian post-communist transition*, Tartu: Tartu University Press.

Lausala, T. (2002) 'The role of energy in the Northern Dimension', in L. Heininen (ed.) *Northern Borders and Security – dimensions for regional cooperation and interdependence*, Turku: Turku School of Economics and Business Administration, Business Research and Development Centre.

Lehti, M. (2004) 'Challenging the "old" Europe: Estonia and Latvia in a "new" Europe', paper presented at the Fifth Pan-European International Relations Conference, The Hague, 9–11 September 2004.

Leito, V. (2002) *Eesti & geopoliitika: iseseisev Eesti Vabariik või Euroopa Liidu uuskoloniseeritud provints?*, Tallinn: OÜ Mandala.

Leito, V. and Silberg, U. (1998) *Euroopa Liit tagantvaates: kõige tähtsamat varjatakse*, Tallinn: TEE toimkond Ei Euroopa Liidule.

Lejinš, A. (2002) 'Latvia and EU enlargement', in H. Hubel (ed.), with A. Bannwart and S. Gänzle, *EU Enlargement and Beyond: the Baltic States and Russia*, Berlin: Berlin Verlag.

Leshukov, I. (2000) 'Northern Dimension: interests and perceptions', in A. Lejinš and J-D. Nackmayr (eds) *The Northern Dimension: an assessment and future development*, Riga: Konrad Adenauer Stiftung and Latvian Institute of International Affairs.

Malcolm, N. (1991) 'The soviet concept of a Common European House', in J. Iivonen (ed.) *The Changing Soviet Union in the New Europe*, Aldershot: Edward Elgar.

Manners, I. (2002) 'Normative Power Europe: a contradiction in terms', *Journal of Common Market Studies*, 40: 235–58.

Marcussen, M., Risse, T., Engelmann-Martin, D.E., Knopf, H.J. and Roschler, K. (1999) 'Constructing Europe? The evolution of French, British and German nation state discourses', *Journal of European Public Policy*, 6: 614–33.

Mariussen, Å. (2002) 'Sustainable fragmentation: regional organizations in the North', in L. Hedegaard and B. Lindström (eds) *The NEBI Yearbook 2001/2002: north European and Baltic Sea integration*, Berlin: Springer.

Marsh, C. (1998) 'Realigning Lithuanian foreign relations', *Journal of Baltic Studies*, 29: 149–64.

Medrano, J.D. (1999) 'The European Union: economic giant, political dwarf', in T.V. Paul and J.A. Hall (eds) *International Order and the Future of World Politics*, Cambridge: University Press.

Medvedev, S. (1998) 'Catholic Europe, marginal Russia, and postmodern north: an essay on the origins and limits of the European project', *Northern Dimensions*, 1998: 44–61.

—— (2001) '[the _blank_space] Glenn Gould, Finland, Russia and the North', *International Politics: a journal of transnational issues and global problems*, 38: 91–102.

Mikkel, E. and Pridham, G. (2004) 'Clinching the "return to Europe": the referendums on EU accession in Estonia and Latvia', *West European Politics*, 27: 716–48.

Miles, L. (1996) 'The Nordic countries and the fourth EU enlargement', in L. Miles (ed.) *The European Union and the Nordic Countries*, London: Routledge.

Miljan, T. (1977) *The Reluctant Europeans – the attitudes of the Nordic countries towards European integration*, London: Hurst.

Miniotaitė, G. (2001) 'The Baltic states: in search of security and identity', *COPRI Working Papers*, 14/2001.

—— (2003) 'Convergent geography and divergent identities: a decade of transformation in the Baltic States', *Cambridge Review of International Affairs*, 16: 209–22.

Moisio, S. (2002) 'EU eligibility, Central Europe, and the invention of applicant state narrative', *Geopolitics*, 7: 89–116.

—— (2003a) *Geopoliittinen kamppailu Suomen EU-jäsenyydestä*, Turku: University of Turku (series C 204).

—— (2003b) 'Back to Baltoscandia? European Union and geo-conceptual remaking of the European north', *Geopolitics*, 8: 72–100.

Morozov, V. (2002) 'The discourses of St. Petersburg and the shaping of a wider Europe: territory, space and post-sovereign politics', *COPRI Working Papers*, 13/2002.

—— (2003) 'The Baltic states in Russian foreign policy: can Russia become a Baltic country?', in M. Lehti and D.J. Smith (eds) *Post-Cold War Identity Politics: northern and Baltic experiences*, London: Frank Cass.

Moshes, A. (1999) *Overcoming Unfriendly Stability: Russian–Latvian relations at the end of 1990s*, with comments by Aivars Stranga, Helsinki and Berlin: UPI-FIIA and Institut für Europäische Politik.

Mouritzen, H. (1996a) 'Unipolar integration continued: a core–periphery Europe', in H. Mouritzen, O. Wæver and H. Wiberg (eds) *European Integration and National Adaptations: a theoretical inquiry*, Commack: Nova Science Publishers.

—— (1996b) 'A core–periphery Europe – but a shortened version', in H. Mouritzen, O. Wæver and H. Wiberg (eds) *European Integration and National Adaptations: a theoretical inquiry*, Commack: Nova Science Publishers.

—— (1996c) 'Comparative and theoretical insights', in H. Mouritzen, O. Wæver and H. Wiberg (eds) *European Integration and National Adaptations: a theoretical inquiry*, Commack: Nova Science Publishers.

—— (1996d) 'Finland', in H. Mouritzen, O. Wæver and H. Wiberg (eds) *European Integration and National Adaptations: a theoretical inquiry*, Commack: Nova Science Publishers.

—— (1996e) 'Polarity and constellations', in H. Mouritzen, O. Wæver and H. Wiberg (ed.) *European Integration and National Adaptations: a theoretical inquiry*, Commack: Nova Science Publishers.

—— (2001) 'Security communities in the Baltic Sea region: real and imagined', *Security Dialogue*, 32: 297–310.

Mouritzen, H. and Wivel, A. (2005a) 'Constellation theory', in H. Mouritzen and A. Wivel (eds) *The Geopolitics of Euro-Atlantic Integration*, London: Routledge.

—— (2005b) 'Comparative analysis meets theory', in H. Mouritzen and A. Wivel (eds) *The Geopolitics of Euro-Atlantic Integration*, London: Routledge.

—— (2005c) (eds) *The Geopolitics of Euro-Atlantic Integration*, London: Routledge.

Mouritzen, H., Haab, M., Miniotaite, G. and Ozolina, Z. (1998) 'Baltic scenarios for the upcoming decade', in H. Mouritzen (ed.) *Bordering Russia: theory and prospects for Europe's Baltic rim*, Aldershot: Ashgate.

Musial, K. (2002) 'Poland as a Baltic state in the process of joining the EU', in H. Hubel (ed.), with A. Bannwart and S. Gänzle, *EU Enlargement and Beyond: the Baltic States and Russia*, Berlin: Berlin Verlag.

Myers Jaffe, A. and Manning, R.A. (2001) 'Russia, energy and the west', *Survival*, 43: 133–52.

Myrjord, A. (2003) 'Governance beyond the Union: EU boundaries in the Barents Euro-Arctic Region', *European Foreign Affairs Review*, 8: 239–57.

Neumann, I.B. (1994) 'A region-building approach to northern Europe', *Review of International Studies*, 20: 53–74.

—— (1997) 'Ringmar on identity and war', *Cooperation and Conflict*, 32: 309–30.

—— (1998) 'European identity, EU expansion, and the integration/exclusion nexus', *Alternatives*, 23: 397–416.

—— (2002) 'This little piggy stayed at home: why Norway is not a member of the EU', in L. Hansen and O. Wæver (eds) *European Integration and National Identity*, London: Routledge.

Niemeläinen, J. (2002) *Kulttuuriseen kotiin: miten Toomas Hendrik Ilves ja Mart Laar rakensivat Virosta pohjoismaata*, unpublished Master's thesis, Tampere: University of Tampere.

Nissinen, M. (1999) *Latvia's Transition to a Market Economy: political determinants of economic reform policy*, Basingstoke: Macmillan.

Oldberg, I. (1998) 'Kaliningrad: problems and prospects', in P. Joenniemi and J. Prawitz (eds) *Kaliningrad: the European amber region*, Aldershot: Ashgate.

—— (2000) 'The emergence of a regional identity in the Kaliningrad oblast', *Cooperation and Conflict*, 35: 269–88.

Østergaard, U. (1997) 'The geopolitics of Nordic identity – from composite states to nation states', in Ø. Sørensen and B. Stråth (eds) *The Cultural Construction of Norden*, Copenhagen: Scandinavian University Press..

Ozhobishchev, S.K. and Iurgens, I.Iu. (eds) (2001) *Rossiia – Baltiia: doklady SVOP: materialy konferentsii*, Moscow: Izdatel'skii tsentr nauchnyh i uchebnyh programm.

Ozolina, Z. (1998) 'Latvia', in H. Mouritzen (ed.) *Bordering Russia: theory and prospects for Europe's Baltic rim*, Aldershot: Ashgate.

—— (1999) 'The impact of the European Union on Baltic co-operation', *COPRI Working Papers*, 3/1999.

—— [Ozoliņa, Ž.] (2003) 'The EU and the Baltic States', in A. Lieven and D. Trenin (eds) *Ambivalent Neighbours: the EU, NATO and the price of membership*, Washington: Carnegie Center for International Peace.

Pabriks, A. and Purs, A. (2002) 'Latvia: the challenges of change', in D.J. Smith, A. Pabriks, A. Purs and T. Lane, *The Baltic States: Estonia, Latvia and Lithuania*, part II, London: Routledge.

Panagiotou, E. (2001) 'Estonia's success: prescription or legacy?', *Communist and Post-Communist Studies*, 34: 261–77.

Parker, N. and Armstrong, B. (2000) 'Preface', in N. Parker and B. Armstrong (eds) *Margins in European Integration*, Basingstoke: Macmillan.

Pavlovaite, I. (2003) 'Paradise regained: the conceptualisation of Europe in the Lithuanian debate', in M. Lehti and D.J. Smith (eds) *Post-Cold War Identity Politics: northern and Baltic experiences*, London: Frank Cass.

Peters, S. (2003) 'Courting future resource conflict: the shortcomings of Western response strategies to new energy vulnerabilities', *Energy Exploration and Exploitation*, 21: 29–60.

Pettai, V. (2003) 'Introduction: historic and historical aspects of Baltic accession to the European Union', in V. Pettai and J. Zielonka (eds) *The Road to the European Union, vol. 2: Estonia, Latvia and Lithunia*, Manchester: Manchester University Press.

Pinder, J. (2002) 'The Union's economic policies towards Russia', in J. Pinder and Yu. Shiskov, *The EU and Russia: the promise of partnership*, London: Federal Trust.

Pynnöniemi, K. (2003) 'Russian foreign policy think tanks in 2002', *UPI Working Papers*, 38/2003.

Raik, K. (1999) 'Estonian perspectives on the Northern Dimension', in H. Haukkala (ed.) *Dynamic Aspects of the Northern Dimension*, Turku: Jean Monnet Unit, University of Turku.

—— (2003a) 'Does the European Union still matter for Estonia's security? Positioning Estonia in CFSP and ESDP', in A. Kasekamp (ed.) *The Estonian Foreign Policy Yearbook 2003*, Tallinn: Estonian Foreign Policy Institute.

—— (2003b) *Democratic Politics or the Implementation of Inevitabilities? Estonia's democracy and integration into the European Union*, Tartu: Tartu University Press.

Raik, K. and Palosaari, T. (2004) 'Tärkeintä on osallistuminen: uudet jäsenmaat mukautuvat EU:n ulko- ja turvallisuuspolitiikkaan', *UPI-Raportti*, 10/2004.

Rengger, N. (2000) *International Relations, Political Theory and the Problem of Order*, London: Routledge.

Rindzeviciute, E. (2003) '"Nation" and "Europe": re-approaching the debates about Lithuanian national identity', *Journal of Baltic Studies*, 34: 74–91.

Romanova, T. (2004) 'EU–Russian energy dialogue and Northern Dimension' in L. Hedegaard and B. Lindström (eds) *The NEBI Yearbook 2004: north European and Baltic Sea integration*, Berlin: Springer.

Ruggie, J.G. (1993) 'Territoriality and beyond: problematizing modernity in international relations', *International Organization*, 47: 139–74.

Ruutsoo, R. (2001) 'A perspective on the Northern Dimension from the Baltic States', mimeo, University of Tartu.

Rynning, Sten (2003) 'A fragmented external role: the EU, defence policy, and new atlanticism', in M. Knodt and S. Princen (eds) *Understanding the European Union's External Relations*, London: Routledge.

Ščerbinskis, V. (2003) 'Looking for neighbours: origins and developments of Latvian rhetoric on Nordic "closeness"', in M. Lehti and D.J. Smith (eds) *Post-Cold War Identity Politics: northern and Baltic experiences*, London: Frank Cass.

Schimmelfennig, F. (2003) 'Strategic action in a community environment: the decision to enlarge the European Union to the East', *Comparative Political Studies*, 36: 156–83.

Schmalz, U. (2000) 'German ambitions and ambiguities: EU initiatives as a useful framework', in G. Bonvicini, T. Vaahtoranta and W. Wessels (eds) *The Northern EU: national views on the emerging security dimension*, Helsinki and Berlin: UPI-FIIA and Institut für Europäische Politik.

Schmitter, P. (1996) 'Imagining the future of the Euro-polity with the help of new concepts', in G. Marks, F.W. Scharpf, P.C. Schmitter and W. Streeck, *Governance in the European Union*, London: Sage.

Scott, J.W. (2002) 'Baltic Sea regionalism, EU geopolitics and symbolic geographies of co-operation', *Journal of Baltic Studies*, 33: 137–55.

Sergounin, A. (2001) 'EU enlargement and Kaliningrad: the Russian perspective', in L. Fairley and A. Sergounin, *Are Borders Barriers? EU enlargement and the Russian region of Kaliningrad*, Helsinki and Berlin: UPI-FIIA and Institut für Europäische Politik.

Sjursen, H. (2002) 'Why expand? The question of legitimacy and justification in the EU's enlargement policy', *Journal of Common Market Studies*, 40: 491–513.

Smith, A. (2002) 'Imagining geographies of the "new Europe": geo-economic power and the new European architecture of integration', *Political Geography*, 21: 647–70.

Smith, A.D. (1992) 'National identity and the idea of European unity', *International Affairs*, 68: 55–76.

—— (1993) 'A Europe of nations – or the nations of Europe', *Journal of Peace Research*, 30: 129–35.

Smith, D.J. (1998) 'Russia, Estonia and the search for a stable ethno-politics', *Journal of Baltic Studies*, 24: 3–18.

—— (2002) 'Estonia: independence and European integration', in D.J. Smith, A. Pabriks, A. Purs and T. Lane, *The Baltic States: Estonia, Latvia and Lithuania*, part I, London: Routledge.

—— (2003) 'Nordic near abroad or new northern Europe? Perspectives on post-Cold War regional co-operation in the Baltic Sea area', in M. Lehti and D.J. Smith (eds) *Post-Cold War Identity Politics: northern and Baltic Experiences*, London: Frank Cass.

Smith, D.J., Pabriks, A., Purs, A. and Lane, T. (2002) *The Baltic States: Estonia, Latvia and Lithuania*, London: Routledge.

Smith, G. (1999) 'The masks of Proteus: Russia, geopolitical shift and the new eurasianism', *Transactions of the Institute of British Geographers*, 24: 481–94.

Smith, K.E. (2003) *European Union Foreign Policy in a Changing World*, Cambridge: Polity Press.

Smith, M. (1996) 'The European Union and changing Europe: establishing the boundaries of order', *Journal of Common Market Studies*, 43: 5–28.

Smorodinskaya, N. (2001) *Kaliningrad Exclave: prospects of transformation into a pilot region*, Moscow: Institute of Economics, Russian Academy of Sciences and Kaliningrad Development Agency.

Sørensen, Ø. and Stråth, B. (1997) 'Introduction: the cultural construction of Norden', in

Ø. Sørensen and B. Stråth (eds) *The Cultural Construction of Norden*, Copenhagen: Scandinavian University Press.

Stanyte-Toločkienė, I. (2001) 'Kaliningrad oblast in the context of EU enlargement', in A. Jankauskas (ed.) *Lithuanian Political Science Yearbook 2000*, Vilnius: Institute of International Relations and Political Science, Vilnius University and Lithuanian Political Science Association.

Stephenson, W. (1953) *The Study of Behavior: Q-technique and its methodology*, Chicago: University of Chicago Press.

Tafel, K. and Raik, K. (2002) 'Teaduslik uurimus "Euroopa Liidu tulevik ja Eesti"', Tallinn: TPÜ Rahvusvaheliste ja Sotsiaaluuringute Instituut and Eesti Tuleviku-Uuringute Instituut.

Thomas, D. and Baas, L. (1992/3) 'The issue of generalization in Q methodology', *Operant Subjectivity*, 16: 18–36.

Tiilikainen, T. (2001) 'Nordic integration policy seen from abroad', *Cooperation and Conflict*, 36: 95–8.

—— (2003) 'The political implications of the EU's enlargement to the Baltic States', in V. Pettai and J. Zielonka (eds) *The Road to the European Union, vol. 2: Estonia, Latvia and Lithunia*, Manchester: Manchester University Press.

Toal, G. (2002) 'Theorizing practical geopolitical reasoning: the case of the United States' response to the war in Bosnia', *Political Geography*, 21: 601–28.

Tonra, B. (2000) 'Mapping EU foreign policy studies', *Journal of European Public Policy*, 7: 163–9.

Trädgårdh, L. (2002) 'Sweden and the EU: welfare state nationalism and the spectre of "Europe"', in L. Hansen and O. Wæver (eds) *European Integration and National Identity*, London: Routledge.

Trenin, D. (2000) 'Security cooperation in north-eastern Europe: a Russian perspective', in D. Trenin and P. van Ham (eds) *Russia and the United States in Northern European Security*, Helsinki: UPI-FIIA and Institut für Europäische Politik.

Tunander, O. (1997) 'Post-Cold War Europe: synthesis of a bipolar friend–foe structure and a hierarchic cosmos–chaos structure?', in O. Tunander (ed.) *Geopolitics in Post-Wall Europe: security, territory and identity*, Oslo and London: PRIO and Sage.

Vaahtoranta, T. and Forsberg, T. (2000) 'Post-neutral or pre-allied? Finnish and Swedish policies on the EU and NATO as security organizations', *UPI Working Papers*, 29/2000.

Vähä-Sipilä, M. (2004a) *Ignalinan tapaus: liettualaiset ympäristöjärjestöt Euroopan integraation ja kansallisen suvereniteettipolitiikan ristipaineessa*, Tampere: Tampere University Press (Acta Universitatis Tamperensis 1050).

—— (2004b) 'Kansallinen identiteettipolitiikka itään laajentuneessa Euroopan Unionissa – liettualaisten ympäristöjärjestöjen tapaus', *Kosmopolis*, 34: 72–89.

Vahl, M. (2003) 'Whither the common European economic space? Political and institutional aspects of closer economic integration between the EU and Russia', paper presented at the workshop 'A laboratory in the margins: the EU's and Russia's policies in northern Europe', Danish Institute of International Studies, Copenhagen, 26–27 September 2003.

Vareikis, E. (2002) 'Lithuania, European integration, and post-Soviet Russia', in H. Hubel (ed.), with A. Bannwart and S. Gänzle, *EU Enlargement and Beyond: the Baltic states and Russia*, Berlin: Berlin Verlag.

Väyrynen, R. (1999) 'The security of the Baltic countries: cooperation and defection', in

O. Knudsen (ed.) *Stability and Security in the Baltic Sea Region: Russian, Nordic and European aspects*, London: Frank Cass.

Veebel, V. (2003) 'Eesti Euroopa tulevikudebatis', in A. Kasekamp (ed.) *The Estonian Foreign Policy Yearbook 2003*, Tallinn: Estonian Foreign Policy Institute.

Vesa, U. and Möller, F. (2003) *Security Community in the Baltic Sea Region? Recent debate and recent trends*, Tampere: TAPRI.

Vetik, R. (2001) 'Euroopa Liit ja Eesti avalik arvamus', in R. Vetik (ed.) *Euroopa Liit ja Eesti avalik arvamus*, Tartu: Tartu Ülikooli Kirjastus.

Wæver, O. (1994) 'Insecurity and identity unlimited', *COPRI Working Papers*, 14/1994.

—— (1996) 'Power(s) and polarity in Europe: 1989–1994 patterns', in H. Mouritzen, O. Wæver and H. Wiberg (eds) *European Integration and National Adaptations: a theoretical inquiry*, Commack: Nova Science Publishers.

—— (1997a) 'Imperial metaphors: emerging European analogies to pre-nation-state imperial systems', in O. Tunander (ed.) *Geopolitics in Post-Wall Europe: security, territory and identity*, Oslo and London: PRIO and Sage.

—— (1997b) 'The Baltic Sea: a region after post-modernity?', in P. Joenniemi (ed.) *Neo-Nationalism or Regionality: the restructuring of political space around the Baltic rim*, Stockholm: NordREFO.

—— (2000) 'The EU as a security actor: reflections from a pessimistic constructivist on post-sovereign security orders', in M. Kelstrup and M.C. Williams (eds) *International Relations and the Politics of European Integration: power, security and community*, London: Routledge.

Wendt, A. (1995) 'Constructing international politics', *International Security*, 20: 71–81.

Wessels, W. (2000) 'Introduction: the Northern Dimension as a challenging task', in G. Bonvicini, T. Vaahtoranta and W. Wessels (eds) *The Northern EU: national views on the emerging security dimension*, Helsinki and Berlin: UPI-FIIA and Institut für Europäische Politik.

Whitman, R.G. (1998) *From Civilian Power to Superpower? The international identity of the European Union*, Basingstoke: Macmillan.

Wiberg, H. (1996) 'Adaptive patterns and their deep roots: a European overview', H. Mouritzen, O. Wæver and H. Wiberg (eds) *European Integration and National Adaptations: a theoretical inquiry*, Commack: Nova Science Publishers.

Wörster, P. (1995) 'The northern part of East Prussia', in T. Forsberg (ed.) *Contested Territory: border disputes at the edge of the former Soviet empire*, Aldershot: Edward Elgar.

Zielonka, J. (1998) *Explaining Euro-Paralysis: why Europe is unable to act in international politics*, Basingstoke: Macmillan.

—— (2001) 'How new enlarged borders will reshape the European Union?' *Journal of Common Market Studies*, 39: 507–36.

Zielonka, J. and Mair, P. (2002) 'Introduction: diversity and adaptation in the enlarged European Union', *West European Politics*, 25: 1–18.

Primary material

Speeches and comments

Adamkus, V. (2000) 'Address by H.E. Mr. Valdas Adamkus, President of the Republic of Lithuania, at the Nice European Conference', 7 December 2000.

—— (2001a) 'Address by H.E. Mr. Valdas Adamkus, President of the Republic of Lithuania, at the International Bertelsmann Forum 2001, session "The EU reform from the East European perspective"', Berlin, 19 January 19 2001.

—— (2001b) 'Remarks by H.E. President Valdas Adamkus in address to the Institute of European Affairs in Dublin', 25 September 2001.

—— (2001c) 'Statement by H. E. Mr. V. Adamkus, President of Lithuania, at the international conference "European integration: economic and security implications for Central and Eastern Europe"', 21 May 2001.

—— (2002a) 'Speech by H.E. Mr. Valdas Adamkus, President of Lithuania, at the 6th Stockholm conference on Baltic Sea region security and cooperation, "Post-enlargement challenges for the Baltic Sea Region"', Stockholm, 24 April 2002.

—— (2002b) 'Address by the President at the Chicago Council on Foreign Relations, "Lithuania's foreign and security policy issues"', 10 September 2002.

—— (2002c) 'Address by the President at the University of Latvia, "Lithuanian–Latvian cooperation in a new Europe"', 3 September 2002.

—— (2002d) 'Address by H.E. Mr. Valdas Adamkus, President of the Republic of Lithuania, at the German Council on Foreign Relations, "Lithuania's future in the Euro-Atlantic community"', 10 October 2002.

—— (2002e) '"Lithuania in an integrated world", speech by H.E. Mr Valdas Adamkus, President of the Republic of Lithuania, at the Royal Institute of International Affairs, Chatham House', London, 27 March 2002.

—— (2002f) 'Statement by the President of Lithuania at the European Council in Copenhagen', Copenhagen, 13 December 2002.

—— (2002g) 'Address by H.E. President Valdas Adamkus of the Republic of Lithuania at the American Chamber of Commerce, "Effects of Lithuania's integration into the European Union"', 26 November 2002.

—— (2002h) 'Speech by the President at the Munich Economic Summit "Europe after enlargement"', Munich, 7 June 7 2002.

—— (2002i) 'Statement by President Valdas Adamkus of Lithuania at Seville European Council', Seville, 22 June 2002.

Alekseev, A. (2001) 'Russia in European politics', *International Affairs* (Moscow), 47: 37–44.

Bērziņš, A. (2000) 'Statement by the Prime Minister of Latvia Mr. Andris Berzins to the European Forum', Berlin, 24 November 2000.

—— (2002) 'Speech by Prime Minister of the Republic of Latvia, H.E. Andris Bērziņš, to the conference "EU enlargement: opportunities and prospects", on "Latvia for Europe and Europe for Latvia"', London, 14–15 March 2002.

Bērziņš, I. (2000a) 'Speech by Mr. Indulis Berzins, the Minister of Foreign Affairs of the Republic of Latvia, EU–Latvia Joint Parliamentary Committee, 5th meeting', Riga, 18 September 2000.

—— (2000b) 'An address of H.E. Mr. Indulis Berzins, Minister of Foreign Affairs of the Republic of Latvia at the conference "Northern and southern dimensions of Europe: challenges for the CFSP"', Rome, 4 December 2000.

—— (2001a) 'Speech by H.E. Mr Indulis Berzins Minister for Foreign Affairs of Latvia, "Latvia – Finland's partner and ally in a greater Europe"', debate on European Union enlargement, Adams Hall, Helsinki, 12 October 2001.

—— (2001b) 'Speech by Mr I. Berzins, Minister for Foreign Affairs, Republic of Latvia at the second foreign minister's conference on the Northern Dimension', Tallinn, 9 April 2001.

—— (2001c) '"Latvia – a reliable partner to Austria in the new European Union", speech by Mr Indulis Berzins, the Minister of Foreign Affairs of the Republic of Latvia, at the Alpbach Forum', 26 November 2001.

—— (2001d) 'Address of the Minister of Foreign Affairs of the Republic of Latvia I. Berzins at the seminar "Latvia in the Europe of the future", "The need to outline a new horizon of thinking"', Riga, 7 December 2001.

—— (2001e) 'Opening remarks by H.E. Mr. Indulis Berzins, Minister of Foreign Affairs of the Republic of Latvia the conference "Strengthening Europe as an area of welfare, social stability and rule of law"', Riga, 16 February 2001.

—— (2002) 'Co-report of the Minister for Foreign Affairs of the Republic of Latvia Mr Indulis Berzins at the 8th Baltic Council', Vilnius, 24 May 2002.

Brazauskas, A. (2004) 'Prime Minister Algirdas Brazauskas about EU enlargement and political challenges'. Online. Available at http://www.lrv.lt/main_en.php (accessed 24 March 2004).

Egorov, V. (2001) 'Kaliningrad: shaping the development strategy: interview with Vladimir G. Egorov, Governor of Kaliningrad oblast', *Baltinfo*, official newsletter of the Council of the Baltic Sea States, 37, April 2001.

Grybauskaitė, D. (2001) 'Statement by Dr. Dalia Grybauskaitė, Deputy Minister of Foreign Affairs, at the European conference "Candidate countries opinion concerning the future of the EU"', Copenhagen, 20 April 2001.

Gusarev, E. (2002) RF Deputy Foreign Minister in the special section 'The European Economic Area: round table discussion', *International Affairs* (Moscow), 48: 179–80.

Hololei, H. (2002a) 'Statement by Mr Henrik Hololei, Alternate Member of the Convention, Government of Estonia, on articles on the architecture of the Constitutional Treaty', Brussels, 7–8 November 2002.

—— (2002b) 'Statement by Mr Henrik Hololei, Alternate Member of the Convention, Government of Estonia, on external action', Brussels, 20 December 2002.

—— (2002c) 'Statement by Mr Henrik Hololei, Alternate Member of the Convention, Government of Estonia', Brussels, 23–24 May 2002.

—— (2003a) 'Statement by Mr Henrik Hololei, Alternate Member of the Convention, Government of Estonia, on articles 43–46 and the final provisions of the draft Constitutional Treaty', Brussels, 24–25 April 2003.

—— (2003b) 'Statement by Mr Henrik Hololei, Alternate Member of the Convention, Government of Estonia on articles 24–33 of the draft Constitutional Treaty', Brussels, 17–18 March 2003.

—— (2003c) 'Statement by Mr Henrik Hololei, Alternate Member of the Convention, Government of Estonia, on articles on external relations of the draft Constitutional Treaty', Brussels, 15–16 May 2003.

Ilves, T.H. (1999) 'Remarks by Mr. Toomas Hendrik Ilves, Minister of Foreign Affairs of Estonia, "The Estonian perspective on EU and NATO enlargement", at the conference on "German and American policies towards the Baltic states: the perspectives of EU and NATO enlargement"', Bonn, 7 May 1999.

—— (2001) 'Article by Toomas Hendrik Ilves, Minister of Foreign Affairs, Estonia, "The common interests of the Northern dimension" (unofficial translation)', *Postimees*, 4 April 2001.

Ivanov, I. (2000) 'Russia, Europe at the turn of the millennium', *International Affairs* (Moscow), 46: 104–10.

—— (2001a) 'Formation of new Russian foreign policy completed', *International Affairs* (Moscow), 47: 1–7.

—— (2001b) 'Baltic Sea co-operation: establishing a new type of a relationship in northern Europe', *Baltinfo*, the official newsletter of the Council of the Baltic Sea States, 40, September 2001.

Kalniete, S. (2003a) 'Speech by the Minister of Foreign Affairs of the Republic of Latvia H.E. Mrs. Sandra Kalniete, the representative of the Latvian government at the Convention', Brussels, 25 April 2003.

—— (2003b) 'Speech by the Latvian Minister of Foreign Affairs at the meeting of government representatives to the European Convention', 21 February 2003.

—— (2003c) 'Speech by the Minister of Foreign Affairs of the Republic of Latvia, H.E. Mrs. Sandra Kalniete to the European Policy Centre seminar "Meet the new member states", "Building the new Europe"', 27 February 2003.

—— (2003d) 'Address by the Minister of Foreign Affairs of the Republic of Latvia Ms. Sandra Kalniete, representative of the Latvian government to the European Convention, concerning the draft articles of the Constitutional Treaty on enhanced cooperation', Brussels, 31 May 2003.

—— (2003e) 'Statement by Mrs. Sandra Kalniete, Foreign Minister of the Republic of Latvia, at the EU–Latvia Joint Parliamentary Committee meeting', Brussels, 17 February 2003.

—— (2003f) 'Speech by the Minister of Foreign Affairs of the Republic of Latvia H.E. Mrs. Sandra Kalniete, the representative of the Latvian government at the Convention, "Intervention on the draft articles of the Constitutional treaty on the EU institutions"', Brussels, 15 May 2003.

—— (2003g) 'Speech by the Minister of Foreign Affairs of the Republic of Latvia H.E. Mrs. Sandra Kalniete, the representative of the Latvian government at the Convention, "Intervention on the draft articles of the Constitutional Treaty on the external actions of the European Union"', Brussels, 16 May 2003.

—— (2003h) 'Amendment form: suggestion for amendment of article 2: part II – title B'.

—— (2003i) 'Amendment form: suggestion for amendment of article 5: part II – title B'.

—— (2004) 'Speech by Latvia's Minister of Foreign Affairs Sandra Kalniete, "Latvia's foreign policy at the crossroads of changes"', at the 62nd Scientific Conference, Riga, University of Latvia, 27 January 2004.

Klepatskii, L. (2000) 'Foreign policy dilemmas of Russia', *International Affairs* (Moscow), 46: 79–87.

Likhachev, V. (2000) 'Russia and the European Union: a long-term view', *International Affairs* (Moscow), 46: 116–26.

—— (2003) 'Russia and the European Union', *International Affairs* (Moscow), 49: 55–63.

Mälk, R. (1998) 'Remarks by Raul Mälk, Minister of Foreign Affairs, "Estonian vision of the European Union", at the international conference "Estonia and the European Union"', Tallinn, 15 November 1998.

Martikonis, R. (2001) 'Address by Mr. Rytis Martikonis, Deputy Minister of Foreign Affairs of the Republic of Lithuania, colloquium "The finalité of European Union: ideas and concepts of the candidate countries"', Centre for European Integration Studies, Bonn, Germany, 16–17 November 2001.

—— (2002a) 'Intervention by Mr. Rytis Martikonis, Representative of the Lithuanian Government in the Convention on the future of the European Union, plenary session of the Convention', Brussels, 22 March 2002.

—— (2002b) 'Intervention by Mr. Rytis Martikonis, Representative of the Lithuanian Government at the plenary session of the Convention on the future of the EU', Brussels, 15 April 2002.

Meri, L. (2000a) 'President of the Republic at the European Conference in Nice', Nice, 7 December 2000.

—— (2000b) 'President of the Republic: "enlargement of the European Union as the motive force of Europe", at the annual meeting of the Swabian Society', Stuttgart, 6 November 2000.

Meshkov, A. (2002) 'Russia and the European security architecture', *International Affairs* (Moscow), 48: 18–22.

Mite, V. (2003) 'Latvia: minority report – EU membership may leave Russian speakers behind (Part 1)', *RFE/RL Report*. Online. Available at http://www.rferl.org/features/2003/08/18082003162129.asp (accessed 21 January 2005).

Ojuland, K. (2002a) 'Address by Ms Kristiina Ojuland, Foreign Minister of the Republic of Estonia, at the European Policy Centre's lecture series "Meet the new member states"', Brussels, 23 October 2002.

—— (2002b) 'Summary of the address by Ms Kristiina Ojuland, Foreign Minister of the Republic of Estonia, at the ninth international conference "Estonia and the EU"', Tallinn, 31 October 2002.

—— (2003a) 'Address by Kristiina Ojuland Minister of Foreign Affairs of the Republic of Estonia at the French Institute of International Relations', Paris, 29 April 2003.

—— (2003b) 'Address by the Minister of Foreign Affairs Kristiina Ojuland to the Riigikogu on behalf of the Government of Estonia, "Main foreign policy guidelines of the Republic of Estonia"', Tallinn, 5 June 2003.

—— (2003c) 'Main guidelines of Estonia's foreign policy: address by the Minister of Foreign Affairs of the Republic of Estonia Kristiina Ojuland to the Riigikogu on behalf of the Government of Estonia', Tallinn, 4 November 2003.

—— (2003d) 'Kristiina Ojuland: cooperation in the Baltic Sea region', Oulu, Finland, 8 September 2003.

Paksas, R. (2003a) 'Address by H.E. Mr. Rolandas Paksas, President of the Republic of Lithuania, to the public congress "Europe our future – current challenges posed by European unification"', 6 November 2003.

—— (2003b) 'Speech by H.E. Mr. Rolandas Paksas, President of the Republic of Lithuania, at the Aleksanteri Institute of the University of Helsinki, "Lithuania in the Baltic Sea region"', Helsinki, 21 May 2003.

—— (2003c) 'Speech by H.E. Mr. Rolandas Paksas, President of the Republic of Lithuania, during the meeting with the Lithuanian diplomatic corps', Vilnius, 27 February 2003.

—— (2004) 'Address by H.E. Mr. Rolandas Paksas, President of the Republic of Lithuania at the meeting with ambassadors residing in Vilnius', Vilnius, 15 January 2004.

Paleckis, J. (2002) 'Statement by Mr. Justas Vincas Paleckis, Vice-Minister of Foreign Affairs of the Republic of Lithuania, Baltic Sea States Sub-regional Co-operation 10th conference', Lillehammer, 24–26 October 2002.

Parts, J. (2003a) 'Peaminister Juhan Parts 23. mail 2003 Toompeal Riigikogu saalis', Tallinn, 23 May 2003.

—— (2003b) 'Märkmed Euroopast', *Eesti Päevaleht*, 27 July 2003.

Prodi, R. (2001) 'Speech by Romano Prodi, President of the European Commission, to the European Parliament, "The enlargement", SPEECH/01/531', Strasbourg, 13 November 2001.

Putin, V. (2001a) 'President V. Putin on priorities for Russian diplomacy', *International Affairs* (Moscow), 47: 1–5.

—— (2001b) 'Vystuplenie Prezidenta Rossiiskoi Federatsii V.V. Putina na otkrytii plenarnogo zasedaniia vstrechi na vysshem urovne Rossiia – ES', 17 May 2001. Online.

Available at http://194.226.82.50/text/appears/2001/05/28535.shtml (accessed 2 September 2003).

—— (2002a) 'Vystuplenie Prezidenta Rossiiskoi Federatsii V.V. Putina na vstreche Rossiia – Evropeiskii soiuz na vysshem urovne', 29 May 2002. Online. Available at http://194.226.82.50/text/appears/2002/05/30092.shtml (accessed 2 September 2003).

—— (2002b) 'Key tasks of Russian diplomacy', *International Affairs* (Moscow), 48: 1–7.

—— (2003a) 'Vstrecha so studentami Kaliningradskogo gosudarstvennogo universiteta', Kaliningrad, 27 June 2003. Online. Available at http://194.226.82.50/text/appears/2003/06/47945.shtml (accessed 2 September 2003).

—— (2003b) 'A state of the nation address to the Federal Assembly of the Russian Federation', *International Affairs* (Moscow), 49: 1–17.

—— (2003c) 'Concluding remarks at the Russia–EU summit', St Petersburg, 31 May 2003.

—— (2005) 'Annual address to the Federal Assembly, The Kremlin, Moscow, April 25, 2005', *International Affairs* (Moscow), 51: 1–15.

Repše, E. (2003a) 'Address by H.E. Mr. Einars Repše Prime Minister of the Republic of Latvia at the cabinet sitting on 19.08.2003', Riga, 19 August 2003.

—— (2003b) 'Speech by Einars Repše, Prime Minister of the Republic of Latvia at Saeima debate on the European Union', Riga, 29 May 2003.

Riekstins, M. (2000) 'Address by Mr. Maris Riekstins, Secretary of State, Ministry of Foreign Affairs of the Republic of Latvia at the conference "Subregional cooperation and integration in Europe"', Athens, 27 November 2000.

—— (2001) 'Remarks by Mr. Maris Riekstins, Secretary of State, Ministry of Foreign Affairs of Latvia, CSIS/SIIA Conference "Enlargement – a priority for the European Union"', Washington, DC, 7 March 2001.

Romanovsky, V. (2001) 'Geography encourages co-operation', in R. Grönick, M. Kulmala and L. Päiviö (eds) *Kaliningrad – Isolation or Co-operation?*, Helsinki: Finnish Committee for European Security.

Rüütel, A. (2002) 'Vabariigi President Euroopa Parlamendi Väliskomisjonis 27. novembril 2002 Brüsselis', Brussels, 27 November 2002.

Songal, A. (2001) 'Will "the disaster island of Kaliningrad" become a success story? Coherent federal policy is a condition *sine qua non*', in R. Grönick, M. Kulmala and L. Päiviö (eds) *Kaliningrad – Isolation or Co-operation?*, Helsinki: Finnish Committee for European Security.

Valionis, A. (2001) 'Statement by Antanas Valionis, Minister of Foreign Affairs of Lithuania, extraordinary session of the Seimas', Vilnius, 23 January 2001.

—— (2002a) 'Statement by Antanas Valionis, Minister of Foreign Affairs of Lithuania, at the European Policy Centre, "Present and future of Europe: Lithuania's view"', Brussels, 10 June 2002.

—— (2002b) 'The opening speech by H.E. Mr. Antanas Valionis, Minister of Foreign Affairs of the Republic of Lithuania, international conference "Building wider Europe"', Vilnius, 30 November 2002.

—— (2003a) 'Address by Minister of Foreign Affairs Antanas Valionis to Association of American Chamber of Commerce in Lithuania, "Lithuania's foreign policy after 2003"', Vilnius, 23 January 2003.

—— (2003b) 'Intervention by Mr. Antanas Valionis, Minister of Foreign Affairs of the Republic of Lithuania, at the ministerial meeting "The wider Europe: co-operation in the

Central-Eastern Europe through the common borders with the enlarged EU", "The EU and eastern neighbours: wider Europe – general remarks" ', Kiev, 10 November 2003.

—— (2003c) 'Interview of Lithuania's Foreign Minister Mr. Antanas Valionis', 13 January 2003. Online. Available at www.urm.lt (accessed 24 March 2004).

Verheugen, G. (2001) 'Speech at the University of Tartu, "Changing the history, shaping the future" ', Tartu, 19 April 2001.

—— (2002) 'Main extracts of Mr Verheugen's speech in Warsaw, Center for International Relations and "Rzeczpospolita", "Learn from history and shape the future" ', Warsaw, 11 July 2002.

Vīķe-Freiberga, V. (2000a) 'Address by H.E. Vaira Vike-Freiberga, President of the Republic of Latvia, to the Foreign Affairs Committee of the European Parliament, "Latvia and the new round of EU enlargement" ', Brussels, 28 November 2000.

—— (2000b) 'Address by Dr. Vaira Vike-Freiberga, President of the Republic of Latvia, at the London School of Economics and Political Science, "Latvia's place in a new Europe" ', London, 27 October 2000.

—— (2000c) 'Address by Dr. Vaira Vike-Freiberga, President of the Republic of Latvia, at the Norwegian School of Economics and Business Administration, "Latvia in the process of regional and European integration" ', Bergen, 21 September 2000.

—— (2001) 'Address by H.E., Dr. Vaira Vike-Freiberga, President of the Republic of Latvia, at the Center for Strategic and International Studies, "Completing the new Europe: the Baltic dimension" ', Washington, DC, 24 April 2001.

—— (2002a) 'Address by H.E. Dr. Vaira Vīķe-Freiberga, President of Latvia, in the workshop organized by the Die Zeit foundation, "Governance in the EU: enlargement in perspective" ', Berlin, 23 August 2002.

—— (2002b) 'Address by H.E. Dr. Vaira Vīķe-Freiberga, President of Latvia, at the Slovenian Association for International Relations, "The future of European integration" ', Ljubljana, 17 April 2002.

—— (2002c) 'Address by H.E. Dr. Vaira Vīķe-Freiberga, President of Latvia, at the Academy of Athens, "Dimensions of European civilization: past, present and future" ', Athens, 27 March 2002.

—— (2002d) 'Address by H. E. Vaira Vīķe-Freiberga, President of Latvia, at the University of Helsinki, "The future of the Baltic Sea region" ', Helsinki, 21 March 2002.

—— (2003a) 'Address by H.E. Dr. Vaira Vike-Freiberga, President of the Republic of Latvia, at the European Parliament', Brussels, 10 October 2003.

—— (2003b) 'Address by H.E. Dr. Vaira Vike-Freiberga, President of Latvia, at the Atlantic Club', Sofia, 4 December 2003.

—— (2003c) 'Lecture by H.E. Dr. Vaira Vike-Freiberga, President of the Republic of Latvia, Warsaw University, "Latvia & Poland: prospects for regional and transatlantic partnerships after Prague and Copenhagen" ', Warsaw, 26 February 2003.

—— (2003d) 'Statement by H.E. Vaira Vīķe-Freiberga, President of the Republic of Latvia, at the New Neighbours Initiative of the European conference', Athens, 17 April 2003.

Documents

Council of Foreign and Defence Policy (2001) 'Russian interests in northern Europe: what are they?', Moscow.

European Commission (1994) 'Communication from the Commission to the Council: orientations for a Union approach towards the Baltic Sea Region, SEC(94) 1747 final', 25 October 1994.

European Commission (1997a) 'Agenda 2000 – Commission opinion on Latvia's application for membership of the European Union, DOC 97/14', Brussels, 15 July 1997. Online. Available at http://europa.eu.int/comm/enlargement/dwn/opinions/latvia/la-open.pdf (accessed 23 January 2005).

European Commission (1997b) 'Agenda 2000 – Commission opinion on Lithuania's application for membership of the European Union, DOC 97/15', Brussels, 15 July 1997. Online. Available at http://europa.eu.int/comm/enlargement/dwn/opinions/lithuania/liop-en.pdf (accessed 23 January 2005).

European Commission (1998) '1998 Regular report from the Commission on Latvia's progress towards accession'. Online. Available at http://europa.eu.int/comm/enlargement/report_11_98/pdf/en/latvia_en.pdf (accessed 23 January 2005).

European Commission (1999) '1999 Regular report from the Commission on Latvia's progress towards accession, LATVIA – Regular Report – 13/10/99'. Online. Available at http://europa.eu.int/comm/enlargement/report_10_99/pdf/en/latvia_en.pdf (accessed 23 January 2005).

European Commission (2000) 'Tables summarizing the allocation of TACIS resources, 1991–1999'. Online. Available at http://www.europa.eu.int/comm/external_relations/ceeca/tacis/figures.pdf (accessed 20 November 2003).

European Commission (2001) 'Communication from the Commission to the Council: the EU and Kaliningrad, COM(2001) 26 final', Brussels, 17 January 2001.

European Commission (2002a) 'General assistance document 2002, D3 D(2002)', Brussels. Online. Available at http://www.europa.eu.int/comm/enlargement/pas/phare/pdf/gad_2002_general_part.pdf (accessed 11 November 2004).

European Commission (2002b) 'EU–Russia partnership on Kaliningrad, MEMO/02/169', Moscow, 12 July 2002. Online. Available at http://www.europa.eu.int/comm/external_relations/russia/russia_docs/js_elarg_270404 (accessed 13 May 2004).

European Commission (2003a) 'Financial assistance'. Online. Available at http://www.europa.eu.int/comm/enlargement/financial_assistance.htm (accessed 22 January 2004).

European Commission (2003b) 'Commission working document: the second Northern Dimension Action Plan, 2004–06, COM(2003) 343 Final', Brussels, 10 June 2003.

European Commission (2003c) 'Communication from the Commission to the Council and the European Parliament, "Wider Europe – neighbourhood: a new framework for relations with our eastern and southern neighbours, COM(2003) 104 final', Brussels, 11 March 2003.

European Commission (2003d) 'Comprehensive monitoring report on Estonia's preparations for membership'. Online. Available at http://europa.eu.int/comm/enlargement/estonia/index.htm (accessed 23 January 2004).

European Commission (2003e) 'Comprehensive monitoring report on Latvia's preparations for membership'. Online. Available at http://europa.eu.int/comm/enlargement/report_2003/pdf/cmr_lv_final.pdf (accessed 11 November 2004).

European Commission (2003f) 'National indicative programme, country: Russian Federation; budget years: 2004–2006'. Online. Available at http://www.europa.eu.int/comm/external_relations/russia/csp/04–06_en.pdf (accessed 20 November 2003).

European Commission (2004a) 'Relations with Estonia'. Online. Available at http://www.europa.eu.int/comm/enlargement/estonia/index.htm (accessed 30 August 2004).

European Commission (2004b) 'European Union and its main trading partners 2000 economic and trade indicators'. Online. Available at http://www.europa.eu.int/comm/trade/issues/bilateral/data.htm (accessed 30 August 2004).

European Commission (2004c) 'Relations with Latvia'. Online. Available at http://www.europa.eu.int/comm/enlargement/latvia/index.htm (accessed 11 November 2004).

European Commission (2004d) 'Relations with Lithuania'. Online. Available at http://www.europa.eu.int/comm/enlargement/lithuania/index.htm (accessed 4 November 2004).

European Commission Delegation in Russia (2003) 'Energy'. Online. Available at www.eur.ru/eng/neweur/user_eng.php?func=coopspec&id=39 (accessed 11 April 2003).

European Commission Delegation in Russia (2004a) 'E-Note: foreign investments in Russia'. Online. Available at http://www.delrus.cec.eu.int/en/images/pText_pict/222/Foreign%20investment_new%20data.doc (accessed 27 September 2004).

European Commission Delegation in Russia (2004b) 'The EU and Russia – economic and trade indicators'. Online. Available at http://www.delrus.cec.eu.int/en/images/pText_pict/216/Economic%20indicators.doc (accessed 27 September 2004).

European Council (1999) 'Common Strategy of the European Union of 4 June 1999 on Russia, (1999/414/CFSP)', Official Journal of the European Communities L 157/1.

European Council (2000) 'Northern Dimension – Action Plan for the Northern Dimension with external and cross-border policies of the European Union 2000–2003, 9401/00', Brussels, 14 June 2000.

Government of Estonia (2003) 'Positions of the Estonian Government on the future of Europe, approved by the Government on 19 November 2002 and on 14 January 2003'.

Government of Latvia (2003) 'Contribution to the drafting of the Northern Dimension Action Plan 2004–2006: Latvia's input'.

Government of Lithuania (2002) 'Guiding principles of the Government of Lithuania on the future of the European Union, presented at the session of the Governmental European Integration Commission on July 1, 2002'.

Government of Lithuania (2003a) 'Non-paper: Eastern Europe and Central Asia, meeting doc. 241/03, origin Lithuania date 27.08.03'.

Government of Lithuania (2003b) 'Position of the Government of Lithuania on the EU institutional reform'. Online. Available at http://www.urm.lt/data/3/EF128115524_position.htm (accessed 24 March 2004).

Government of the Russian Federation (2003a) 'Non-paper: EU Northern Dimension: Russian approach', 14 January 2003.

Government of the Russian Federation (2003b) 'Non-paper: Further steps in areas covered by the Northern Dimension of the EU: Russian proposals', 17 February 2003.

Inter-Governmental Conference of the European Union (2004) 'Treaty establishing a Constitution for Europe'. Online. Available at http://www.europa.eu.int/constitution/en/lstoc1_en.htm (accessed 17 November 2005).

'Joint statement on EU enlargement and EU–Russia relations', Brussels, 27 April 2004. Online. Available at http://www.europa.eu.int/comm/external_relations/russia/russia_docs/js_elarg_270404. (accessed 20 May 2004).

'Joint Statement, EU–Russia Summit, 13990/03 (Presse 3 13) 2'.

Ministry of Foreign Affairs of Lithuania (2004) 'Co-operation between Lithuania and the European Union: de-commissioning the Ignalina nuclear power plant'. Online. Available at http://www.urm.lt/data/3/EF22613417_ignal.htm (accessed 18 November 2004).

Republic of Latvia (2000) 'Strategy for the integration into the European Union'.

—— (2002) 'The National Security Concept', unofficial translation, adopted by the *Saeima* on 24 January 2002, Riga, 24 January 2004.

'Russia–European Union Permanent Partnership Council (PPC) meeting in Luxembourg,

921-28-04-2004', Luxembourg, 28 April 2004 (unofficial translation from Russian, Ministry of Foreign Affairs of the Russian Federation).

Russian Federation (1999) 'Russia's Middle-Term Strategy towards the EU (2000–2010)'.

Russian Federation (2000) 'Foreign policy concept of the Russian Federation', *International Affairs* (Moscow), 46: 1–14.

News sources

Eesti Ekspress 2003
Helsingin Sanomat 2002
Helsingin Sanomat 2003
Helsingin Sanomat 2004

Rosbalt (2001) 'The Lithuanian Government won't mind Yukos taking over Mazeikiu Nafta'. Online. Available at http://www.rosbaltnews.com/print/print?cn=22626 (accessed 4 November 2004).

Rosbalt (2002) 'US Williams, Russian Yukos conclude Mazeikiu Nafta deal'. Online. Available at http://www.rosbaltnews.com/2002/04/12/450555.html (accessed 4 November 2004).

Rosbalt (2003a) 'Russia declares petroleum blockade against Latvian port'. Online. Available at http://www.rosbaltnews.com/print/print?cn=61323 (accessed 7 September 2004).

Rosbalt (2003b) 'Latvia protests to Russia over oil pipeline'. Online. Available at http://www.rosbaltnews.com/print/print?cn=61478 (accessed 7 September 2004).

Rosbalt (2003c) 'Transneft may buy Latvian oil terminal Ventspils Nafta'. Online. Available at http://www.rosbaltnews.com/print/print?cn=63538 (accessed 7 September 2004).

Rosbalt (2003d) 'Buy, Russia, buy'. Online. Available at http://www.rosbaltnews.com/print/print?cn=64145 (accessed 7 September 2004).

Rosbalt (2003e) 'Oil-short Ventspils looks to Kazakhstan as new source'. Online. Available at http://www.rosbaltnews.com/print/print?cn=64801 (accessed 7 September 2004).

Rosbalt (2003f) 'TNK-BP overtaking weakened Yukos'. Online. Available at http://www.rosbaltnews.com/2003/12/14/65076.html (accessed 7 September 2004).

Rosbalt (2003g) 'German Gref: foundations for better living standards in Kaliningrad region have already been laid'. Online. Available at http://www.rosbaltnews.com/print/print?cn=63632 (accessed 14 November 2004).

Rosbalt (2003h) 'High-speed rail link to connect Kaliningrad and Russia'. Online. Available at http://www.rosbaltnews.com/print/print?cn=63184 (accessed 14 November 2003).

Rosbalt (2003i) 'Kaliningrad Parliament asks for direct financial Aid from EU'. Online. Available at http://www.rosbaltnews.com/print/print?cn=61887 (accessed 14 November 2003).

Rosbalt (2003j) 'EU to spend EUR 5 million on Kaliningrad transit database'. Online. Available at http://www.rosbaltnews.com/print/print?cn=61887 (accessed 14 November 2003).

Rosbalt (2003k) 'Governor of Kaliningrad region: travel to "mainland Russia" is now problem-free'. Online. Available at http://rosbaltnews.com/print/print/print?cn=64168 (accessed 14 November 2003).

Rosbalt (2003l) ' "A different kind of Russia" for Russians, "a different kind of Europe" for

Europeans'. Online. Available at http://www.rosbaltnews.com/2003/02/12/61351.html (accessed 18 November 2003).

Rosbalt (2003m) 'We are entering into a conflict with the EU without giving any thought to the consequences', Rosbalt interview with Valery Ustyugov. Online. Available at rosbaltnews.com/2002/09/28/50305.html (accessed 20 November 2003).

Rosbalt (2004a) 'Acceptance of Russia into WTO called cowardly betrayal of Latvia'. Online. Available at http://www.rosbaltnews.com/print/print?cn=66704 (accessed 7 September 2004).

Suomen Kuvalehti 2003

Other sources

Altogether thirty-six Q methodological experiments conducted in Estonia, Finland, Latvia, Lithuania and Kaliningrad, thirty-four followed by interviews, during November–December 2002, except one in February 2002; four additional interviews in Estonia and Lithuania during May 2002–February 2003.

Central Statistical Bureau of Latvia (2004) 'Basic socio-economic indicators, foreign trade'. Online. Available at http://www.csb.lv//Satr/grada03.cfm?akurs=Karek (accessed 9 September 2004).

Köll, J. (2002) 'North European and Baltic statistics', in L. Hedegaard and B. Lindström (eds) *The NEBI Yearbook 2001/2002: north European and Baltic Sea integration*, Berlin: Springer.

Köll, J. (2003) 'North European and Baltic statistics', in L. Hedegaard and B. Lindström (eds.) (2003) *The NEBI Yearbook 2003: north European and Baltic Sea integration*, Berlin: Springer.

Statistics Lithuania (2004a) 'Main partners of exports'. Online. Available at http://www. std.lt/web/main.php?parent=525&module=525&action=page&id=426&print=y (accessed 4 November 2004).

Statistics Lithuania (2004b) 'Main partners for imports'. Online. Available at http://www. std.lt/web/main.php?parent=525&module=525&action=page&id=427&print=y (accessed 4 November 2004).

Statistical Office of Estonia (2004) 'Main social and economic indicators of Estonia, 7/04'. Online. Available at http://www.stat.ee/122318 (accessed 30 August 2004).

Index

www.ingramcontent.com/pod-product-compliance
Ingram Content Group UK Ltd.
Pitfield, Milton Keynes, MK11 3LW, UK
UKHW020858280225
455677UK00006B/88